Th.077

The**Blaikie**
REPORT

An Insider's Look at
FAITH AND
POLITICS

To Canadian
Food Grains Bank!

Bill.

by**Bill Blaikie**

The Blaikie Report
An Insider's Look at Faith and Politics
Bill Blaikie

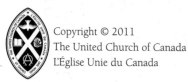

Copyright © 2011
The United Church of Canada
L'Église Unie du Canada

Library and Archives Canada Cataloguing in Publication

Blaikie, Bill, 1951–
    The Blaikie report : an insider's look at faith and politics / by Bill Blaikie.

Includes index.
Issued also in electronic format.
ISBN 978-1-55134-188-0

    1. Blaikie, Bill, 1951–. 2. Politicians—Canada—Biography. 3. Politicians—Manitoba—Biography. 4. New Democratic Party—Biography. 5. Canada—Politics and government—20th century. 6. Canada—Politics and government—21st century. 7. Religion and politics—Canada. I. Title.

FC601.B53A3 2011   971.064'5092   C2011-906272-0

United Church Publishing House
3250 Bloor St. West, Suite 300
Toronto, ON
Canada M8X 2Y4
1-800-268-3781
www.united-church.ca/sales/ucph

 UCPH is a ministry of The United Church of Canada, supported by the Mission and Service Fund and readers like you.

Design: Diane Renault-Collicott, Graphics and Print
Cover image: Peace Tower © Pichunter | Dreamstime.com

Printed in Canada
5 4 3 2 1   15 14 13 12 11

Also available as an

UCRDstore.ca

100181

This book is dedicated to my wife, Brenda,
to my children, Rebecca, Jessica, Daniel, and Tessa,
and to the memory of my parents, Robert and Kathleen Blaikie

Contents

Foreword. vii

Acknowledgements. ix

Introduction. 1

1. The God Squad 5

2. The Social Gospel 14

3. Culture Wars 23

4. Growing Up Political in Transcona. 37

5. The Prophetic Tradition 49

6. Seeking the Welfare of the City 59

7. First Peoples and Constitutional Debates 71

8. An Effective Electorate 85

9. The Medicare Crisis 98

10. Parliamentary Reform. 109

11. Our Environmental Deficit. 127

12. Hope in the Post–Cold War Era 143

13. A Willingness to Turn the Page. 156

14. The Gulf Wars and Parliamentary Diplomacy. 169

15. Free Trade—A Chosen Powerlessness 183

16. Globalization and the WTO. 198

17. A Passion for Justice. 215

NDP Members of Parliament, 1979 to 2008. 225

Notes 227

Index 229

Foreword

For those in the Canadian public who find themselves a little jaded by politics and politicians, Bill Blaikie's memoir is a refreshing antidote. The long-time MP from Winnipeg–Transcona, who went on to serve as a provincial minister in the Manitoba NDP government, recounts his career as an elected public servant. He came to Parliament in the service of a social cause, steeped in the teachings of the social gospel, the experience of serving in a ministry in Winnipeg's North End, in addition to an abiding faith in the rightness of social democracy.

One of the most fascinating parts of the book is his discussion of the interplay between faith and political action, decrying that today this is seen only as an issue prompted by the powerful influence of conservative Christian evangelicals, forgetting the important religious roots of the Canadian left. It is perhaps no coincidence then that Blaikie is a graduate of the University of Winnipeg, whose association with the religious political left in Canada includes seminal social gospel figures like Salem Bland, J.S. Woodsworth, and Stanley Knowles.

Overall he gives the reader a perspective of many important decisions of the last 30 years as seen from the opposite benches, showing a particular distaste for Liberal tactics on free trade, the Charter, and social policy. It is a useful chronicle to have and a reminder of just how many important issues have been fought out in the halls of Parliament.

Blaikie retired from the House of Commons after three decades of service, as the first NDP Deputy Speaker, a sign of respect held for him by his peers for his integrity and parliamentary performance. Those qualities shine through in his book. It is an honest account of a man who served Parliament well and a welcome, distinctive contribution to the annals of contemporary Canadian politics.

Lloyd Axworthy
President, University of Winnipeg
Minister of Foreign Affairs, 1996–2000
Member of Parliament from Winnipeg, 1979–2000

Acknowledgements

The first person I want to acknowledge and thank is my wife, Brenda, who has not only put up with the dozens of evenings lost to writing this book, but also had to act as on-call tutor, adviser, and troubleshooter as I learned how to use the computer, and, in stages, came to be able to make more and more things happen on my own. She was no doubt as glad to see the end of the book as I was.

Gratitude is also due to all those who initially encouraged me and seemed excited about the idea that I might write a book, including, very importantly, the editorial staff of United Church Publishing House. In particular I would also like to mention the Rev. Dr. James Christie, former Dean of Theology at the University of Winnipeg, and Dr. John Badertscher, retired Professor of Religious Studies at the University of Winnipeg, who not only encouraged me but also took the time to read the manuscript and make gentle suggestions and corrections. Thanks to my daughter Rebecca, who did some initial typing for me, and to theology student Jamie Watt, for her typing of several chapters before I got the hang of it myself. The latter's admonitions to not let my new provincial political responsibilities get in the way of finishing the book were not forgotten.

I would also like to thank all the people who worked for me over the 29½ years that I was a member of Parliament. Long-service awards of appreciation go to Jean Gaudet, who was in my Ottawa office from the beginning in 1979 to the end in 2008, to Marilyn Sime, my constituency assistant for 22 years, and to Sharon McLaughlin, who worked in both offices for a total of 14 years. Others who worked for a time in my office and then went on to other challenges were Joanne Cerilli, Randy Schulz, Jeanne Bell, Joe Masi, Rick Huizenga, Alec Connelly, Paul Badertscher, Paul Degenstein, Michael Parasiuk, David Dubinski, Paul Labun, Lloyd Penner, Chad Semain, Jonathan Weier, Jean-Guy Bourgeois, Jamie Burgess, Adam Hodgins, Scott Harris, Peter Dueck, Matt Wiebe, Jeff Hook, and Josina Robb.

None of it would have been possible without the continuing support of the voters of Winnipeg–Birds Hill, Winnipeg–Transcona, and Elmwood–Transcona. I am grateful for their loyalty through good times and bad, and for never falling for the argument that they should put their principles aside and vote for whoever they thought would be on the government side of the House. I am grateful to all those who worked in my campaigns. You are too numerous to name, but you all have a special place in my political memory. And I am grateful beyond measure to grandparents Bob and Kay Blaikie and Bill and Isobel Bihun for being such a wonderful and helpful extended family to Brenda and the kids while I was routinely away in Ottawa.

Finally, it was a privilege to work with all the other NDP MPs who served in the nine Parliaments I sat in, a band of brothers and sisters who consistently chose the more difficult path of challenging established ideologies, interests, and values in the name of greater justice and equality. Our demise was hoped for, and predicted, many times. But you cannot kill a dream, and the dream lives on as I write these words on the eve of the first Parliament in which the NDP will be the Official Opposition.

––––––––

Tragically, as this book was going to print, Canadians were universally saddened by the untimely death of NDP leader Jack Layton. Jack was one of those who encouraged me to write a book, and one of the last conversations I had with him, early in July 2011, was about the book. Though Jack and I were once rivals for the NDP leadership, we became friends and allies, even though we did not completely agree with each other on everything. I will miss him, personally and politically. I was truly excited about the prospect of Canadians making him prime minister in 2015.

Introduction

On March 15, 2007, under the impression that an election would be triggered within a week or so, I announced that after nearly three decades in federal politics, I would not be seeking re-election. I had just returned from Greece, where I had been part of a parliamentary delegation led by Speaker Peter Milliken, a Liberal, who had nevertheless been re-elected Speaker after the Conservatives formed a minority government in January 2006. He had appointed me Deputy Speaker of the House of Commons after consultation with the new Prime Minister, Stephen Harper. I was the first New Democrat to serve in this capacity, and I enjoyed my time in the chair immensely. I was pleased with the reputation for being both fair and firm that I acquired with all parties, and further enjoyed working with the staff of the House of Commons in a way that had not been possible before, particularly with the Clerk and Deputy Clerk, respectively, Audrey O'Brien and Marc Bosc.

It wasn't the first time I had thought of stepping down. I had considered not running in the election of 2004, following the 18 months I had spent as the New Democratic Party's Parliamentary Leader, while our new party leader and my rival in the recent leadership race, Jack Layton, waited for the general election to obtain a seat in the House, which he did. I was persuaded to stay on at that time by Layton, on the grounds that the 2004 election might well produce a minority Parliament in which my experience would be very valuable to him and to the new caucus. Paul Martin's Liberals were indeed reduced to a minority government, but not one in which the NDP held the balance of power in the way we had hoped. And although we attained significant extra spending on social priorities in the 2005 budget, the key hope for that Parliament, real progress on proportional representation, proved to be elusive. The Liberals were not willing to really go down that road.

That fall I again considered not running, in an election that I thought would probably come the following spring or summer. But when the NDP decided in November 2005 to precipitate the fall of the Martin minority, I was caught with no time for an announcement, and ended up running again. My party's decision to risk that election was taken in the hope that it would produce a Parliament in which the Liberals were forced to work more consistently with the NDP. The Liberals, for their part, had hoped to put more distance between themselves and the bad name that they were getting thanks to the sponsorship scandal. They did not want an election until at least the spring of 2006, when they hoped to win back a majority.

Having the power to cause an election is not the same as having the power to determine its outcome. Instead of the Liberals winning the 2006 election, but not by too much, as we had hoped, they lost. Harper's Conservatives formed a minority—and the rest is history. The Liberals blamed the NDP instead of themselves, and blamed us in particular for their inability to implement their commitments on the Kyoto Accord on climate change, on the Kelowna agreement with First Nations, and on the national child care plan negotiated by Toronto MP Ken Dryden. The first two were deathbed repentances, after many years of not acting on the files. Even the child care plan was a promise long overdue, but could have been saved if the Liberals had followed our advice to put it into legislation, which would have put it beyond the destructive grasp of a Conservative minority.

Although it seemed that the 21st-century NDP would never get to relive the glory days of the minority Parliaments of 1963–68 or 1972–74, when we were really able to make things happen, the opportunity briefly presented itself again in the late fall of 2008 when the plan for a Liberal-NDP coalition government supported by the Bloc Québécois almost came to be. For a moment, I thought that I had retired from federal politics one election too soon. But Prime Minister Harper's inflammatory, irresponsible language about the alleged evil of this perfectly legitimate parliamentary procedure, and a spurious prorogation of Parliament, combined with the inefficacy of Liberal leader Stéphane Dion, soon put an end to such thinking. In 2011, when as a result of an incredible breakthrough in Quebec, the NDP formed the Official Opposition, I was tempted to think that I had retired two elections too soon.

The election called for October 14, 2008, by Stephen Harper left me doubly irritated. Politically I could hardly believe that Harper had the nerve to declare Parliament dysfunctional, even before it sat that fall. Especially when it was widely known that the Conservatives had been operating out of a manual for their MPs on how to make committees dysfunctional. Personally, it meant that I would miss the opportunity for a time in the House of Commons when—as is sometimes the case when a person is retiring—comments are offered about the departing one and, unlike at a funeral, there is also a chance to respond. I had participated in many of these occasions over the years, speaking for the NDP when, for example, Jean Charest and Jean Chrétien were leaving. I always enjoyed the collegiality, the humour, and the better side of politics that these occasions could reveal. I had turned down the suggestion of such a time in May 2008, arguing that the fall would be time enough. Bad call.

During the exit interviews that I did in the media around my retirement, I was sometimes asked if I was going to write a book about my 30 years in federal politics, from nomination in 1978 to retirement in 2008. I replied that I had certainly thought about doing so, and took such questions as encouragement. This book is the result of that encouragement, plus the interest of United Church Publishing House in making it a reality. I have endeavoured to write something that may interest a variety of readers, from the strictly political to those who may take a special interest in the interface between faith and politics, as I understood it in my own life, and as I encountered it in others. Part autobiography, part theological and political analysis, and part political memoirs and anecdotes, I have highlighted some of the main issues and responsibilities that presented themselves during that time.

I first began drafting this book just after the 2008 election. As it turned out, the book would have to wait a while yet as the opportunity for a new political venture presented itself. Manitoba Premier Gary Doer suggested to me that I consider running for the provincial NDP in a by-election that had to be held within the boundaries of my old federal riding. The Premier made it clear that he wanted me in his cabinet if I won, and invited me to sample the joys of governing, after so many years in opposition. After reflecting on whether this was properly perceived as a call, or as a temptation, and after canvassing the membership of the Elmwood NDP, I decided to run and was elected to the Manitoba legislature on March 24, 2009, and appointed Minister of Conservation on November 3, 2009. Book writing would have to take a back seat.

As would, to some degree, my other post-parliamentary project, the Knowles-Woodsworth Centre for Theology and Public Policy. The centre was the culmination of an idea that I had discussed with Lloyd Axworthy, President of the University of Winnipeg, and Jim Christie, its Dean of Theology. The purpose of the centre, now in its infancy, is to create and support events and resources that shed helpful light on the relationships, past, present, and future, between faith and politics, and on the diversity of these relationships. In the context of the University of Winnipeg, which has a strong association with the social gospel tradition, not least through Stanley Knowles and J.S. Woodsworth themselves, one of the goals is to counter the common perception of the relationship between religion and politics as primarily a right-wing phenomenon.

A week is a long time in politics, and we are all quick to judge or to predict the future. Perhaps we need more often to take the view attributed to former Chinese premier Zhou Enlai, who when asked what he thought about the effects of the French Revolution replied that it was too early to tell. Early or not, I offer this snapshot of Canadian politics as I experienced it in one of the greatest privileges a citizen can have, the opportunity to represent fellow citizens in Parliament. I have heard both former prime ministers John Diefenbaker and John Turner refer to public life as a calling not unlike the call to ministry. In my case I felt called to both.

The God Squad

What was right or what was wrong with my own
faith-based politics, I wondered, that they had
caused so little offence all those years?

At a candidates' debate for the New Democratic Party leadership in the fall of
2002, I referred to the social gospel as one of the traditions that inspires and
informs the NDP. In the question period that followed, an audience member
took me to task. *Gospel* is a Christian concept, she objected, and by using
the word I was engaging in a form of Christian imperialism that left non-
Christians out of the conversation.

I wasn't sure what to make of it: Was this an overreaction to my objective
description of the origins of the party? A plant by one of the other campaigns?
A brilliant flash of multicultural sensitivity? Wherever the question was
coming from, it did raise an important point. In the early 20th century, the
social gospel movement offered a Christian critique of the capitalist world
view that continues to inform the left to this day. In a 21st-century secular,
pluralist Canadian context, with a widespread touchiness about anything
Christian and about the role of religion in politics in general, how are we who
see ourselves in the social gospel tradition to speak of what we believe?

This touchiness about religion manifested itself most obviously in the stormy debate about faith and politics occasioned by the arrival of Stockwell Day on the federal scene in 2000. Although Day himself did not make his Christian orientation a central part of his campaign, it was certainly part of the basis for his popularity with elements of the newly formed Canadian Alliance party. His personal beliefs attracted intense media attention and much public discussion. For some, the thought of Day wielding power in Parliament raised the spectre of the worst excesses, real and imagined, of the American religious right.

Political considerations aside, I welcomed the public discussion that Day's arrival occasioned. I gave more interviews about the relationship between faith and politics in the wake of Day's election than ever before. Yet as a United Church minister who had been in Parliament for over 20 years when Day arrived, I was a bit mystified by the sudden attention the religious beliefs of Canadian politicians were getting.

What was right or what was wrong with my own faith-based politics, I wondered, that they had caused so little offence all those years? Indeed, why is all the attention given to certain religious beliefs of certain Canadian politicians? Why isn't the attention more universal? Or is the attention given to certain views the tip of the iceberg of hostility to any expression of religion in politics that should be of concern to all people of faith?

In an October 2006 issue of the Canadian magazine *The Walrus*, the cover headline was "Jesus in the House." The feature story, entitled "Stephen Harper and the Theo-cons: The Rising Clout of Canada's Religious Right," raised concerns about the influence of the Christian right on the Harper government. Around the same time, an article entitled "Called into the House: Why Christians Are in Ottawa," appeared in *Faith Today*, the magazine of the Evangelical Fellowship of Canada. In it, I was described as bristling at the current Canadian controversy about mixing politics and religion: "What am I? Chopped liver? We've been mixing politics and religion on the left for a long time."

I was glad to be interviewed for the *Faith Today* article, and glad to be counted among the sheep and not the goats. Too often both magazines, though hardly similar in any other respect, are alike in noticing or naming as Christians only those who fit a certain stereotype. Left-leaning Christians sometimes have a hard time even being acknowledged as Christians.

After the 2006 election, *Christian Week*, an evangelical Canadian weekly newspaper, published an article called "Christian Candidates Prepare to Serve Ottawa." I looked in vain for any reference to me or any other New Democrat.

Even those NDP members of Parliament whose strong Catholic commitment and involvement in their church had been highlighted in the media in the aftermath of the same-sex marriage vote, along with the various ways their parishes and bishops had reacted to their vote, did not merit recognition as Christians.

As much as I welcomed the chance to explain how my own political and religious beliefs were connected, the media frenzy and public debate that surrounded Day's faith were curiously unfocused. Too much of the discussion centred on whether having strongly held religious views should disqualify a person from political service. For his part, though he stood accused of a host of sins, ranging from theocratic ambition to creationist naïveté, Day himself never seemed to feel the need to give an account of how his faith informed his politics. In fact, the debate largely ignored what should have been the central question about him or anyone else who professes a connection between their politics and their faith perspective: What exactly did his political stance have to do with his religious convictions, and how did one flow from the other?

Stockwell Day eventually fell on better political times. His political life was redeemed and he developed a reputation as a competent and relatively non-controversial cabinet minister, before he retired in 2011. I will also always remember with appreciation the personal phone call that I received from him when my mother died in June 2008. But as a Christian who is a Conservative, and as a conservative Christian, he unintentionally became the poster boy of a stereotype that misleads Canadians by suggesting that Christian politics can be of only one sort.

———

In my first five years in the House of Commons, 1979 to 1984, I worked with five other Christian clergy in the NDP caucus: fellow United Church ministers Stanley Knowles and Jim Manly, Roman Catholic priests Bob Ogle and Andy Hogan, and Anglican priest Dan Heap. Other lay members of caucus also saw themselves in continuity with the social gospel tradition of Tommy Douglas and J.S. Woodsworth, which had contributed to the formation of first the Co-operative Commonwealth Federation and then the New Democratic Party.

When I was first elected in 1979, the same election brought to Parliament the NDP candidate in Saskatoon East, Father Bob Ogle, who became a dear friend and colleague. Ogle became the party's Health Critic and I was the Social Policy Critic. We did some touring together across the country to meet with various groups, and the press dubbed us the God Squad.

Our tour had a particularly humble, or humbling, beginning. The press conference to announce it was held in room 130 in the basement of the Centre Block, where press conferences are often still held. It was the first such event for both Ogle and me, and we were anticipating the challenge of answering questions with some nervousness. All for naught. No one from the media showed up. We were humbled, and perplexed. All subsequent press conferences have had to meet a very low bar in order to be deemed a relative success. Later on room 130 would have broadcasters' pool cameras covering the event, so that even unattended press conferences would still be covered electronically. It is surely something close to theatre to speak to an empty room like someone is there, just in case someone is watching through the camera from somewhere else. Although come to think of it, speaking in the House of Commons can be like that on occasion.

Later that day we learned that our press conference had been scheduled at exactly the same time that the details of legendary parliamentarian and former Tory prime minister John Diefenbaker's estate were being revealed across town. We learned a lesson about timing that day. Diefenbaker had died in mid-August of 1979. I was a colleague of his in the 31st Parliament, but I never sat in the House with him, which I regretted. Sidling up to Dief for a chat in the chamber would have been an enviable opportunity. As it was, I only saw him once after my election, in the parliamentary restaurant. Not long after that, in mid-August, his funeral train was to be crossing the country on the way to Saskatoon and I was offered an NDP spot on the train. I turned it down because my family and I were still very much in a state of acute mourning for my 20-year-old brother Bobby, who had been killed on his motorcycle on August 4. The train would have been a memorable event, and no doubt a source of some good political storytelling. As time passes, the political junkie in me sometimes second-guesses the decision to pass on the opportunity. Diefenbaker's seat went to the NDP candidate Stan Hovdebo in a subsequent by-election. Hovdebo had run in the general election in May, and was only in the House for a week or so after the by-election when he was back on the campaign trail for the third time in less than a year. He served the people of Prince Albert, Saskatchewan, until 1993.

At the time that Ogle and I went on our tour, the moniker God Squad was used in an affectionate way. Twenty years later there were groups of MPs who, because of their combination of conservative faith and conservative politics, were also referred to as the God Squad. But the term was used with a kind of derision or hostility. The transition of this phrase from affectionate nickname to negative epithet is indicative of what has happened to the relationship between faith and politics over that period of time.

Father Bob Ogle died in 1999. We had a strong connection, born out of our common faith and common political commitment, but also out of a common connection in Saskatchewan. He grew up near Rosetown, a town not far from Biggar, Saskatchewan, where my dad grew up, and knew a nearby Scottish family that the Blaikies visited on occasion.

Ogle had been a missionary in Brazil, six years that changed his life and created in him a strong commitment to justice for what was then often called the developing world. He served on the North/South Parliamentary Task Force, authored an autobiography titled *North/South Calling*, and finished his life trying to establish Broadcasting for International Understanding, a non-profit attempt to get more information about global realities into the media. One of Ogle's pet peeves was the way the national news often told viewers what was happening with the stock market or the gross domestic product, as if they were the only important indicators—or, given the realities they hid or omitted, as if they were important at all.

If Ogle had had his way, viewers would also be regularly reminded of how many kids were dying of preventable diseases, or of how much money was being made or spent on the arms race that could have been spent on food and water for the hungry and thirsty of the world. Bob Ogle had a talent for storytelling and compelling images. He memorably compared the nuclear arms race to two guys up to their knees in gasoline. One guy has one match, the other has two. The guy with two matches thinks he's safe.

Our common faith, however, did not extend to a common view of ecclesial authority. When he was told by the Vatican that he could not run for re-election in 1984, I suggested that he should run anyway, especially given that in his own interpretation of canon law it was up to his bishop, who had given him permission. Ogle said to me, "Blaikie, that's what I would expect from a heathen United Church guy like you." He chose not to run. He was a priest, and he was obedient. I guess you could say that I came from the same school of disobedience as Tommy Douglas. The story is told of how Douglas, a Baptist minister, did not really make up his mind to run for Parliament in the election of 1935 until his superiors in the church told him not to.

I was angry that Canada was losing one of the best MPs we ever had.

I was angrier still that the papal directive had its origins in opposition to the political role that some priests were playing in Central America, priests like Miguel D'Escoto, the Minister of Foreign Affairs in the Sandinista government of Nicaragua who many years later would become President of the General Assembly of the United Nations. And I was puzzled. I had admired Pope John Paul II for the support he had given to Solidarity, the free Polish trade union movement led by Lech Wałęsa that in the 1980s successfully challenged the country's authoritarian communist government.

Many of those involved in Solidarity were confident that what they were doing was living out their Catholic faith, and that their struggle had the blessing of the Holy Father. This was clearly a mix of religion and politics that found favour in Rome. Indeed, one Polish priest was killed by the regime for his activities. Add to this the 1981 papal encyclical *Laborem Exercens*—On Human Work, which was profoundly critical of capitalism, and telling Father Bob to stop being an NDP MP just did not add up for me.

I was anxious to see and hear the Pope when he came to Winnipeg in June 1984. The event was at Birds Hill Provincial Park, just outside my then-riding of Winnipeg–Birds Hill. In the end, I was discouraged from attending, as were others, by the exaggerated predictions of how crowded it would be. Fortunately for me, earlier that week I had had a conversation with Father Fred Olds, priest at Blessed Sacrament parish in my constituency, in which I told him of my plans to go see the Pope. Father Fred was commenting on the event for CJOB, one of the most listened to radio stations in Winnipeg, and innocently probably did me a great political favour when he told listeners that he knew his MP Bill Blaikie was somewhere out there in the crowd. The only other time I remember being of a mind to go hear a visiting religious celebrity of such stature was when I went to hear Billy Graham when I was about 16.

The God Squad that Bob Ogle and I represented was perhaps patronized, to a degree, as idealistic, mushy headed, think-the-world-can-be-a-better-place kind of people whose lack of realism was to be tolerated. The more recent kind of God Squad is seen as authoritarian, judgmental, and out of sync with the times. The paragraph on the token lefty in the Christian crowd in the House in the *Faith Today* article ended by posing the question why there is so much more controversy when the mix is on the right. But the question was left unexplored. The task for the faithful politician is to sort out the two God Squads, and articulate a third kind that is challenging for the right reasons.

———

The spectrum of Christian belief in Canada is much more varied than the furor over the religious right suggests. There are conservative Christians on the political left and liberal Christians on the right, and various combinations in between. People are often more flexible in their politics than their pastors or churches are. Once, having been invited to an evangelical congregation in my riding, I was pleasantly surprised when I looked out from the pulpit to see many folks who had put up signs for me in the last election. I also had Catholic families tell me not to worry about the Liberal or Conservative sign on their lawn—it was there to please their priest, but on election day the secret ballot would be cast for me. Similarly, despite the alignment between United Church policy and most NDP policy, many United Church people vote Liberal or Conservative.

Another time that stereotypes were usefully smashed for me was when I was invited to address a Pentecostal congregation that was meeting in a local school. I went with some trepidation, but with a determination to give a full account of how I thought the gospel called Christians to a life of fighting for social and economic justice. I need not have worried. This congregation consisted of Caribbean Canadian Christians who had no trouble relating to such an understanding of the Christian life. They were no strangers to injustice or discrimination. The chorus of amens that accompanied my various pronouncements was inspiring. I still await this kind of enthusiastic feedback from United Church congregations. What I experienced with that congregation was similar, though not identical, to the combination of theological conservatism, evangelical fervour, and prophetic justice-seeking religion that can be found in the African American Christian tradition.

Even what passes for the secular may be the product of religion. Roger Hutchinson, former principal of the United Church's Emmanuel College in Toronto, properly argues that the liberal consensus on many social issues is a product not just of secular politics, but of years of action in the public domain by mainstream churches and associated Christian activists. What today passes for secular consensus is partly a consequence of previous religious influence in the public realm.

Not long ago, many political speeches were peppered with references to a Christian society—what it should look like and what its obligations should be. Former CCF and NDP leaders like M.J. Coldwell and Tommy Douglas used such language frequently in the mid-20th century. Increasingly, though, the public realm is not a particularly welcoming place for explicit Christian discourse, no matter what the theology.

Nor is it generally welcoming of other religions. Interestingly, an exception is sometimes made for Aboriginal religion. When the Constitution was patriated in 1982, conferences on Aboriginal rights were committed to. At one of these conferences, Prime Minister Trudeau did an unusual thing. The Aboriginal leadership began each conference day with prayers to the Creator. One morning, after the Aboriginal prayers, Pierre Trudeau broke with the usual pattern and, instead of proceeding with the conference, recited the Lord's Prayer. This was around the same time, incidentally, of Trudeau's rebuke to the Canadian Conference of Catholic Bishops for its bold pronouncements on the injustices in the economy; he had joined with the business community in telling the bishops to butt out.

By the 1980s, Canada was well into the secular, multicultural, and pluralistic society that Trudeau himself had been so instrumental in defining. Alongside that definition, the privatization of religion and culture had rapidly accelerated. Religion and ethnicity could be acknowledged and even celebrated, individually and collectively. But preferably that was to happen in the private sphere under an overarching secular umbrella, and eventually, under the values entrenched into the Canadian Charter of Rights and Freedoms. Religion was to be particularly private. God remained in the Constitution, or had even been added to the Constitution at that time, but the less said about God the better.

The Aboriginal leaders, by beginning with prayers, ignored this privatization of religion and insisted on ceremonially integrating their religious consciousness with the political tasks at hand. It seemed to irritate Trudeau. Many years later, he would be eulogized as one with a profound Catholic faith. Trudeau's pique may have foreshadowed a later time, now partly arrived, in which people from many perspectives would long for a world where their religious consciousness could be liberated from the purely private realm. And not only liberated, but also validated, in a context where diverse religious viewpoints can be publicly confessed or even debated without feeling that one is breaking a taboo.

––––––––––

Given the historical influence of religion on Canadian life and the continuing presence of Christianity and other religions, it is essential to find an appropriate way for believers to publicly express their faith in the midst of a secular society. Religion is not an evolutionary curiosity or a vestigial clue to a less-enlightened past. Nietzsche is dead; God isn't. For many, religion is an inspiration that instructs, sustains, and nourishes daily life.

It is impossible—and, in my opinion, undesirable—to banish religion from the public or political spheres. Yet the interface between faith and politics is different in the 21st century, much different than it was in the world of the early social gospel a century ago, and different even than it was 25 years ago. A contemporary pluralist vision would allow religious voices to speak authentically in public life, without implying undue deference to religious authority.

Religion should not be treated preferentially, but neither should there be a negative prejudice against it on principle. There can be a positive, mutually beneficial relationship between faith and politics. And this relationship should not give offence to those who truly wish to broaden the conversation.

Affirming a relationship between faith and politics is not the same as affirming any kind of relationship between religion and the state. In Canada there is no state religion, and in the United States, the disestablishment clause in the constitution forbids one. But too often discussions about faith and politics are dismissed out of hand by some uncritical assertion about the need for separation of church and state. The separation of church and state is a good idea. However, it was designed to protect religion, not eliminate it. Freedom of religion, too, was intended to protect religion, not morph into freedom *from* religion.

People will come to politics with some view of what is ultimately real and true, about the universe and about human existence. No doctrine about church and state should keep us from reflecting on how such views can be properly incorporated into political debate. Religious faith rightly has a role in shaping political values and the policies that flow from them.

The Social Gospel

God is as concerned with the world and with
justice in the here and now, as with the eternal
salvation of individual souls.

What is this social gospel that has so influenced the Canadian left? The
subject's pre-eminent scholar is Richard Allen, the author of *The Social Passion*,
who practised a faith-inspired politics of his own. He became a provincial
NDP cabinet minister in the 1990–95 Ontario legislature, and has recently
completed *The View from Murney Tower*, a lengthy biography of Salem Bland,
the controversial early-20th-century Winnipeg theologian of the social gospel.
Allen writes of the social gospel as a distinct historical period extending from
the 1890s to the 1930s. But the social gospel continues to this day as an
inspiration and an approach to faithful politics.

The social gospel is a name for the vision of all those who, out of their
Christian faith, perceived and articulated the need for fundamental changes
in the capitalist world view and in capitalism itself. Not all of them were
socialists per se, but they held many social justice ideals in common.

Social gospellers shared a profound belief that the ideology of competition
is a lie about the nature of a truly human society. They rejected the profit
motive as a sanctification of vice and a recipe for exploitation. They rejected
the concentration of incredible economic powers in the hands of a commercial
corporate minority, and saw the challenge to our democratic self-image and to

individual freedom that it posed. They shared a belief in the value of economic co-operation as the true expression of our life together. And, in their belief in the necessity of co-operation, not merely its desirability, they were realists about the need for structural restraints on human selfishness.

Social gospellers continue to seek not only to minister to the immediate needs of victims of injustice but to eliminate the causes of injustice as well. They believe that God is as concerned with the world and with justice in the here and now, as with the eternal salvation of individual souls.

However one may decide to speak today out of the social gospel tradition, it is historically the case that something called the social gospel informed and informs the political left in Canada. This was recently reaffirmed in a book by Ian McKay of Queen's University. In a chapter of *Rebels, Reds, Radicals* devoted to "redefining the left" in Canada, he names spiritual awakening and the social gospel as one of several paths to leftist politics in Canada. He also points out the discomfort of many on the secular left when confronted with the fact that "many leftists in Canada have been believers, rooting their resistance to capitalism in religious values."

That discomfort is part of the larger process by which the Christian left has become far less visible over the last 25 years, while the Christian right has come to be the dominant public face of both Christianity and Christian politics. Even the global celebrity status of Pope John Paul II (from 1978 to 2005) conformed to this paradigm; it was only his conservative views that attracted attention, not his critiques of capitalism, capital punishment, or the invasion of Iraq. This analysis is even more true in the United States. And it should be a matter of concern, not just to Christians on the left, but to other progressives who want their way of looking at things advanced.

In a time when religion is largely characterized in the political arena as a conservative force, we need both to diversify the face of religion in the political realm and to reclaim territory that was once held in common by religion and the left. We need to re-establish in the public mind that there are faith-informed progressive perspectives on a variety of issues. There is not only a debate between faith and non-faith. Often what is really going on is a debate among Canadians of the same faith, or a debate between conservative faith communities and a secular liberalism that owes its values in part to Christianity.

Faith should be associated in the public mind with a diverse group of people who, though they may share particular beliefs, arrive at different conclusions about contentious public policy issues and, as a result, support different parties or argue within political parties about these issues. Thirty years ago, I was focused on infusing my fellow Christians with the need for democratic socialism. Today, I find myself focusing on a need for left-wingers to appreciate the importance of a Christian tradition different from that of the high-profile right, a tradition that should not disappear from the narrative of the left.

It is not in the best interests of Canadians to have religion caricatured as narrowly focused on only a few issues or, even worse, to have "faith" or "religious argument" come to be seen as inadmissible in public discourse about public policy options. Questions of peace and war, the economy, and the environment are also issues to be informed by faith. But the task, for both the faithful and for non-believers, is to discern appropriate ways of speaking in an explicitly faith-informed way in the public square. A fundamentalist secularism is not the answer either: dismissing views purely because they are "religious" throws out the wheat with the chaff. Fundamental beliefs—whether secular or religious—will inevitably inform one's political views.

One reason that the left in Canada has been as successful as it has, whether in forming or in influencing governments, is that historically Canadians would often hear in what the left was saying the practical expression of what they heard from scripture and from their church's teachings on Sunday mornings. Nor should we forget the key role in the civil rights movement played by religious leaders like Martin Luther King. In a post-Christendom context, this resonance may be more difficult to achieve, but the Christian left and centre must not abandon the public square to a brawl between secular fundamentalists and the religious right.

Probably the most famous of all Canadian social gospellers is J.S. Woodsworth, the first leader of the Co-operative Commonwealth Federation, the political predecessor of the NDP. An early influence on Woodsworth was Walter Rauschenbusch, whose time as a minister serving the needs of the poor in New York City's Hell's Kitchen led him to a new appreciation of the gospel as a call for transformation of the here and now. As his great-grandson Paul Rauschenbusch wrote in the 100th-anniversary edition of Rauschenbusch's

Christianity and the Social Crisis, first published in 1907, Walter Rauschenbusch saw that Jesus wanted a world based on love, service, and equality. Jesus's disciples could not do otherwise than set themselves against a system, such as capitalism, that was based on coercion, exploitation, and inequality.

Rauschenbusch's seminal *A Theology for the Social Gospel*, based on a series of lectures he gave in April 1917, articulates the basic tenets that came to be associated with the movement. In the chapter on "The Super-personal Forces of Evil," Rauschenbusch presciently describes the current corporate model of globalization:

> Predatory profit or graft, when once its sources are opened up and developed, constitutes an almost overwhelming temptation to combinations of men. Its pursuit gives them cohesion and unity of mind, capacity to resist common dangers, and an outfit of moral and political principles which will justify their anti-social activities.

Rauschenbusch cites numerous groups down through history that have extorted their fellow human beings in this way and notices, correctly, that such groups tend to resist political liberty and social justice. As he says, "liberty and justice do away with unearned incomes." He saw the solution as the creation of "righteous institutions to prevent temptation," institutions that would seek to redeem the "sinfulness of the social order" that had to take a "share" in the sins of all individuals within it. The word *share* is significant here. It wasn't, at least for Rauschenbusch, a simple question of social determinism; individual responsibility plays an important part. What he called "the lust for easy and unearned gain" had to be contained.

In the wake of the Great Depression, and in the post–Second World War economy, it is fair to say that many "righteous institutions" were established, at least in the so-called developed world. They aimed to prevent temptation, to inhibit exploitation, and to protect most people from predatory profiteering of the worst kind. Such measures went hand in hand with others designed to promote equality and to empower the powerless. Social gospellers worked alongside trade unionists, farmers, activists on the intellectual left, humanists, and Canadians from other religious traditions. For example, David Lewis, a key figure in the building of the CCF and leader of the NDP from 1971 to 1975, credits in his autobiography the inspiration of the Jewish Bund, an Eastern European socialist movement that had been founded in the late 1800s.

So it was that in Canada by the 1970s we had achieved our own unique, though partial, version of the world that social gospellers dreamed of. It was also in the 1970s that capital, in the form of powerful corporate forces, began to rebel against the postwar social contract and its righteous institutions.

In the postwar era, Canada had enacted child labour laws, and many other labour laws, to regulate the relationship between employers and workers, establishing collective bargaining as a right and promoting workplace safety and health.

We built kindergartens, and schools, and a public education system that provided opportunities previously unavailable to working people.

We brought many necessary utilities under public control in the fields of transportation, communication, energy, automobile insurance, and water.

We developed orderly marketing systems in many sectors to take the cruel rough-and-tumble out of the marketplace for primary producers.

We created a relatively progressive tax system in which, at one time, the corporate sector paid a much larger share of the tax load than it does now.

We put in place a public pension system and a family allowance system, whose cornerstone was the concept of universality: the important symbolic and practical insight that some social benefits ought to come to us because we are members of the community, not because we are charity cases.

We enshrined the notion that foreign investment should have to show how it would benefit the community.

We had housing policies that made good housing affordable for most, and homelessness unknown.

We enacted generic drug legislation that speeded up affordable access to new drugs.

And last but certainly not least, because we have done it better here than almost anywhere else, we took health care out of the marketplace with the establishment of medicare.

All this was done, largely by the nation-state, in the context of a Cold War where a certain economic stability prevailed in the West under the umbrella of the Bretton Woods agreement, a postwar international financial management agreement by which the money-changers, if not driven out of the temple, were at least held in check. Today the money-changers have been set loose upon the world with a vengeance, and are just the latest stage in a process that has brought down or is bringing down all the "righteous institutions" that the social gospel helped to create.

In the Canadian context, it is instructive to remember that a more just world was created not by ideas alone, but by political action. It is no coincidence that many of the things I have listed as accomplishments of the postwar era—

notably medicare—had their decisive moments when the CCF, or later the NDP, held the balance of power in Parliament, were threatening to form a federal government, or pioneered changes when they did take power at the provincial level.

This world that I am describing was the world I wanted to improve on when I first ran for office in 1979. For all its achievements, it was still a very imperfect world. On the environment, justice for Aboriginal peoples, and the nuclear arms race, for example, it cried out for redemption in new ways.

Walter Rauschenbusch talked about the social gospel as a form of "expectation." This sense of expectation distinguished earlier generations of social gospellers: history was on their side. They might be ahead of their time, but with education, economic growth, and assorted other things associated with progress, the world would eventually conform to their views. Not for them the gloomy critique of modernity, of the consumer society, technology, and growth, of reason itself and its ability to save. They were not bothered by nightmares about ecological disaster and global climate change. There were setbacks, but they were setbacks on the way to ultimate victory.

The spirit of optimism and progress that characterized the social gospel came together in the ecumenical movement of the early 20th century. Leaders of the movement decided that the 20th century would be Christianized. Though the First World War represented a failure of modern civilization and of 19th-century optimism, hope persisted nonetheless.

In 1925, the union of the Methodist, Congregationalist, and Local Union Churches and 70 percent of the Presbyterian Church in Canada was formalized. Proponents of the social gospel saw the formation of The United Church of Canada as a big step toward Christianizing the social order. Essential to this hope for some was the national character of the United Church, a new uniting and truly Canadian church that provided a way to reach all Canadians.

These social goals were political in their implications, and through the creation of the CCF in 1933, the left wing of the new national church and the social gospel found a political ally in Ottawa. But even as the political successes of the social gospel accumulated, the theology of the social gospel faced harsh criticism. From neo-orthodox theologians such as Reinhold Niebuhr came the critique that the self-righteous hopes of the 19th century needed to be tempered by a renewed sense of human limitations. Further, the pacifism associated with elements of the social gospel was seen as especially unrealistic, and as evidence of an inability to appreciate the ambiguities of historical existence and, particularly, the moral ambiguity of collective human behaviour.

Early in his life, Niebuhr had embraced the enthusiasm of American left-liberal Protestants for Eugene Debs's Socialist Party. Later Niebuhr was the chief articulator of a critique of the left, forged in the context of the need to deal with Nazi Germany, that came to be known as Christian realism. Yet according to biographer Richard Fox, by the end of his life, Niebuhr regretted the way in which Christian realism was being used and abused to justify the Vietnam War, a form of American *realpolitik* that he ultimately rejected. There is, after all, a difference between realism and nihilism.

Domestically, the social gospel was accused of an unrealistic demand that our economic and social life reflect the law of love. The concept of justice was demoted from the concrete expression of love to a secondary, more pragmatic order that one worked toward by balancing power with power, and doing as best as one could within the prevailing liberal paradigm.

To me, the claim that the social gospel lacked an appreciation for the full depth and scope of human sinfulness is largely unfair. The social gospel saw that sin was not just an individual reality, but a social reality, and it had to be responded to socially as well as individually. The social gospel saw that those who longed for the kingdom of God contended with powers and principalities as well as with flesh and blood. Thus, it could be argued that it recaptured a fuller and more biblical sense of the reality of sin than had generally been the case for many years.

Many social gospellers saw a connection between war and capitalism, even those who were not pacifists on absolute principle. They saw that wars are not the outcome of momentary, unoriginated decisions by evil people or their evil leaders, but are often the outcome of exploitative and competitive international economic and political relationships in which all nations are culpable. The social gospel was ahead of its critics in its appreciation and identification of sin, the tragedy of the human condition rather than its perfectibility, and the underlying geopolitical realities of conflicts too often only dressed up as matters of principle.

———

The social gospel ran into difficulty and division when the Second World War broke out, as it had in the context of the First World War. The reality of war challenged national loyalties, and in 1939, the pacifism of even the most stout pacifists, when they were confronted with the radical evil of Nazism. Speaking of stout pacifists, J.S. Woodsworth was at odds with the rest of his caucus when he was the lone voice against the declaration of war in the House of Commons on September 10, 1939. Though the war was a tragedy in which both sides were not without historical fault, one side certainly held out exceedingly more positive possibilities for humanity than the other. Yet many still found it difficult to take a hard look at the war and its immediate causes and make a decision. What was absent was a political theology that would be less vulnerable to easy caricature and criticism as wishful moralistic thinking.

The theology of Dietrich Bonhoeffer and the Confessing Church in Nazi Germany would prove fertile. Many Christians were looking for a theology that would enable them to make choices in difficult historical contexts, to take sides, to be prophetic as well as pastoral toward their neighbours and their nation. Bonhoeffer, who was ultimately executed for taking sides against Hitler, wrote of the need for Christian political choices to be both provisional and concrete. Provisional choices remain open to change, to the instruction of experience, context, praxis, and failure. But the choices must be concrete; uttering general principles isn't good enough.

The gospel, said Bonhoeffer, becomes concretized in the ears of the hearer. You either hear the good news of the forgiveness of sins or you do not. But the command, what you are to do with the freedom of the gospel, can only become concrete if it is related to the real possibilities of the here and now. The church cannot just say, for instance, "War is bad, but some wars are necessary." Rather, it must say, "Participate in this particular war" or "Do not participate in it." The church cannot just say that it is wrong for people to starve, but then say nothing definite about what form a solution might take. It must, according to Bonhoeffer, dare to say things like "now be socialists" when that's what the situation calls for.

Living from the same forgiveness of sins, individual Christians can make provisional political choices in given historical situations. Christians can choose to be in solidarity, sympathetically but self-critically, with historical movements that work for a world in which the fellowship intended by God for human life is more fully realized, and where the injustice done to the poor and the powerless is overcome. Social gospellers were Christians who made the choice to take sides, to be associated in various ways and to different degrees with the democratic opposition to and critique of capitalism, and with the dream of the world articulated in the Magnificat of Mary (Luke 1:46–55), where the arrival of Jesus is praised and welcomed as the scattering of the proud, the putting down of the mighty, the exalting of those of low degree, the filling of the hungry, and the sending of the rich away empty.

Twentieth-century Swiss theologian Karl Barth's view that all human endeavours are relative is sometimes cited to devalue a commitment to political life, somewhat in the same way as Niebuhr was used against the social gospel. But that's a misunderstanding of his position. Barth, a democratic socialist, is said to have observed that a preacher should always preach with the Bible in one hand and the newspaper in the other. Rather than devalue political action, Barth's theology frees us up to engage in politics *as politics*. We are freed to participate in a fully human activity in which political commitments, because they are distinguished from religious commitments, are able to be provisional.

Many critics of socialism oppose it not on socialism's merits but because their ideological commitments have taken on a religious dimension to such an extent that they are not able to consider the socialist political option without feeling like an apostate. Religious socialists can make a similar mistake. When a concrete historical expression of the socialist hope—a specific political party, for example—falls far from perfection, they immediately disassociate themselves from the movement and seek higher ground. It would be better to persist, according to Barth, because as inadequate as any particular movements might be, they still want what Jesus wants. Papal encyclicals grant Roman Catholics this freedom to engage in politics. They may support particular socialist movements as long as they do not embrace a total world view. That is to say, as long as they continue to make a distinction—not a separation, but a distinction—between their faith and their politics.

Critics of capitalism see the disparities that capitalism creates and express the same passion of Jesus against this inequity. This is not crass materialism, as some would have us believe, unless they wish to say of Jesus, too, that he was a despicable materialist because he wanted the hungry to be fed and the naked clothed. It is a materialism that wishes a life abundant that enables each person to pursue the higher goals of creativity, self-fulfillment, mutual love, and respect for creation that are possible within real community.

CHAPTER

3

Culture Wars

I was often caught in the middle, wishing for
the kind of certainty that others seemed to possess
·in such abundance.

Early one Sunday morning, two days before my first federal election on May
22, 1979, I was awakened by my campaign organizer, Ron Bailey. He wanted
me to know that church parking lots in the riding were being visited by pro-
life activists. On every windshield, tucked under a wiper, was a pamphlet
urging people to vote for my opponent, Dean Whiteway. "Stop the Slaughter,"
screamed the pamphlet. Vote for Dean Whiteway, who will "continue to fight
for the lives of these babies," not for Bill Blaikie, who will "vote to continue
aborting unborn children."

Whiteway was the Progressive Conservative MP I was running against. In
the federal election of 1972, he had come close to unseating Doug Rowland,
the NDP MP for the riding of Selkirk, which stretched all the way from
suburban northeast Winnipeg to towns like Gimli in Manitoba's Interlake
region. Whiteway never stopped campaigning during the minority Parliament
of 1972–74, and in 1974 he won the riding. In 1979 boundary redistribution
forced him to choose between running in the newly created and totally
suburban riding of Winnipeg–Birds Hill or in the northern, rural part of his
old riding. He chose the former, which now included Transcona, where I was
the NDP challenger.

Whiteway was the kind of conservative who would be a prime candidate for recruitment into the Reform Party in the early 1990s. He was pro-life, pro–capital punishment, a critic of bilingualism, unions, and deficits, and a born-again Christian. And indeed, he actually did become a Reform candidate in 1993, running against his fellow evangelical Christian Jake Epp in the riding of Provencher. Epp, a Progressive Conservative first elected in 1972, had the misfortune of seeing the wisdom of a parliamentary compromise on the abortion law after the Supreme Court decision in 1989 struck down the law that had existed since 1969. For this, Epp would experience in his local faith community the kind of self-righteous questioning of his identity as a Christian that one might say was normally reserved for United Church ministers.

Running against Dean Whiteway, I had hoped for a grand theological debate over the politics that flowed from the biblical tradition. But it didn't happen, a foreshadowing of a strange reluctance I would often encounter on the part of evangelical Christians to make a biblical argument for their politics, instead of just acting like the biblical grounding of their politics was self-evident. In any event, I will never forget arriving on the Hill right after the 1979 election, and seeking Whiteway out. I found him in his office packing boxes and looking quite dejected, and at that moment, I felt bad about winning. Whiteway asked if I would feel all right about prayer, which I did, and he prayed for me as I started my new life in Ottawa. It was not the last time that I would feel that the demonization of the Christian right by the left was somehow off the mark—but seeing so many fine people on the Christian left constantly demonized by the Christian right generally kept the emotion of such moments to a minimum. At last report, Whiteway had become the principal of a private Christian school in the United States.

I was outraged at being demonized that Sunday morning in 1979. The pro-life people had not even talked to me; they had been told that I had argued for easier access to abortion. I had actually argued for more-equal access to legal abortions for all Manitoba women, especially those in remote areas where a therapeutic abortion committee was not available. For a group that called themselves non-partisan, it all seemed pretty partisan to me. To my great relief, their campaign seemed to backfire in my case, especially at my home church, Transcona Memorial United Church. Many people at Transcona Memorial told me, or my mother, who was very active in the United Church

Women, that they had not firmed up their intention to vote for me until they saw the pro-life literature. They knew that I was no baby killer. And they wanted no part of any campaign that said I was.

The counterproductivity of such tactics continues to be lost on certain anti-abortion activists. As recently as October 2007, some of them threatened to picket a Catholic Conference on Faith and Justice in Winnipeg because I was one of the invited speakers. They also objected to James Loney speaking at the conference—and succeeded in getting him uninvited. Loney, a gay man and one of four peace activists taken hostage in Iraq in 2005, had been invited to speak about peace, but because of his open disagreement with his church on homosexuality, his invitation was revoked at the last minute by the Archbishop of Winnipeg, the Rev. James Weisgerber.

This provided a fleeting opportunity for "gotcha" journalism. My invitation had not been revoked. Would I now boycott the conference to protest what had happened to Loney, or did I not care enough about the issue? Fortunately, I had met Loney when he and I were speakers at the first workshop of the NDP Faith and Justice Committee, so I simply called him and asked what he thought I should do. My inclination was to go anyway, and that was also his advice to me. When I mentioned this conversation to inquiring reporters they had a tendency to look disappointed and change the subject.

So, with Loney's blessing, I went ahead. Earlier that month I had spoken to the Forum on Ecumenical Dialogue sponsored by the Canadian Council of Churches about the challenges of Christian diversity in doing public theology. The conference James Loney could not attend was another occasion to reflect on how badly Christians deal with diversity among themselves on particular issues. The picketers, however, never showed.

As a candidate in 1979 I had not given much thought to abortion as a religious or a political issue. In the inner-city ministry in which I was active, we were preoccupied with the well-being of children after they were born. Politically I was focused on such issues as the inordinate power of the multinational corporations, the environment, justice for Aboriginal Canadians, and the abolition of nuclear weapons. Abortion had not been on my personal or political radar, something I suppose could be criticized by pro-life and pro-choice advocates alike.

One thing is for sure. With the pamphlets on that Sunday morning in 1979, I had been rudely introduced to what have been called the culture wars, culture wars that would use up a lot of political oxygen for decades. These wars would most obviously be fought over reproductive issues, over sexual orientation, over marriage, over end-of-life issues, over stem cell research. The culture wars were also about questions of crime and punishment, most notably, early in my parliamentary life, about the question of capital punishment. Later they would be about the nature and severity of sentencing. I embraced the view that the solution was to be as tough on the causes of crime as on crime itself. But the argument for prevention is always the harder argument to make, even if it is the right one, because it does not have the air of urgency about it that comes with dealing with known criminals. Those who are saved from a life of crime are very seldom known by name, and quantifiable. And, although it is really in a category all by itself, a different kind of culture war would be fought over gun control and the long-gun registry.

———

The challenge in reflecting on these issues is to sort out the nature of the disagreement as experienced by decent folks on both sides, while at the same time being clear about how the issues are manipulated for political purposes to get people to vote for an agenda or a political party that they would otherwise keep their distance from. This was certainly the case in the United States. The culture wars there enabled the political right to win all kinds of votes from blue-collar and working-class voters whose economic and social well-being would be devastated by free market fundamentalism and globalization. Those workers' well-paying jobs would be exported to cheap labour markets in the name of competition, which is often just another name for higher profits at the expense of the unemployment of your fellow citizens.

So far, Canadian versions of this political phenomenon have played out on a smaller scale. In the 2006 election, a survey by Ipsos Reid suggested that the vote of evangelical Christians and Catholics who attend church weekly was a deciding factor, no doubt largely motivated by the debate over same-sex marriage, in the election of the Conservative minority. In the 2008 election, these voters may still have voted the same way, but they would have had a right to feel disappointed, and to some degree used and misled.

Despite having deliberately gathered votes from those against same-sex marriage in 2006, the government's strategy was to have a vote early in that Parliament on whether to revisit the issue. Parliament voted not to, and this is one parliamentary decision that we can expect Prime Minister Harper to respect. Why? Because he knows, and he knew when he was pretending otherwise, that the issue had already been decided by the courts and by the reality of the hundreds of same-sex couples already married. Using the notwithstanding clause of the Constitution to declare the married unmarried is not really on. Especially when the ban would have to be renewed every five years.

Another interesting decision in the 2006–08 Parliament was Justice Minister Rob Nicholson's decision to disown Alberta Tory Ken Epp's private member's bill C-484, which, in the event that a pregnant woman is killed, would have required an unborn child to be treated as a person for the purpose of a double murder charge. Although the bill was not technically about abortion, it was seen to be. Support for it, or opposition to it, mirrored the two sides of the established abortion debate. Nicholson's decision came at a time when the pro-life movement was once again demonstrating a capacity for tactics unclouded by better judgment by going ballistic about the appointment of Dr. Henry Morgentaler to the Order of Canada. Whatever one's position on the abortion issue, it seems to me that recognizing a doctor who has been willing to go to jail for providing what he saw as a fundamental women's health service is not entirely out of order.

The decision on Epp's bill was significant, and it was more than just a tactic on Nicholson's part. It seemed to reflect a judgment by the Conservatives that a debate about abortion in Canada, even of a vicarious nature, was not only not in their political interest but also could probably not be won in any event. The pro-life political base would have to be satisfied in some other way, as it was in 2010 when Prime Minister Harper's global plan for better maternal health ruled out support for abortions in other countries.

In the debate over abortion, as in other debates that fell into the general category of the culture wars, I was often caught in the middle, wishing for the kind of certainty that others seemed to possess in such abundance. Yet the word *middle* does not do justice to my experience. It wasn't just a question of trying to find a compromise in the middle of some continuum. It was also a question of there being something wrong, something not properly identified or articulated, about exactly what or where the disagreement really was.

Part of the problem lies with the limits of what is sometimes called the "rights discourse," and the difficulty that that discourse often has in distinguishing between a debate about what is or should be a right and what is right. This is the problem with modern liberalism and its contractual concept of justice that

Canadian Red Tory philosopher George Grant paid so much attention to in his writings. Grant is famous for his book *Lament for a Nation*, which he wrote after Prime Minister Diefenbaker's defeat in 1963, in no small part because of Diefenbaker's resistance to complying with the Kennedy administration's views of what Canadian nuclear policy should be.

Grant's lament for Canadian sovereignty won him much praise on the political left. He was also a fierce critic of capitalism and its values. But that same way of thinking led him to critique the moral pluralism of modern liberal societies, in which the question of what is a right comes before the question of what is the good, with the state seen to be at its best when it remains neutral on controversial moral issues.

Another great Canadian philosopher, Charles Taylor, made a related observation in *The Malaise of Modernity* (1991), when he talked about the need for a moral horizon, in the light of which the increasing choices available in an individualistic society need to be made, if choice is to be meaningful. The mere act of choosing—of being able to choose, of exercising a right to choose—is an occasion for freedom, but is that the end of the discussion? In the context of the abortion debate, a hint of an answer to this question is suggested by the fact that the same people who say they are against abortion on demand would also say, if asked the question differently, that the decision is up to the woman and her doctor, which amounts in practice to the same thing. One way of putting it has the ring of amorality to it. The other has the ring of a concern about privacy, dignity, and an assumption that good reasons will still be expected, if not enforced.

Insofar as the culture wars centre on an argument about individual rights, both sides have internal contradictions. Many of those who would argue against choice in one context are, ironically, all for the economic freedom of individuals and corporations to choose self-interested policies in the global marketplace, even if those policies contribute to disease and death for millions. The profit strategies of the multinational drug companies come to mind. On the other hand, those who exalt the right to choose in reproductive and other personal matters might be better off making the argument from the point of view of what is good policy in a pluralistic world, as opposed to what is an absolute right. Lest a wide-ranging ethos of choice end up bolstering those who would argue for the right to choose private over public health care, for example. In any event, the right to personal choice or freedom may become an increasingly inadequate framework for dealing with all the choices that the future will make available. The abortion debate started when the only choice was whether or not to have a baby, not what kind of baby to have.

The challenge in society at large is to have such a debate in a context that transcends the debate between pre-modern or pre-liberal positions and modern or postmodern liberalism. Within the Christian community, the challenge is to have such debate without excommunicating or demonizing the other, and without the kind of selective biblical literalism that is categorical about issues like abortion and homosexuality, which Jesus never referred to, while being accepting of the proliferation of divorce, a topic Jesus did have something to say about. A biblical literalism on the latter issue might not be such a political winner, even with the conservative political base. And taking seriously the hundreds of biblical passages that would make the rich and powerful uncomfortable would certainly not be a political winner. Ask social gospellers.

The culture wars deserve a book all to themselves. A representative sample of the letters I received on these issues as an MP would certainly be an interesting chapter. They ranged from the thoughtful to the outrageous and even threatening—some threatening in this life and some, particularly from certain fellow Christians, explaining in graphic terms the threat to me in the next life. The letters I found most difficult were those from Catholics involved in social justice advocacy who agreed with the NDP on so many issues but found the party's approach to abortion to be a stumbling block. I always hated the way that such issues got in the way of building the support that would have been needed to challenge the dominant economic paradigm, something only the NDP wanted to do. One wonders how much of what only the NDP was advocating was sacrificed on the altar of issues that were going to turn out a certain way anyway.

At the end of the day, I came to the view that abortion should be safe, legal, and rare. Safe is a matter for doctors. Legal is a matter for Parliament. I am still somewhat bothered by the fact that there is no law on the matter, however permissive, but the absence of a law can quite fairly be blamed on pro-lifers, who could not agree amongst themselves. And rare is a matter primarily of social and economic policy, of decent incomes, of generous maternity leave, and of adequate child care, the latter being something Conservatives seem resolutely opposed to. Indeed, the debate over child care is another ongoing culture war, with the political right obviously perceiving the idea of a state-funded national child care program as cultural anathema. Witness the Conservative cancellation of the Liberal plan in 2006, and its replacement with a meagre subsidy to families that created no new daycare spaces. What is required are policies that are pro-child and pro-family, rather than pro-life or pro-choice. Abandoning children to the vagaries of the market after they are born is the antithesis of a solution.

————

The fact is that on issues like abortion and same-sex marriage, I was always a step or two behind my own church, The United Church of Canada, which had in effect been pro-choice for years and which called for legalized same-sex marriages in 2003. On same-sex marriage, I preferred the view that same-sex civil unions should be allowed, with the word *marriage* reserved for heterosexual couples, but I didn't see the matter as a question of right and wrong. This view on marriage was a very common one that was easy to find on all sides of the political spectrum up until just a few years before it became an issue, which is why I was uncomfortable with rhetoric that characterized all opponents of same-sex marriage as "homophobic." I understand the view I held to be still the view of U.S. President Barack Obama, hardly an unprogressive person. In any event, by the time the debate over marriage became intense, my church, my party, and the Supreme Court of Canada had all weighed in with a view that went further than my own.

When the vote finally came in the House of Commons in July 2005, I did not see it as an opportunity to demonstrate my now superseded preferences. I saw it as an occasion in which one had to vote on whether or not the House of Commons should bring federal marriage law into conformity with the legal reality that had been created by Prime Minister Chrétien's decision not to appeal a lower court ruling to the Supreme Court, and into conformity with the profoundly human reality that so many gay and lesbian couples had already married. It was also a matter of respecting what had been determined by the Supreme Court to be a Charter right in its judgment on the Chrétien government's reference to it of the issue of marriage and what would constitute a violation of the Charter.

On the same-sex marriage vote, it is important to correct a common misunderstanding of what happened within the NDP caucus. It is often wrongly claimed that Bev Desjarlais, the NDP MP for Churchill, Manitoba, was thrown out of the caucus because of her decision to vote differently than the rest of us. A version of this error is to be found in Marci McDonald's book *The Armageddon Factor.* The vote on marriage was not a free vote for the NDP caucus, although I thought that there were good reasons for seeing it as an occasion for one. We had had a free vote on the issue before, when Alexa McDonough was leader, and the caucus was divided. But that was before there was a clear party policy; indeed, the clear party policy was adopted at the next convention after the free vote, in order to prevent this division from happening again. This was the party reality that Jack Layton had to deal with when he became leader.

The lack of a free vote still leaves room, however, for discretion as to how dissent is dealt with, and although Desjarlais was sanctioned, she was not thrown out. She withdrew from caucus voluntarily, and honourably so, when she lost the nomination in Churchill. Having decided to run anyway as an independent against the nominated candidate, she felt the right thing to do was to remove herself from the caucus.

It is important to distinguish the debate over same-sex marriage from earlier federal debates about prohibiting discrimination against gays and lesbians, adding sexual orientation to human rights legislation, and legislation affecting sentencing. In all these cases there was no significant division or debate to speak of within the party. But when the Manitoba NDP government led by Premier Howard Pawley was the first provincial government in English Canada to legislate against discrimination on the basis of sexual orientation in 1987, it was not done without significant internal debate. Pawley gives a frank and helpful account of how he achieved this milestone in his 2011 political memoir, *Keep True.* Worthy of note is his observation that after he heard the venomous quality of the speeches against the legislation, he was more certain of the rightness of the legislation than he had been at the beginning. I know what he means.

When it comes to certain other issues that can be categorized as belonging to the culture wars, the left-right distinctions get more blurred, or perhaps as blurred as some of the more mature issues were in earlier stages. I hope they do not become sorted out along left-right lines, as this too often makes people choose not what they think is right but rather what company they want to be in. In this regard, the religious right has been particularly unhelpful to the side it takes on various issues by using overly judgmental and self-righteous language. Reform Party founder Preston Manning now runs an institute to train budding religious conservative activists how not to turn people off. He claims to be operating out of the scriptural injunction to be "wise as serpents and innocent as doves" (Matthew 10:16). I am not convinced that this was what Jesus had in mind when he gave such advice to his disciples.

Two themes that have not broken out on left-right lines yet, and may not, are the questions of embryonic stem cell research and end-of-life issues like euthanasia, physician-assisted suicide, and how to regard actions like those of Robert Latimer, who killed his daughter Tracy to put an end to what he judged to be her intolerable suffering. There are conservatives who take the view that the potential benefits of embryonic stem cells to the living outweigh the concern about destroying embryos. There are people on the left, particularly those who either as parents or as family members have experienced the value of the life of a disabled child, who resist any way of thinking that says certain lives are not worth living.

My intention herein is not to go any further on these subjects, except to say that once again I find myself, as I suspect many others do, caught between two points of view. From the perspective of individual rights, I might conclude one thing. But I am pulled in another direction when I take into account the way such rights are exercised in an imperfect world, where individual decisions can be influenced by other than purely compassionate reasons, and by social forces and norms that pressure individuals to regard one set of choices as superior to others.

––––––––

Another issue associated with the culture wars is that of gun control and, particularly, of the long-gun registry. This issue took centre stage once again, after my departure from the House, when in the fall of 2010 a private member's bill that would have ended the long-gun registry, which had been established in 1995, was narrowly defeated in the House of Commons. I had first dealt with gun control in my first federal election in 1979, when the gun control laws brought in two years earlier were still an issue with many voters. Some of these people were predicting that the ultimate goal was a registry, and some went further, predicting that a registry would be followed by confiscation. My response was to defend the 1977 legislation, but I also said then that I would not support the idea of a long-gun registry.

Following the tragic massacre at Montreal's École Polytechnique on December 6, 1989, there was a call for stricter gun control, a call that was answered by the Justice Minister of the day, Kim Campbell, with further regulations and rules governing the purchase, possession, and use of firearms. Along with my NDP colleagues in the House of Commons, I supported these measures, again declaring to constituents opposed to the measures, and to those who predicted a long-gun registry as the next step, that that was a step I would not support should it ever arrive.

In April 1994 the gun control debate resumed after a woman was killed with a shotgun in the Toronto restaurant Just Desserts. This is important to remember, as it helped to frame the debate as something caused by an event in Toronto that led to consequences for gun owners all across the country. Too often the registry is portrayed as a response to the Montreal massacre. Some might argue that a registry should have followed the massacre in Montreal. But it did not. In any event, the relatively new Liberal government's response to the Toronto event was to bring in legislation to create a long-gun registry, and the debate has raged on ever since.

The gun registry was passed by Parliament in 1995 during what I often call the Babylonian Parliament, when the NDP was in exile, having lost party status by virtue of not having the 12 seats required for such status. Arguments for treating us better than our numbers merited fell on deaf ears, whether of the Speaker or the leadership of the other parties. We were not able to serve on committees, which meant that over 90 years of accumulated opposition experience was excluded. The governing Liberals had a heyday as they ran roughshod over the rookies assembled before them without benefit of institutional memory. The nine NDP MPs looked longingly at the American system, where seniority meant something.

Another serious problem was that we got to ask our few questions in the last minute of question period, when the press gallery was already empty. This guaranteed that left-wing criticism of the Liberals was never reported, which was great for them because all they had to do to look progressive was be more progressive than the Reform Party—a challenge they met daily with their eyes closed. Unfortunately it also caused many New Democrats to constantly bemoan the failure of caucus to attract the attention they seemed to think was easily available. The living envied the dead, or at least the defeated, who did not have to suffer being treated as losers by their own party as a result of winning when everybody else lost.

One incident related to party status had to do with the annual national prayer breakfast. After the 1993 election, I was unceremoniously evicted from the office in the Centre Block that I had occupied for 14 years. One day a Bloc Québécois MP showed up and told me it was his office. After briefly considering barricading myself in and doing a parliamentary Alamo, I ended up with a room in the West Block, which had once been a lounge, or a smoking room perhaps. It had a cloakroom, and a bathroom with three urinals, two stalls, and three sinks.

The room was just down the hall from 200 West Block, where many events were held. When I moved in I was informed that should Her Majesty the Queen ever have a walkabout in room 200, I would be expected to cede my office to her as required. The fancier seat on one of the toilets—for which I declined several media requests for pictures over the years—attested to the reality of this possibility.

In any event, one day in early 1994 I received a call from Speaker Gib Parent's office requesting that my office be available for the dignitaries as they assembled before the breakfast. I mentioned this to Audrey McLaughlin, the NDP leader, asking what role she was playing at the breakfast, as party leaders generally read a scripture or offered a prayer. She had not been contacted. I refused the use of my office. Closer to the event I got a call from the obviously irritated Speaker, who in a somewhat lecturing tone told me that they had always used that office. I replied that the leader of the NDP had always been invited to participate. The conversation was short, and ended with me hanging up after saying that although Parliament might have a rule about 12 members, I wasn't aware that God did.

Gib Parent's Speakership was itself a product of the culture wars. With the Liberals split between him and Jean-Robert Gauthier in the election for Speaker following the 1993 election, it was Parent's pro-life political history and involvement with the prayer breakfast that gave him the Reform votes he needed to win.

———

The decision of the federal NDP caucus to vote against C-68, the bill that enacted the long-gun registry in 1995, was a product in part of the nature of the ridings represented by the nine NDP MPs. Five were from Saskatchewan, where the provincial NDP was also opposed to the registry. Another was from the interior of British Columbia. The leader, Audrey McLaughlin, was from the Yukon. I was from Manitoba, where the provincial NDP under Gary Doer was also lining up against the registry, and I had already committed to not supporting a registry in previous elections. Not only that, but I was a genuine skeptic about the efficacy of the registry, a skepticism reinforced by many police officers I knew. And I did not have a hard time relating to the anger of ordinary long-gun owners that they were somehow being portrayed as part of a problem that they felt they had nothing to do with.

The implicit—and often explicit—attitude of registry proponents betrayed a patronizing view of long-gun ownership. I had grown up hunting ducks with my father and uncles, in a house where the shotguns were displayed over the bar in the basement rec room. They were never a problem, because they were treated with due respect. My father was a hunter safety instructor. Thus I felt, but did not always give public voice to, what many others were feeling and expressing. After the vote, I would experience even more serious caricaturing of those who opposed C-68, as a torrent of self-righteousness poured over the NDP caucus, particularly from party members. This was helped in no small part by the active dissent of the only MP who did not vote with the caucus.

Svend Robinson voted for C-68, and many in the party thought he had done the right thing. What was wrong about what followed was the vilification of those who had voted otherwise. I received letters from people I had worked with for years that basically wrote off anything I had ever done as meaningless and without merit. I was now some combination of a collaborator with misogyny and a person with no principles. It was the only time that letters from the left matched the toxicity of letters from the cultural and religious right. It was very disheartening, and affected my judgment about running for leader in 1995, something I had been actively exploring. I remember going to the annual United Church regional Conference that year and being taken aback by the vehemence of the delegates about the issue. In both my party and my church, the culture wars had supplanted the class warfare that I much preferred. It was not long after that that I decided to drop the idea of running. I did not like the idea of changing my position, especially in the face of what I regarded as hysterical and unreasonable criticism.

The two leadership candidates on the final ballot in the fall of 1995, Svend Robinson and Alexa McDonough, both made an issue of how they thought the caucus had gone astray and that they would lead us back to virtue. My view was that we had to accept a certain amount of respectful disagreement on such issues, that issues like the gun registry are not core issues for the left, and that too much is sacrificed in treating them as though they are. My vote on the gun registry was used against me when I did take part in the leadership race of 2002–03. But at this writing the argument for finding a way to disagree constructively where we can in the culture wars, rather than one side seeking to vanquish or purge the other, seems to me still to be a good idea.

Growing Up Political in Transcona

This was a political party willing to challenge the powerful, to be critical of popularly held positions or prejudices, and to critique the mentality and the ethic of the market.

I was brought up attending Transcona Memorial United Church, in the working-class Winnipeg suburb of Transcona, where one didn't usually inquire where your father worked, but rather what he did at the Canadian National Railway. My father was a machinist. The CN shops in Transcona employed over 3,000 people in the 1950s and '60s. Today there are less than 500 employed, thanks in part to technological change and contracting out. But more painfully, it is thanks to CN's privatization and then to its merger with Illinois Central, an egregious case of foreign ownership of a vital Canadian asset that is an affront to Canadian sovereignty and a front for establishing a labour-management culture in this country that is hostile to the well-being of working people.

As a student, I worked for CN myself off and on from 1969 until 1974. I was a dishwasher and third cook on the diners and a labourer in the shops doing assorted forms of sorting, stacking, and cleaning, especially sweeping. When I first showed up at the shop gate to campaign as a politician, there was many a quip about how my broom and wheelbarrow were waiting for me if things didn't work out. The morning after my first election I went with

Stanley Knowles to the shop gate to say thank you, as was his custom. As the men went by on their way in, they more often than not said something like "Congratulations, Mr. Knowles," followed by "Good luck, kid."

In 1981, at a dinner with the University of Winnipeg's President, the late Henry Duckworth, I learned of his own connection to Transcona. The dinner at Dr. Duckworth's house was an opportunity that came with giving the Religion and Life lectures at the university in 1981. He had lived in Transcona as a boy in the 1920s when his father was the town's Presbyterian minister. The description of the shops in Duckworth's autobiography matches my own memories of several decades later: "When the workday at the CN shops ended, the men poured forth like lava from an erupting volcano, breaking into rivulets as they made their way to their respective streets and homes." Indeed, long before the current promotion of "active transportation," dozens of men came to work on bicycles. I soon learned the art of handing off a political pamphlet to someone whizzing by on a bike.

———

Transcona is located seven miles east of Winnipeg, and was created as a community to serve the railway shops that began to take shape there in 1909. It was similar to the North End of Winnipeg, but different in significant ways. There was, unlike the North End, no numerically significant Jewish community, and thanks to Transcona's proximity to St. Boniface, it had a French Canadian component. Otherwise, the town was easily nearly half Ukrainian, with immigrants from Poland, Italy, and Holland complementing the English, Irish, and Scottish remainder. In elementary school I remember being envious of the Ukrainian kids who got to stay home from school on Ukrainian Christmas.

Like the residents of the North End, the Ukrainian community in Transcona was very supportive of the Co-operative Commonwealth Federation and later the New Democratic Party. As I once had it explained to me, Ukrainian immigrants who came to Canada before the First World War were primarily anticzarist and left wing in their politics, whereas those who came after the Second World War were primarily anticommunist, and therefore often adamantly against anything on the political left. It made for interesting congregational politics when a priest from the second wave served a congregation made up of families from the first wave, as was the case in Transcona for a while. My experience was that the priest was politely tolerated, but ultimately had no effect on the voting habits of his parishioners. They knew who their real friends were, despite preaching to the contrary.

Provincially, Transcona has voted for the CCF and then the NDP almost continuously since 1945. Federally, as part of the riding of St. Boniface, it was represented mostly by Liberal MPs, with the exception of the Diefenbaker years when it had a Tory MP. It was only when Transcona was removed from St. Boniface in 1979 and joined with other neighbourhoods that had a history of voting NDP in the new riding of Winnipeg–Birds Hill that it was able to be represented by one of its own. But I grew up in the United Church in Transcona, surrounded by CCF-NDP voters, without ever knowing, even loosely, about the social gospel, about the connection between Christian activism and left-wing politics in Canada, about prophetic Winnipeg personalities in the United Church tradition like J.S. Woodsworth, founding leader of the CCF, and the Rev. Stanley Knowles, who represented our neighbours in Winnipeg's North End.

One reason for my ignorance of the tradition may have been that our long-time provincial NDP incumbent, Russ Paulley, also a railroader, was Anglican. Paulley, MLA for Transcona from 1953 to 1977, and leader of the Manitoba NDP throughout the 1960s, became Minister of Labour in Premier Ed Schreyer's government. Or it may also have had something to do with the fact that my mother was a Progressive Conservative. In fact, she was a delegate to the Tory provincial leadership convention in 1967, although I hasten to report that she later became a New Democrat. But most of all, I didn't know about the political dimension of the gospel because I was brought up in a Christian world view that saw itself as apolitical.

I did absorb the biblical tradition, get to know the foundational stories of Judeo-Christian civilization, and learn hymns and songs that still stand me in good stead. In fact, I would wager that many United Church men and women who, over the years, have run for the NDP in hopeless ridings have gone to their political doom humming "Dare to Be a Daniel," rather than citing various political or religious tracts.

Parallel with my life in the church, in Cubs and Scouts, and in youth pipe bands, I had a precocious interest in politics. I always had a sense that something very important and interesting was happening in politics. As Tory legend Dalton Camp put it in his memoirs, politics is really the only game in town. The stakes are higher, and the plays and the players are more complex than anything sport has to offer.

I remember watching the Kennedy-Nixon debates in 1960 when I was nine, and attending Transcona City Council meetings with a friend when we were 12. We would usually be alone in the public gallery, watching six aldermen and the mayor. It was pretty boring at times, but some of the arguments were entertaining and interesting. Years later, two of the aldermen I used to observe, Bill Dzyndra and Jack Perry, would support my campaigns for Parliament.

I ran for president of Arthur Day Junior High and learned a political lesson or two in the course of losing and winding up vice-president. Later at Transcona Collegiate, I led a successful fight against joining the Greater Winnipeg Students' Union, because I felt it would be run by the big-city high schools while claiming to speak for all of us. Instead we formed the Transcona Springfield Student Advisory Committee, which I chaired, and in this capacity met regularly with the superintendent of schools, Bobby Bend, to express whatever grievances students had. This was the first but not the least time that I would defend Transcona from absorption. Just a few years later, I organized a protest against one of the few policies of the Schreyer government that I disagreed with, the amalgamation of Transcona into a single Winnipeg city, sometimes referred to as "Unicity."

In the spring of that school year, Bend won the leadership of the Liberal Party of Manitoba, a race precipitated by the resignation of Gil Molgat. Whatever his virtues, Bend was seen as a political throwback to an earlier era. He helped set the stage for the NDP, under newly elected leader Ed Schreyer, to surprise everyone by forming the government in June 1969.

Bend had beat Bernie Wolfe for the Liberal leadership. Wolfe, a successful municipal politician from Transcona who was later appointed to the Canadian Transport Commission, would be a source of advice and encouragement in my early years as an MP. Molgat became a senator, and when I went to Parliament, we would tease each other about our competing regimental loyalties, his to the Royal Winnipeg Rifles and mine to the Queen's Own Cameron Highlanders of Winnipeg, in which I served as a militiaman and piper from 1967 to 1972.

I participated in the Transcona Jaycee Junior Parliament from 1966 to 1971, and in Tuxis and Older Boys Parliament, a United Church–sponsored predecessor of the Manitoba Youth Parliament. I was prime minister of the Transcona parliament in 1970. I remember 1968 as a formative political year, but primarily in a sad way. It was the year that Martin Luther King and Robert F. Kennedy were assassinated. I had had high hopes for Kennedy as someone who would make a difference on the war in Vietnam. I think I may have had more than the usual interest in American politics because of an elective course I took in grade 10 from a teacher by the name of Harry Zentner, whose quick wit and sometimes humorous political analysis made for an interesting year. Other teachers that contributed to my interest in politics were my British history teacher Monty Lowe and my Canadian history teacher Gary McEwen.

The prime minister of my first Tuxis parliament in 1968 was Tom Axworthy. Forty years later, Axworthy and I would be the panellists at an event in Ottawa examining reforms to rejuvenate and recivilize the Canadian Parliament. A lifelong Liberal and currently CEO of the Walter and Duncan Gordon Foundation for public policy development, Axworthy once was principal secretary to Pierre Trudeau and later a professor at Harvard and then Queen's.

I am pleased to note that the Transcona Junior Parliament admitted girls many years before the provincial youth parliament did. This happened when Willie Parasiuk was its prime minister, in no small part due to the persistence of his then-girlfriend, Wilma Hewitson. Later Parasiuk would become a prominent minister in the NDP government of Howard Pawley. Wilma Parasiuk would continue her activism, leading the party committee on the status of women.

I first met Willie Parasiuk when I came home from my studies in Toronto in the spring of 1977 just in time to make the nomination meeting where he would be chosen as Transcona's provincial NDP candidate. It took place during a particularly nasty strike at the Griffin Wheel plant in Transcona, a strike that had made the national news when I was still away at school. The story showed footage of a police officer I knew from Transcona hauling away a striker whom I also knew. I have walked dozens of picket lines in the last 30 years, but luckily never had to deal with a situation that bad.

When I ran for the federal NDP nomination in 1978 in the new riding of Winnipeg–Birds Hill, Parasiuk would nominate me. Stanley Knowles, whom I would meet at the event for the first time, was the guest speaker. Willie and Wilma Parasiuk became close friends. Unfortunately, Willie was defeated in the 1988 provincial election and subsequently they moved to Vancouver. The silver lining in that cloud is that my wife, Brenda, and I have enjoyed many wonderful visits with them on the West Coast. The Liberal who won in Transcona in 1988 did not last long. In 1990 Transcona was returned to the NDP fold when Daryl Reid, an electrician with CN, was elected.

———————

In the spring of 1971, after taking a year off university to work at CN, travel, and reflect, I watched the federal NDP leadership convention on TV. Listening to speeches by M.J. Coldwell, Tommy Douglas, and David Lewis, I heard what I had been looking for—a prophetic politics. This was a political party willing to challenge the powerful, to be critical of popularly held positions or prejudices, and to critique the mentality and the ethic of the market. That fall, I joined the New Democrats. Years later when Douglas and Lewis were held up by the "left" of the party as icons of what the NDP should be, it was instructive to remember that at that time they had been regarded by the same folks as far too pragmatic and not radical enough.

Up until 1971 I had been active in the Progressive Conservative Party of Canada, as president of the St. Boniface Federal Young Progressive Conservatives and briefly on the provincial executive of the senior party. My Progressive Conservative past was something that Joe Clark used to take delight in reminding me of from time to time in the House of Commons. Starting in 1968, I had worked with another prime minister of the Transcona parliament, Leonard Domino, to create an unusually large YPC group in Transcona, simply by making the argument for involvement rather than any particular argument for being a Tory. We were very active in the provincial Tory campaign against Russ Paulley in 1969. With our controlling numbers at the nomination meeting, the YPC had assured Ken Gunn-Walberg's selection over Peter Graham, then editor of the *Transcona News*. Gunn-Walberg turned out to be a radical libertarian of sorts who wanted to privatize everything. Graham would have been the better candidate, and years later we crossed paths again, when Graham was mayor of the Polish pavilion one year in Winnipeg's famous Folklorama festival, both of us now New Democrats.

In 1970 I ran for president of the Manitoba Progressive Conservative party—coming in third out of four after Robert Steen, who later became mayor of Winnipeg, and Graeme Haig, a lawyer and party stalwart, who won on the first ballot. I ran on the idea of changing the name of the party by eliminating the word *conservative*, arguing that the real threat to democracy was the multinational corporation, not government, and calling for a leadership convention. Little did I know that many years later, in what has to be a tragedy of Canadian politics, the opposite would happen and the word *progressive* would be eliminated when Stephen Harper, as leader of the Canadian Alliance, and Peter MacKay, as leader of the Progressive Conservatives, merged their two parties in 2003 to form the Conservative Party of Canada.

Many times I counselled Peter MacKay to be patient, and not do the merger, arguing that he might be prime minister someday if he resisted the temptation. MacKay and I had become friends in the course of working together after 1997 as House Leaders for our respective parties. I had served in the House with his father before him, as I did with a number of other MPs, including Jack Layton and Justin Trudeau. I am not sure of everything that was involved, but I always believed that the timing of the merger of the two conservative parties was not unrelated to the pending expiry of corporate Canada's ability to finance it, as corporate donations to political parties were slated for extinction by new campaign fundraising rules. Financially, it may have been a question of now or never for the political right.

I have fond memories of many fine people I met in the Progressive Conservative Party in the late 1960s and early 1970s: of Lincoln Alexander, the first Black MP, elected in 1968 in Hamilton, Ontario, who was the guest speaker at a YPC retreat in 1969. Linc-baby, as he encouraged us to call him, became Minister of Labour in Joe Clark's short-lived government and later the Lieutenant-Governor of Ontario. Of Walter Dinsdale, a long-time Manitoba MP who was elected the year I was born and was responsible for my first visit to the House of Commons in 1969, when I was attending a Tory national convention. Of federal PC leader Robert Stanfield, with whom at another Ottawa convention I walked over to Parliament from the Château Laurier. Of John Diefenbaker, whom I piped in more than once and with whom I once had quite a heated discussion about Sir John A. Macdonald and Louis Riel at a Tory banquet I attended with my mother when I was 16. Of Walter Weir, Premier of Manitoba from 1967 to 1969, whom I accompanied on a couple of trips to rural constituencies, thereby learning a bit about politics, as I did when I canvassed one Saturday for Duff Roblin in the federal election of 1968.

Roblin, who served as premier from 1958 to 1967, had brought in the provincial sales tax the year before. The anger of some over the tax had not subsided, causing them to be quite direct about what I could do with the brochures I was handing out. The rest of the 1968 election I spent working for Vaughan Baird, the Tory candidate in St. Boniface. I have met Baird many times over the years at various events, and he has always been encouraging and generous in his comments about my subsequent life on the political left.

During the many cab rides that I would later share with Senator Duff Roblin from the Ottawa airport to the Hill from 1979 to 1992, I had plenty of opportunity to kid him about the early political lessons that I had received at his expense. He was a true gentleman, and had kind words to say about the integrity of Russ Paulley, who had been CCF and NDP leader during Roblin's time as premier. In June 2004, I was part of the Canadian delegation to the 60th anniversary of D-Day with Roblin, who had been chosen to represent Manitoba veterans at the ceremony on Juno Beach. It was also the occasion for me to meet Smokey Smith, Canada's last surviving recipient of the Victoria Cross. Sadly, both Roblin and Smith are no longer with us.

With other YPCers, I was active in ensuring the election in early 1971 of Sidney Spivak as the leader over Harry Enns, something Enns acknowledged in a 2002 tribute in the Manitoba legislature on the sad occasion of Spivak's death. Enns, who died in 2010, was the dean of the Manitoba legislature, but I will always remember him for a comment he made to a meeting of YPCers in his early years as an MLA. He appreciated our concern about the environment, but he doubted that enough people would really want to do anything significant about it till people were dropping dead in the streets from pollution. He may have been too close to the truth, I fear. Sid Spivak was definitely a *progressive* conservative, as was his wife, Mira Spivak, who served in the Canadian Senate from 1986 to 2009. Mira Spivak refused to join the Conservative Party created in 2003.

———

Fond memories aside, by the fall of 1971, I realized I was in the wrong party. Fortunately, Russ Paulley had been a good friend of my grandfather, Alex Taylor, who had been chief of police in Transcona when Paulley was mayor. Grandpa Taylor was a Tory, a political orientation he may have brought with him from Northern Ireland, where Liberals were associated with home rule, an unpopular position in rural County Antrim. But the family often voted for Paulley just the same.

Paulley always told me that I would come over to the NDP one day. He was right, and when I was ready he made it easy for me. I will never forget him telling the first NDP meeting that I went to that the success of the party would depend on the ability of people to change their minds, and as that is what I had done, I should be warmly welcomed. That night I was elected to the local executive. Thereafter I learned a lot from Paulley's special assistant, Art Wright, a former politician himself who was also a railroader and an active member of Kildonan United Church in northwest Winnipeg. Wright was steeped in the history of the CCF, the Independent Labour Party, and the role of various church folk in left-wing politics, like Lloyd Stinson, a United Church minister who was the leader of the party before Russ Paulley.

Later on I would learn my NDP history from party elders like David Orlikow, MP for Winnipeg North from 1962 to 1988, who was part of the great left-wing Jewish tradition in the North End of Winnipeg, another important strand in the history of the CCF-NDP. Not to mention NDP City Councillor Magnus Eliason, whose experience in the party went right back to a 1932 conference in Calgary, a year before the CCF was created. Eliason was an Icelandic Canadian and a Unitarian, not unlike one of his political contemporaries, the Rev. Philip Petursson, who was an NDP MLA from 1966 to 1977.

Many who were in the Transcona YPC made the journey with me at that time, including my friend Richard Greenaway, who would be the NDP candidate in the rural Provencher riding in the federal election of 1979, taking on Tory incumbent Jake Epp. Greenaway would go on to serve the cause of justice for working people through his work with the United Transportation Union, as a strong advocate for his fellow workers at the Canadian National Railway. Another Transcona YPCer of that era was John Reshaur, also a long-time friend, who has lived in Denmark for the last 30 years and been very involved in the environmental movement there. Reshaur recently served a term as a councillor on the island of Samso, an island globally recognized for its ecological innovation and energy policies. He sat for a party that is to the left of the Danish social democrats. The exception to this leftward mobility at the time was Leonard Domino, who was elected the Tory MLA for the provincial constituency of St. Matthews for a term in 1977.

Significant to the development of my political thinking at the time was that from 1969 on, I constantly found myself supportive of policies that the newly elected provincial NDP government of Ed Schreyer was introducing, over Conservative opposition. Schreyer was a young, articulate, and powerful spokesperson for a new way of looking at the world that I was increasingly ready to embrace. By the time he was re-elected premier in June 1973, I was very active in the NDP. The victory party in the basement of St. Joseph the Worker Catholic Church was particularly sweet, as the Conservatives and Liberals had co-operated to run only one candidate against Russ Paulley, to no effect.

It was at that 1973 victory party that Ken Collier, a Transcona NDP stalwart who worked as a carman at the CN shops, first suggested to me that I should think of myself as a potential NDP candidate. I got my public political feet wet that fall by running for the school board. The whole campaign—two big signs, one on each main drag in Transcona, and one pamphlet—cost less than

$300. I came in second out of four candidates. I have often reflected on how important losing that election proved to be. Had I won, I might never have gone to seminary in Toronto as I did only a year later, and life would have been much different. The year before that, I had racked up another electoral defeat when I unsuccessfully ran for external vice-president of the University of Winnipeg Students' Association.

At a Transcona NDP social in 1973, when Ed Schreyer was premier and I was a philosophy student at the University of Winnipeg, I asked him why there were never any government ads for philosophers. He replied with a grin that there was only room for one philosopher in any one government. In 1977, now leading the opposition, Schreyer was encouraging when I approached him about trying for the federal NDP nomination. But he warned me that if I was serious about getting elected I would have to shave my beard off. Needless to say, I did not heed this advice. Almost 30 years later, the tables were turned when Schreyer phoned me to see what I thought about him running federally in the riding of Selkirk–Interlake. When I ran for the leadership of the federal NDP in 2002–03, I was honoured to have the support of all four NDP premiers of Manitoba—Ed Schreyer, Howard Pawley, Gary Doer, and Greg Selinger.

Another helpful meeting in the fall of 1977 was a lunch organized by fellow United Church minister Bill Millar, who thought I should get advice from his friend Dave Chomiak, a former assistant to Schreyer. Chomiak encouraged me to get in touch with young people like Joanne Cerilli and Randy Schulz, both of whom would come to work for me after I was first elected. Joanne's uncle, Al Cerilli, was someone Schreyer had pointed me to. Al Cerilli was with the Canadian Brotherhood of Railway Trainmen and General Workers, the union that I belonged to when I worked at CN, and after my election we worked together for years on many issues of importance to my constituents who worked for CN. Cerilli and I also shared a passion for the promotion of passenger rail. He is still active with the Congress of Union Retirees.

I think Brenda would think it important to note that she was never a YPCer. She came from an NDP family. Brenda's father, Bill Bihun, was the political education officer for Local 142 of the CB of RT&GW. I belonged to Local 142 myself, at first when I worked at Symington Diesel Shop, and throughout most of my jobs at the CN, with the exception of the two summers I worked on the dining cars, when I belonged to a different local. The CB of

RT&GW was a good union and it was a shame that it, along with many other rail unions, was eventually absorbed into the Canadian Auto Workers.

The CAW, otherwise an extremely good union, just never got rail into its heart and soul, and it showed. I was particularly upset with its lack of opposition to the privatization of the Canadian National Railway. For someone who liked to lecture everybody else about how they weren't left wing enough, union President Buzz Hargrove might as well have been Michael Walker of the right-wing think tank the Fraser Institute for all the concern he showed about privatizing such a huge chunk of publicly owned infrastructure. The CAW was used to dealing with large private corporations, and Hargrove saw the new privatized CN as just another big corporation, instead of the travesty that it really was.

Brenda and I had both gone to Transcona Collegiate and then to the University of Winnipeg. But her first recollection of me is her father exclaiming "Probably that damn Blaikie kid!" when, camping at Moose Lake Provincial Park in 1965, they wondered where the sound of the bagpipes was coming from so early in the morning. He was right: I was waking up the troops at a Scout camp down the road. Our first date was on October 17, 1970, which is tragically carved in Canadian history as the date that Pierre Laporte's body was found during the October crisis in Quebec. Brenda and I heard the news over the radio in my 1962 Pontiac at the local A&W drive-in.

I had an NDP family, too, but it was in Saskatchewan. My paternal grandfather, Bob Blaikie Sr., was a CCF supporter in Biggar, Saskatchewan, as was most of that side of the family. My dad's sister, my Aunty Bea Gray, introduced me at a rally in Biggar during the leadership race of 2002–03. Historically, Biggar, a rail town, was a CCF and NDP stronghold, sending such political giants as national CCF leader M.J. Coldwell and Premier Woodrow Lloyd to Parliament and the legislature, respectively. My dad always joked that his only contact with Lloyd, who was a local schoolteacher and principal, was when he got the strap from him once.

My Grandpa Blaikie might have acquired some of his political inclinations before he got to Canada, coming from Cambuslang, Scotland, part of greater industrial Glasgow and a traditional labour stronghold. The year 2011 marks the hundredth anniversary of his arrival in Canada in 1911 with his older brother, Jim. They were 18 and 21 years old, and arrived first in Winnipeg where they worked on the construction of the Manitoba legislative building, before going to Biggar where they were employed as railway carmen. My Grandpa Blaikie joined the Brotherhood of Railway Carmen in Biggar in 1913.

Just months after my future Grandma, Helen Boag, came from Scotland to marry him in June 1914, he and his brother were heading back across the sea with the 1st Canadian Mounted Rifles as part of the Canadian Expeditionary Force in World War One. My Grandpa Blaikie was a piper, and it was from him that I received the initial encouragement to take up the pipes, when he sent me the chanter that he had had with him in the trenches. I played the lament at his graveside in 1966.

Bob Blaikie Jr., my father, was resolutely apolitical until after he retired from senior management at CN. He wasn't always happy with my mom's political activism, but she wasn't to be deterred. She was certainly quite unlike many women I would meet while knocking on doors at election time, who would often say that the political decisions were up to their husbands. In the election of 1988, after his retirement from the railway in 1986, my dad was my sign chair, and one day when we were working on signs in his garage, he told me that he had been a closet New Democrat for years. I believe this was not unlike many in CN management at the time, who had started at the bottom and never forgot where they came from. In my dad's case he had started out in 1942 shovelling coal in Biggar, came to Transcona in 1943 as an apprentice machinist, and retired as the Assistant General Superintendent of Equipment Department, Prairie Region, in 1986.

My dad was a tough but fair supervisor, who had the respect of his peers and the union leaders he negotiated with. Being Bob Blaikie's son was always a credit to me, even with those who had sometimes been on the losing end of a dispute with him. My dad was a Canadian nationalist, and when he sent me to buy a new bicycle tube at Blostein's hardware in Transcona, he always gave me the extra money to buy the one made in Canada. A veteran of the Canadian Navy in the Second World War, he would accompany me in 1995 to the christening of the HMCS *Winnipeg* at Esquimalt, British Columbia. We shared a laugh when, as we stood under the bridge of the ship while going for a cruise, a big wave came over the bow and drenched him. He hadn't been that wet with his clothes on since 1945.

5

The Prophetic Tradition

The prophets were criticizing kings and kingdoms
on the basis of how they were treating their people,
whether the vulnerable were being looked after,
whether justice was being done.

When I arrived at the University of Winnipeg in 1969, I was part of a generation that was questioning our obligation to uncritically accept whatever the United States or others were doing in the name of containing communism, somewhat in the same way as we are now expected to accept whatever is done in the name of security or fighting terrorism. Indeed, one of my first experiences of politics was at a Progressive Conservative meeting at the Marion Hotel in St. Boniface, Manitoba, that my mother had taken me to as a teen. MP Bud Sherman was speaking about his recent trip to Vietnam, and I challenged him on being far too uncritical of the American position. On the way home my mom said she would think twice about bringing me to meetings again, though she later relented. Years later, at a peace conference in Nelson, British Columbia, in 2006, I would have the great pleasure of meeting Senator George McGovern, who had run on an antiwar ticket against Richard Nixon in 1972.

My first inkling that something was wrong had come as a schoolboy in October 1962, when I thought the world was going to end in a nuclear war over Cuba. I will never forget that day in grade 6 when I went back to school after lunch knowing that the Russian ships were meeting the American blockade that afternoon, unsure whether I would ever see home again. It was an experience that made me a lifelong advocate of nuclear disarmament. That said, it is ironic that my father's life may have been one of the Allied lives that were saved by the atomic bombs that led to Japan's surrender in 1945. He and his twin brother, Bill, were on leave from the navy before heading to the Pacific when the war ended.

In my university days, it was the war in Vietnam that was creating what could be called a mass prophetic consciousness. The prophetic perspective dares to imagine that one's own side might be wrong, sinful, or motivated by something other than what we are officially being told. This perspective didn't always come easily to an older generation steeped in the righteousness of the Allied cause in the Second World War, a righteousness that I do not question. And it didn't come easily to the generation that had fought that war to have its children become cynical about Western foreign policy, the source of so much idealism. But no one, least of all the Hebrew prophets, ever said being prophetic was a pleasant business.

I hadn't yet encountered the prophetic tradition in the United Church. To use theologian H. Richard Niebuhr's famous typology of the relationship between Christ and culture, there wasn't a lot of *Christ against culture* in my upbringing, more the *Christ of culture*. The only opposition to the prevailing culture I'd encountered was opposition to sinful behaviour like alcohol abuse, sexual infidelity, swearing, lying, or stealing. It was an ethic limited to the personal behaviour of individuals, rather than addressing the political and economic behaviour of institutions and corporations and those powerful enough to run them. Or addressing those with the potential—which, in a democratic society, means voters—to challenge and regulate the behaviour of the powerful. When the church deliberates on how to relate to power, it is far too common for voters to be omitted from the analysis. Perhaps more time should be spent talking to citizens and less time preaching to the choir or trying to get the attention of governments.

Arriving at university, I had yet to learn that, as someone once said, the Canadian left owes as much to Methodism as it does to Marx. As John Wesley, the founder of Methodism, said in a sermon he gave on the Sermon on the Mount, in 1748, "Christianity is essentially a social religion, and to turn it into a solitary one is to destroy it."

I did not yet see that salvation might involve being saved not just from destructive personal behaviour, but also from destructive environmental policies, dangerous workplaces, and oppressive relationships. Nor had I encountered the economy as a moral or theological issue. More and more research and reflection—I am thinking here of what I have learned from reading the works of biblical scholars like Marcus Borg and John Dominic Crossan—points to the original economic meaning of many of Jesus's parables and teachings, and to the original political and subversive significance of confessing Jesus as Lord in an imperial context that used identical language to describe the Roman emperor.

It was against the non-prophetic Christianity that I had grown up with that I was rebelling when in my first year at the university I took a religious studies course from Charlie Newcombe, who for many years had been Old Testament professor at United College, which became the University of Winnipeg in 1967. Newcombe taught the politics of the biblical stories. He made us see that the prophets were criticizing kings and kingdoms on the basis of how they were treating their people, whether the vulnerable were being looked after, whether justice was being done. I learned that God takes sides. It stirred in me a hope that I could bring biblical faith and my real-world experience into a helpful dialogue.

That same year, in Phil Wright's philosophy class, I was introduced to Socrates, and to a critical take on technological rationality, that is, the perils of separating the pursuit of knowledge from the pursuit of wisdom. I would also be grateful a few years later to philosophy professor Brian Keenan, who through his courses—and through informal seminars over the years around the campfire—kept me conscious of the limits of liberalism and the social sciences; and to Carl Ridd and John Badertscher, religious studies professors who also went from being teachers and mentors to friends and supporters over the course of my political life.

In my second year at the University of Winnipeg, 1971–72, John Badertscher invited the visiting William Stringfellow to speak to his religious studies course entitled Technology, Humanism and Nature. The course featured books like *The Technological Society* by Jacques Ellul and Theodore Roszak's *The Making of a Counter Culture*. Stringfellow was active with the Berrigan brothers in opposing the draft in the United States and had even harboured Father Daniel Berrigan when he was being sought by federal authorities for acts of civil disobedience. Stringfellow's book *An Ethic for Christians and Other Aliens in a Strange Land* described America as Babylon and Christians as exiles. I embraced this way of thinking on one level, but was in tension with it on another. I didn't want to give up on the political process, or on America.

From Stringfellow I learned that to be prophetic in the 20th century didn't mean putting the Bible aside after gleaning some social ethic from it. Being prophetic meant picking up the Bible, discerning who the principalities and powers were in the current age, and standing up to them. This was neither religious liberalism nor evangelical authoritarianism, both of which for him were ways of not dealing with the world. Stringfellow, who died in 1985, was also associated with the Sojourners Community in Washington, D.C., from which evangelicals like Jim Wallis challenge Christian colleagues to a more biblically based activism.

John Badertscher had been a Methodist minister and civil rights activist in the United States before coming to the University of Winnipeg to teach religious studies. Brenda had also taken a course from Badertscher, and when we were married on June 29, 1973, we had him co-officiate at our wedding. When I taught a theology course on faith and politics at the University of Winnipeg in the fall of 2009, I invited John to speak about his experiences in the civil rights movement.

———

After Brenda and I were married at Transcona Memorial United Church in June 1973, we bought a very small old house in Transcona, for $5,500, and settled in. We had both graduated with BAs in the spring and Brenda was off to the University of Manitoba to get her teacher training. I was doing a fourth year in Honours Philosophy, a degree that I am still one course short of qualifying for. Student bursaries and loans ran out by January and I ended up working midnights at the CN rail welding plant not far from where we lived. Staying awake in class was sometimes a challenge, and I never finished a directed individual study I was doing on the philosophy and nature of humour.

In the meantime, Carl Ridd and John Badertscher persuaded me to apply, with their support, for a fellowship called Trial Year in Seminary, sponsored by the Rockefeller Foundation, designed for those who were uncertain about ministry but willing to explore the possibility. I was one of 60 successful applicants out of 600 throughout the United States and Canada. With the fellowship, I could have studied at any one of several prestigious American schools. But I wanted to study in Canada, and at that time, only the Toronto School of Theology and McGill University in Montreal were accredited with the American Theological Association. I chose Toronto and TST's United

Church seminary, Emmanuel College, because, among other reasons, Toronto was the place where Brenda had the most likelihood of getting a job teaching, which she did, although it was half-time the first year.

In 1976, activist Phil Berrigan visited a small house church community that we were part of at Emmanuel. This community included Peter Short, who would later become Moderator of the United Church (2003–06); Doug Martindale, who would succeed me in a few years in working at Winnipeg's North End Community Ministry and be elected to the Manitoba legislature in 1990; Chris Levan, who has authored several books on religion and social ethics; Randy MacKenzie, who would run for the NDP in 1980 in the Saskatchewan riding of Assiniboia, where he was serving his first pastoral charge as a United Church minister; and Bill Cantelon, who now serves Cordova United Church in Victoria, British Columbia. With the exception of Martindale, who was a dedicated fan, we all played on the Emmanuel intramural hockey team, the Big E. The contact with the Berrigans came through another member of our group, Ken Hancock. Hancock was not only the best player on the Emmanuel team but, perhaps ironically, given the physicality of the game, also the most committed to non-violence as a Christian calling.

Phil Berrigan was convinced of the futility of conventional, electoral politics. I didn't agree with him, although there are days when I wonder. Part of our difference of opinion may be a difference between the Canadian and American context. Policies, positions, and perspectives that are hard to find, even on an individual basis, in the U.S. Congress are represented in the Canadian Parliament by the NDP. Canada does have a different social and economic ethos, although it's eroding. And Canadian governments sometimes abstain from military initiatives like George W. Bush's invasion of Iraq or his Ballistic Missile Defense plan, even if they then can't bring themselves to criticize the very same initiatives. And if the free market is the false god, the idol that we have all been compelled to worship, then Canada has had distinctive features that we should cherish and defend. We have not done all things by the free market—in culture, in health care, in supply management (for example, through the Wheat Board), in post-secondary education, to name a few.

Phil Berrigan spent the last few years of his life in prison for engaging in civil disobedience. I wrote him just before his death in 2002 to remind him of our conversation, and to let him know what I'd been up to. He was kind enough not to suggest, in reply, that I had been wasting my time.

———————

When I graduated from the Toronto School of Theology in 1977 it was at the height of the debate about the Mackenzie Valley Pipeline. Ecumenical justice coalitions abounded, and a new critique of our way of life and energy consumption habits was being developed. Just before the impending era of deregulation and market fundamentalism put off facing ecological realities for a generation, it seemed that we were on the brink of really doing something different. It turns out we weren't, but we will be someday, because we are running out of oil and the sooner we get busy on the alternatives the better. I once heard comedian Dick Gregory say that we won't get the solar power we need until the multinational corporations figure out how to install a meter on the sun. I'm sure they are working on it, but in the meantime there will be a role for other approaches.

My three years at the Toronto School of Theology were a life-changing experience. In order to be ordained, I had to become a member of The United Church of Canada; unlike a lot of the people I had gone to Sunday school with, who were automatically confirmed and then subsequently never really had much to do with the church, I had taken a pass on confirmation, somewhat to my parents' frustration.

Brenda and I were both confirmed into the United Church at what was then Trinity United Church on Bloor Street in Toronto. The minister at Trinity was a young guy by the name of Bill Phipps, who had gone into ministry after being a lawyer. Little did I know that someday Phipps would be the Moderator of the United Church (1997–2000), and that the night before an Ottawa press conference that got him into hot Christological water, with a report of his alleged uncertainty about the divinity of Jesus, he would be having dinner with me in the parliamentary dining room. Phipps's term as Moderator, otherwise wonderfully focused on the idea of the "moral economy," got off to a bad start in terms of reaching the parts of the Christian community who needed to hear his message most. He was a clear victim of "gotcha" journalism.

Toward the end of my time in Toronto I spent more time at Bloor Street listening to minister Cliff Elliott, from whom I had taken a half course at Emmanuel. The other half course that year was from Howie Mills, for whom I wrote a paper on the nature of violence and non-violent resistance. Mills had distinguished himself as a key person in the grape boycott in the early 1970s that supported the organizing of grape workers in California by union activist César Chávez. In 1993 when Chávez died, I would make a statement in the House of Commons about Chávez's life and work.

Mills, as head of Ministry Personnel and Education for the United Church, defended my right to be ordained in 1978 against a few who questioned my "call" on the basis that I was also a nominated NDP candidate for the imminent election. I did not see my call to ministry as something that contradicted my call to public life. One was a vocation that I could pursue in the church. The other was a call that would depend in large part on voters. One can commit to a lifetime in the ministry; committing to a lifetime as an elected politician is somewhat presumptuous. Not to mention that in 1978 when I was to be ordained, my election to Parliament was anything but certain. It became possible in part because so many fellow United Church ministers joined many others in coming out to work in my campaign. One of them was Doug McMurtry from Immanuel United Church in my riding, with whom I had worked on Aboriginal issues and Project North. In 2009 I attended his 90th birthday celebration. He was not only a great supporter, but also my unofficial pastor. When things were rough in Ottawa, I could usually count on a helpful and encouraging letter from Doug.

Immanuel United Church was not the only United Church in the riding that early on and throughout was a source of support. First and foremost was my home church, Transcona Memorial United, where the clergy team of Roger Coll and Lynette Miller, along with too many others to name, were solidly behind me, as were the clergy couple that succeeded them in 1988, Jeff Cook and Carol Fletcher. Grey St. United in Elmwood was also a place where I found solidarity and support. The minister there when I was first elected was Jim Uhrich, who had been my Sunday school teacher at Transcona Memorial when I was a teenager. Other United Church ministers who come to mind as sources of support in the riding were Gordon Fulford and Bill Hickerson.

That Winnipeg already had in 1978 an MP who was a United Church minister, in the form of Stanley Knowles, was a helpful basis for arguing in favour of my ordination that year. Howie Mills, who later went on to become the United Church's General Secretary, successfully argued that no distinction should be made between the two of us, and none was.

———————

In a liberation theology course at St. Michael's College with Father Tim Ryan, I was inspired by a guest lecture by Dom Hélder Câmara of Brazil, who lamented the fact that when he helped the poor he was called a saint, but when he asked why they were poor he was called a communist. Bishop Câmara was critical of capitalism and communism, but most of all he was critical of the well-established strategy of branding anyone who dared to imagine that there was an alternative to injustice as an enemy of freedom. In his 1971 book *Revolution through Peace*, Câmara urged Christians to break free of the negative stereotypes of socialism. Socialism is no more linked to materialism than are certain kinds of capitalism, does not necessarily imply an oppressive regime, and indeed can also describe a government that serves the community and humankind.

I was also inspired by the public theological comments of Canadian Bishop Remi De Roo, and count Roman Catholic theologian Gregory Baum as one of my mentors. In my student years, dreams of substantial ecumenical unity and action on justice issues by mainline Protestants and Catholics were both real and expected to grow. As a guest speaker at a course on ecumenism I took at TST from renowned Canadian church historian John Webster Grant, Baum told the class that what increasingly divided Christians was not the differences between denominations, but rather their attitude toward Christendom and its demise. The division was between those who welcomed Christendom's demise and saw it as an opportunity for a more authentic Christian life, and those who resisted the demise.

Toward the very end of my formal theological education I started to be inspired by the work of United Church theologian Douglas John Hall. With ideas reminiscent of Baum's, Hall argued for the real relevance of Christian faith in today's world. But he also said that Christians could no longer interpret humanity's salvation as their own special prerogative, rather than the prerogative of all people of goodwill.

My most important theo-political education centred on the great blessing I had in being invited to have lunch on a regular basis with Gregory Baum and Roger Hutchinson. John Bädertscher had told me to look Hutchinson up when I got to Toronto. At that time he was a professor of religious studies at Victoria University in Toronto; now he is the retired principal of Emmanuel College. Baum was at the Institute for Christian Thought, and is now professor emeritus at McGill. Hutchinson's thesis had been on the Fellowship for a Christian Social Order, which was active in Canada in the 1930s. Nowadays we'd expect an organization with such a name to be politically right wing, but in the halcyon days of the social gospel, it was the left that was openly calling on Canada to be more Christian. I received an honorary doctorate of divinity from Victoria University in May 2009; I was pleased that Hutchinson and my professor of Christian Ethics at Emmanuel, Douglas Jay, were speakers at the event.

While studying at TST, I was also influenced by the work I did under the supervision of Ernie Best, on the mid-19th-century English theologian and Christian socialist Frederick Denison Maurice. Maurice advocated co-operation, based on the law of love revealed in Jesus Christ, and argued strenuously against the prevailing economic ethic, especially what he called the lie that competition is the law of the universe. In a time when proposals for a co-operative approach based on a critique of capitalism were caricatured as anti-Christian, Maurice was one of the first to point out that such proposals were actually more in keeping with the will of God for human life than the established "Christian" economic status quo.

The study of F.D. Maurice led me into reading others of the English Christian left, such as William Temple, who wrote *Christianity and Social Order* in 1942. Archbishop Temple, though acknowledging that the church cannot speak with authority on the purely economic effect of certain proposals, nonetheless argued that it was legitimate for the church to speak out on economic matters:

> [The church] is, however, entitled to say that some economic gains ought not to be sought because of the injuries involved to interests higher than economic.... We all recognize that in fact the exploitation of the poor, especially of workhouse children...was an abomination not to be excused by any economic advantage thereby secured; but we fail to recognize that such an admission in a particular instance carries with it the principle that economics are properly subject to a non-economic criterion.

I was also influenced by Dr. Best himself, although I never embraced the position that had caused him to be a conscientious objector in the Second World War. In this sense, I have always been more of a Tommy Douglas social gospeller than a J.S. Woodsworth social gospeller. Woodsworth stood alone in Parliament against the declaration of war in 1939. Douglas tried to join up.

This is a long-standing source of division on the left, particularly the religious left. To what extent can the use of force be justified, and if justified, to what extent should it be used in any given context? And what is the appropriate political and personal response to policies that perpetuate militarism and war? For my part, for example, I have never been supportive of those who wish to divert their taxes from being spent on defence, although this may be more a quarrel about the nature of politics than an argument about defence. If you want a different policy, there is no individual way out by virtue of diverting your taxes. There is only the call to involvement in the collective political task of electing a government with different policies.

My years at Emmanuel College and TST were a time in my life when I learned a lot from many great teachers, and I look back on it with enormous gratitude. Final mentions must go to church historian John Webster Grant, who warned me against the kind of sweeping historical generalizations that I still delight in; to Old Testament professor Vernon Fawcett, for whom I did a paper on the Hebrew concept of justice; to Heinz Guenther, who gave me an appreciation of the complexity and importance of understanding the historical context of the gospels; and to pastoral theology professor Greer Boyce, whose sermon on Matthew 10:34 ("I have not come to bring peace, but a sword") helped me to come to terms with the fact that my emerging understanding of Christian faith would put me in situations where conflict rather than harmony might be the rule.

CHAPTER

6

Seeking the Welfare of the City

The world may start with a garden but it ends with a city, the New Jerusalem.

Toward the end of my theological studies, I had an opportunity to become acquainted in a whole new way with the roots of the social gospel in Canada. As part of the requirements for ordination, I spent a summer at Sutherland Mission in the North Winnipeg neighbourhood known as Point Douglas. That summer-student placement in 1975, and my subsequent ministry at North End Community Ministry from 1977 to 1979, introduced me to the struggles of the inner city.

A favourite text of mine at the time came from Jeremiah 29:7, where the prophet says to the exiles in Babylon, "seek the welfare of the city where I have sent you...and pray to the Lord on its behalf, for in its welfare will you find your welfare." Another one was Habakkuk 2:9–12, where we hear:

> "Alas for you who get evil gain for your houses, setting your nest on high to be safe from the reach of harm!" You have devised shame for your house by cutting off many peoples; you have forfeited your life.... "Alas for you who build a town by bloodshed, and found a city on iniquity!"

North End Community Ministry, operated out of Stella Avenue Mission, is the same place that J.S. Woodsworth worked out of when he wrote his seminal social-justice work *My Neighbour* in 1911, and when Stella Mission was part of the larger ministry of All People's Mission. There is a plaque on the outside of the building recognizing its historical significance. All People's was a ministry of the Methodist Church that expanded greatly under Woodsworth. Allen Mills, in his biography of Woodsworth, *Fool for Christ,* writes:

> Under [Woodsworth] the mission expanded both the size and type of its operations so that it became much more of a settlement house *cum* social welfare agency. Its work included many aspects: kindergarten, language and home-keeping school, and a centre of political education and agitation. Pre-eminently Woodsworth saw its function as ministering to the social needs of the thousands of immigrants then crowding into the north of the city.

Sutherland Mission was another remnant of All People's; it is now the home of the Manitoba Indigenous Cultural Education Centre. One of my tasks at Sutherland was to get to know the community well enough to make a recommendation about the viability of the church's ministry there. In this task I was joined by a group of concerned church folk from Westworth United Church in River Heights, an affluent area of Winnipeg. My supervising pastors, Ian Macdonald and Fred McNally, were from Westworth, and my former professor Carl Ridd was also part of the Westworth group.

Ridd was a well-known and well-liked professor of religious studies at the University of Winnipeg. I had taken his most famous course, Religious Quest in the Modern Age. As I would later joke at his retirement roast, after studying Dostoevsky, Camus, Kafka, and Conrad in his class, I was moved to read Arthur Koestler's *Darkness at Noon* for comic relief. That summer was the beginning of a great relationship with Carl and his wife, Bev. When I got elected, he subscribed to Hansard and over the years provided me with much comment on my interventions and those of my fellow MPs. My kids have fond memories of our annual summer visit to the Ridd cottage on Lake of the Woods. I always looked forward to the time in the visit when Carl and I would leisurely swim across the bay and back, all the while discussing the latest in politics and theology. The last time I would see him was on the steps of the Manitoba legislature in February 2003; we were both speaking at a rally protesting the American invasion of Iraq. Carl Ridd was an Olympic basketball player in his day and kept in very good shape. All of us who cherished his presence in our life and the life of our city were shocked when he died of leukemia later that year.

The Westworth group also included two other people who would become an important part of my personal and political life, Dudley and Eleanor Thompson. They distinguished themselves by being the only ones to accept my recommendation that the best thing people could do for Point Douglas was move there and become an active part of the community. The Thompsons lived in Point Douglas for several years and did a lot of great work there. Eleanor retired in 2007 as executive director of Urban Circle, a very successful institution created to train First Nations people in Winnipeg for employment opportunities. Dudley is a well-respected architect who was well ahead of his time in allowing the ecological to instruct the architectural.

———

Sutherland Mission, as I said, was in Point Douglas, where a young Tommy Douglas had lived. His mother, Anne, had been a volunteer at the mission, and Tommy, though he never spoke to the man at that time, remembered the powerful presence of the mission's superintendent, the Rev. James Shaver Woodsworth. Some years later, as a teenager, Tommy Douglas would personally witness Bloody Saturday, June 21, 1919, when mounted police fired on the crowds of the Winnipeg General Strike. Later in the same day police arrested Woodsworth and charged him with sedition for editing the strike newspaper, in which he had quoted the prophet Isaiah in support of the strikers' demands for labour rights. The first editor, the Rev. William Ivens, had already been arrested. The people would have their turn to speak very soon. Some of the strike leaders were elected to political office while they were still incarcerated and some shortly thereafter.

Tommy Douglas didn't know then that J.S. Woodsworth would be elected to Parliament in 1921, and that he would join him there in 1935. When I was at Sutherland Mission I had no idea that I would later be a friend of both Douglas and Stanley Knowles, who replaced Woodsworth in 1942, and speak at their memorial services in 1986 and 1997, respectively.

In 1986 I officiated at Tommy Douglas's memorial service in Ottawa, a very special responsibility because I knew that Tommy had specifically requested that I do so. I learned of Tommy's request two years before his death when in the early summer of 1984, near the start of the federal election called by the new Prime Minister, John Turner, Tommy Douglas was hit by a bus. I got a call from Tommy's son-in-law, Ted Tulchinsky, husband of Tommy and Irma's adopted daughter Joan. Tommy was in a coma. I was told that he had always spoken quite highly and affectionately of me, and they thought I might be able to help bring him out of the coma. I flew to Ottawa and spent the better part of a day with Tommy, holding his hand, recalling Burns Nights on the Hill that we had shared, and telling him about the election campaign. I will never know if my presence made a difference, but I was glad to hear the next day that he had come out of the coma.

When Tommy Douglas died in February 1986, I was further honoured to share the front of the church with King Gordon, one of the founders of the CCF, who gave the eulogy. At the end of the service, after we sang the great Welsh hymn "Guide Me, O Thou Great Jehovah," the song the miners had sung in the streets when the U.K. mines were nationalized, I stepped down from the pulpit and played the lament on the pipes. There had been much scripture shared at the service, but also the poetry of Robert Burns. I remember quoting from one of Burns's most famous poems, a poem that is no doubt one of the bedrocks of the Scottish egalitarian tradition that Douglas was brought up in. In the poem we are enjoined to long for the day that is coming yet when

> Man to Man, the world o'er,
> Shall brothers be for a' that.

Brian Mulroney attended the service at Dominion-Chalmers United Church in Ottawa. It was the only time I got to lecture him on the virtues of the left without retort. Instead, when I got back to my office there was a nice handwritten note waiting for me in which he complimented me on the service and on my remarks. When I ran for the federal NDP leadership in 2002–03, one of my most enthusiastic supporters was actor and activist Shirley Douglas, Tommy's daughter, and a great defender of causes like medicare in her own right.

After Tommy Douglas's service, Stanley Knowles always told me that I would have to be involved when his time came. And I was, in June 1997, at both the service in Ottawa and the one in Winnipeg. The Winnipeg service was held at Westminster United Church on June 16, two days short of Stanley's birthday on the 18th. At the end of my address, I held the very Bible that Stanley had read from in Westminster United Church in 1942 at J.S. Woodsworth's memorial service, and ended with the prayer tucked away in its pages with which he had ended that service:

Thou hast shown us, O God, what is good, and what it is that Thou dost require of us. Hear us in the prayer of our inmost hearts, that we, like him who we honour today, may do justly, love mercy, and walk humbly with Thyself. Amen.

———

During my two years at North End Community Ministry I had the good fortune to work with Deaconess Verna McKay. Verna was married to Stan McKay Sr., an Elder in the Aboriginal Christian community from Fisher River Cree Nation in Manitoba, and much respected for the work that he and his late first wife, Dorothy McKay, had done in creating a place for people to stay when they came into the city from the reserves. Stan and Verna McKay led a lot of cross-cultural workshops to help people understand each other's ways. One of my most treasured possessions is the pipe that Stan presented to me when I left for Parliament.

At North End Community Ministry we had a clothing depot and drop-in centre, where I had many conversations with local women about the problems they were facing in the neighbourhood. At the seniors' drop-in centre I looked forward to my weekly lunch and game of pool with a group of elderly Ukrainian men who filled me in on the way that some of them had been treated during the First World War and in the dirty thirties because they were regarded as aliens. From the young Aboriginal kids in the after-school program I learned the joys of endless floor hockey in a dusty old basement. And from a man on welfare who had phoned us for help with food for him and his family, because moving from one house to another had used up what he had, I learned how a political message of austerity and sacrifice is sometimes surprisingly embraced by those whose lives are already austere and who have little to sacrifice.

In those days, before food banks and before the need for food banks exploded, we used to pay a pastoral visit to homes that made such a request. When I asked him, sitting there in obvious poverty, how he felt about his welfare rates being so low, he replied, "We are living beyond our means. Something has to give." The fact that the poor do not always vote with their wallets, but see themselves as part of the larger community project, is too often lost on the left and taken advantage of by the right.

Speaking of the left, or far left, perhaps one of my most unusual experiences during my time in inner-city ministry came in the summer of 1975, when

Saigon was being evacuated and the Americans were conceding defeat in Vietnam. Posters began to appear in Point Douglas inviting people to a victory party at the Labour Temple on Pritchard Avenue. Although I had been opposed to the war in Vietnam, like many Canadians, I found the idea of a victory party to be outside the pale of my imagination. Yet such was the politics of Winnipeg's North End that such a party could be contemplated, a party at which all the promise of a fully communist Vietnam could be celebrated.

The future would not be kind to the ideological hopes that I witnessed that evening when, out of political curiosity, I briefly dropped in on the event. Probably just long enough to go on some RCMP file as a suspected commie, although I had learned through a family friend in the reserve army intelligence corps that I was already on a list of possible subversives for my participation in a 1969 rally outside Winnipeg's Centennial Concert Hall where Prime Minister Trudeau was speaking to a Liberal fundraiser. I had had the subversive nerve, as a YPCer at the time, to carry a poster expressing concern about the possible voyage of the oil tanker *Manhattan* through the Northwest Passage in the Arctic. There had been an oil tanker spill in Chedabucto Bay, Nova Scotia, a few years previous and many were concerned about a similar event in the Arctic, a concern that is even more relevant today as a result of global warming.

The 1970s was a time for renewed hope for the city. When I was at Emmanuel College, Brenda and I had volunteered in the campaign to re-elect to Toronto City Council Dan Heap, who would become my NDP colleague in the House of Commons in a 1981 Toronto by-election that, up until the votes were counted, was portrayed in the media as a Liberal-Tory contest. The 1970s was also a time of renewed interest within the church about ministry in the city and particularly in the inner city. Canadian Urban Training courses in social activism were being offered in many venues, and there was a lot of emphasis on the need for systemic change in order to finally deal with the issues. The cry was for something beyond charity and closer to justice.

At the Christian Resource Centre in Toronto I met a United Church minister by the name of Barry Morris, with whom I would later work in Winnipeg when he was at St. Matthew's–Maryland Community Ministry. Morris later went to First United in Vancouver and is now with that city's Longhouse Council of Native Ministry. Over the years, we've talked about how the hope we had in the 1970s seems remote now. There isn't the cry for justice that we remember from that time.

Sometime in the next decade the city got onto the back burner again, just as the neo-conservative (also called neo-liberal) socio-economic model was kicking in. Idol worship of the false promises of the marketplace and deregulation were creating all kinds of new victims, many of whom showed up at the door of inner-city ministries.

Remember the days before the neo-conservative revolution when the minimum wage was worth more, when welfare was worth more, when more people were covered by unemployment insurance, when in the name of de-institutionalization, many Canadians with mental health challenges hadn't yet been thrown into the streets to look after themselves, when there were no food banks, when the government thought it had a responsibility for housing, and when gun and gang violence were the exception rather than the rule? After 25 years of free trade, privatization, and deregulation, it's hard to remember a moment when, with real systemic change, we might have been able to go to a higher level of social and economic equality than we dare to even dream of now.

Today, cities are creeping back onto the agenda, but it isn't always easy to get attention to important issues. Personally, as an opposition MP, I was always prepared to declare a moratorium on talk of government scandals, if it meant that the more important scandals of poverty, war, discrimination, and environmental degradation would be dealt with.

The preoccupation with scandal serves the cause of those who prefer mutual character assassination, however justified in some cases, to challenging the present-day powers and principalities who stand in the way of God's kingdom and its justice. I've searched the Bible high and low and I can't find the passage that justifies putting a priority on tax cuts for the rich and powerful instead of meeting the needs of the poor and powerless. And yet the tax cut narrative continues to be a structural prejudice in the way that the established paradigm would have us approach the politics of taxation.

From 1990 to 1993 I was the Tax Critic of the NDP and devoted much energy to exposing various tax loopholes that enable the rich to avoid paying their fair share of the load. My fondest memory of that responsibility was in June 1993 when the Fraser Institute did its usual personal tax freedom day press conference on the Hill. I commandeered the microphone after Executive Director Michael Walker was done, and reminded those present that corporate tax freedom day comes in January. It was not appreciated. The other memory of that responsibility is the ambiguity I felt about uncritically joining the chorus against the GST. I felt that we were contributing to an antitax ethos that was ultimately inimical to our view of the role of government and the need for a reliable tax base to finance the policies we advocated. It is no coincidence that the social democratic countries most admired by many New Democrats have high consumption taxes.

In a similar vein, I never felt so keenly ever again the class differences between myself and my constituents on the one hand, and in this case the Tories on the other, as I did in May 1985. Michael Wilson, Minister of Finance in the recently elected Mulroney government, brought down his first budget. When he read out the passage that announced a lifetime personal capital gains tax exemption of $500,000, the Tory caucus exploded in an expression of sheer personal and political ecstasy. I couldn't think of anybody I knew who would be positively affected in the least.

The only time I was ever on Wilson's team was in the winter of 1983–84 during the annual hockey game between the government and opposition MPs. Wilson was the goalie for the opposition, and Jean Chrétien was the goalie for the governing Liberals. Recounting how I managed to knock down three oncoming Liberals at the opposition blue line is still one of my favourite stories, even if I did end up with some bruised ribs.

———

According to French theologian Jacques Ellul, the city poses a problem for God in the biblical tradition. The city is a place where all humanity's greatness, vanity, and false sense of security are gathered together in a self-sufficiency that tries to exclude God. Nevertheless, from the building of the first cities by Cain, whom God marked for protection, to the weeping of Jesus over Jerusalem, there is a constant indication in the Bible that God cares for cities, in spite of their sin. From Sodom and Gomorrah to Nineveh, from Babylon to Jerusalem, God's will is to save and to make fully human not just individuals, but communities. British Prime Minister Margaret Thatcher may have believed that there was no such thing as society, but such a belief is not grounded in the biblical tradition.

As Ellul reminds us in *The Meaning of the City* (1970), the world may start with a garden but it ends with a city, the New Jerusalem. The primary relationship of God is with and to the world. "For God so loved the world..." (John 3:16). It is in that context that I understood the work of the church and its outreach ministries in the city.

At North End Community Ministry we saw ourselves as a ministry *to* the church as well as a ministry *of* the church, calling on the faithful to seek also the welfare of the city. We saw ourselves as part of the prophetic ministry of the church, challenging people to embrace a politics of engagement with the needs of the inner city rather than a politics of disengagement and abandonment. I would guest preach at United Church pulpits around the city and warn people that Winnipeg was developing into a city that looked like a doughnut; a cluster of communities arranged according to economic categories, around a deteriorating middle.

In a sermon at Fort Garry United Church in April 1978, I described two ways we were working for long-term change. First, by working with allied groups that could pressure the government on housing, rent controls, Aboriginal issues, daycare, and so on. Second, by bringing the concerns of our ministry in the inner city—where despair, woundedness, and need were so evident—back to the rest of the church, offering the whole people of God in Winnipeg the possibility to act for justice and health in the here and now. I concluded, "We want to help the church to be the church. This offering of ours is intended to be and ought, it seems to me, to be received as a gift, rather than as a demand."

My sermons weren't always received as welcome gifts. Around this time the Progressive Conservative Premier of Manitoba, Sterling Lyon, was known to be critical of the United Church for spending too much time on social, economic, and Aboriginal issues and not paying enough attention to saving souls. The cutbacks in resources and services to the poor initiated by Lyon's government when it took office in 1977 were part of the reality that our inner-city ministry had to deal with.

Since our work was funded by the church and therefore free of the threat of government funding cuts, I was often called on to speak out on behalf of the concerns of organizations that had to be more cautious. At times there were many hats to wear, and meetings to attend, from the Housing Action Coalition, the Anti-Sniff Coalition (seeking action against the sale of glue as an inhalant), the Associated Tenants Action Committee, the Inter-Agency Committee, and a group organized to oppose a major overpass through an inner-city neighbourhood. I also enjoyed a good relationship with Hank de

Bruyn, a Christian Reform pastor who ran the Indian Family Centre a few blocks away. De Bruyn was a fine theological sounding board and we had many great discussions.

It was during my work with the Sherbrook-MacGregor overpass group that I had the good fortune to work with Sister Geraldine MacNamara. Sister Mac, as she was known, was the founder of Rossbrook House in Winnipeg's inner city, a drop-in centre. Her philosophy was that "no child who does not want to be alone should ever have to be." Sister Mac died prematurely in her forties, but her legacy continues in the good work that still goes on at Rossbrook House.

I was also privileged to work against the overpass with George Heshka, then-principal of Dufferin School and, since 1980, principal of Sisler High School in Winnipeg's North End. Heshka refuses to retire and is renowned for the quality of his leadership and of the education his students receive. He had been my physics teacher at Transcona Collegiate; in grade 12 he agreed to pass me providing I promised to never take physics again anywhere, a promise I have honoured. It was also during this time in the inner city that I first met Greg Selinger, then a community activist, now the Premier of Manitoba.

In Winnipeg, we were also grappling with the reality that the challenges faced by a growing Aboriginal population were not the same as the challenges faced by the traditional immigrant communities. Therefore, inherited models of ministry in the community would have to change, and indeed much change has taken place in the church's relationship with Aboriginal peoples since that time.

At a national prayer breakfast in the 1990s, an MP who was active in the prayer breakfast movement said, "Some people say it's up to government to get the poor out of the slums. But we in the prayer breakfast know that if we get Jesus into the hearts of the poor, they will get themselves out of the slums." This is a clear-cut example of a divide that exists within the Christian community. This statement contained not a hint of what I consider to be the fundamental insight of the biblical tradition, both in the prophetic tradition of the Old Testament and in the teachings of Christ: what is needed in so many circumstances down through the ages, in order for the poor not to be poor, is for the rich and powerful to have Jesus in their hearts. Or to put it in a more modern way, also for governments—and in a democracy, for the voters—to have Jesus in their hearts. If Jesus were Lord in the hearts of the affluent and the powerful, and Lord in the hearts of voters, governments that wanted to would have a much freer hand in setting the right priorities.

Did Jeremiah, Hosea, Amos, and other biblical prophets bemoan the spiritual life of the orphan, the widow, the stranger, and the needy, and say that if only they turned to God, they would be all right? Or did they address the inadequacies and injustices of the king, and the elite, and the court prophets who told the powerful what they wanted to hear?

The social gospel tradition in Canada, in the United States, in the United Kingdom, and elsewhere has its roots in the inner cities of Toronto, Winnipeg, Chicago, Detroit, and London. There the raw and cruel face of capitalism was bared for all to see, and Christians with eyes to see and ears to hear could discern that the central social and economic ethic of the biblical tradition was one that stood in stark contrast to the conventional wisdom of the world. It was at the Mansfield House inner-city mission in London's East End that J.S. Woodsworth's comfort with the world was first shaken.

———

In this 21st-century, pluralistic, secular Canada, any dialogue between politics and religion writ large must transcend older paradigms. In this sensitive environment, even language like the "social gospel" can be heard as residual Christian imperialism if it is not used properly. There is a need to make the same connection between social democratic principles and the prophetic traditions in all the major faiths as was made by an earlier generation between progressive politics and social gospel theology.

What better place to begin this task than in the inner cities of our country? There we find both the diversity and the need for a new prophetic unity in that diversity that speaks out of, and to, all the faith traditions present among the Canadians who live there. Jesus cried over Jerusalem, and it is tempting for those who have been actively seeking the welfare of their city for years to cry over Canadian cities. I certainly felt this way when, in preparation for a sermon I recently gave, I dug through my files and looked at presentations my colleagues and I had made 30 years ago concerning Winnipeg's inner city, and what would happen if we did not invest massively on a number of counts to deal properly with the growing Aboriginal population in Winnipeg. Today we are reaping the whirlwind, having sown our current state with various stages of inaction over the years, or in some cases, the wrong actions, like the damage that was done by residential schools.

Seek the welfare of the city you are in, says Jeremiah to the exiles in Babylon. Build houses and live in them, plant gardens, raise children, for in the city's welfare you will find your own. The faithful are not asked to leave Babylon, or to destroy it, but to seek its welfare. This is sound biblical advice to those who experience the city as a place of exile from the world that they would like to be living in.

Note that the prophetic instruction is not to *build* the city, to take part in any vain attempt at immortality and fame. The welfare or peace that we seek for the city will not always be what the city seeks for itself. If the city seeks more and more luxurious housing developments, while affordable housing for low-income families goes unbuilt, the biblically instructed will beg to differ. The Christian calling, I believe, is to live in the city, speaking individually and collectively, as the church, to the pretensions of the city. It is to speak a discerning word to the city, when the real welfare of the city is ignored in favour of powerful interests or entrenched ways of looking at it that keep us from doing what we need to do to build just, sustainable communities.

CHAPTER

7

First Peoples and Constitutional Debates

If we could not agree or reach a compromise
for our own sakes, then we needed to do it
for the sake of the world.

Because of my recent experiences in inner-city ministry, when I was elected to the House of Commons on May 22, 1979, Aboriginal issues were top of mind.

That February, I had preached at the service of thanksgiving for Robertson House, which was sold when North End Community Ministry decided to consolidate the work that had been going on there and at Stella Mission. I spoke of the grand history boasted by Robertson House, a Presbyterian ministry founded in 1912 that became part of the United Church in 1925, and all the good work that went on there. It was hard to go anywhere in Manitoba without running into someone who had played basketball or attended Sunday school at Robertson House. But I also spoke about the changes that were happening in Winnipeg's inner city and North End, including the massive influx of Aboriginal people coming into the city. "They are the new immigrants," I said, "or to be more accurate, migrants, commuters from one culture and place to another…where cultural differences, prejudice, and difficulty in adjusting to urban ways pose serious economic and personal problems."

How these difficulties were dealt with would be crucial to the future of life in Winnipeg. We couldn't rely on ways of ministry developed for immigrants to the city from a faraway country. Native peoples, to use the language of the time, were indeed, as we now say, First Peoples who were here before us.

I'm embarrassed to admit that at the time I knew next to nothing about the role that residential schools had played in contributing to the social and personal problems that continue to trouble the Aboriginal community. Many years later in March 2000, as an MP, I would speak to this issue in the House of Commons, both to acknowledge the culpability of the churches that participated, but also to urge the government to accept its full share of responsibility; the churches, after all, ran the schools for the federal government.

The United Church, in 1986, would be the first church to publicly apologize for its treatment of Aboriginal peoples; in 1998, the church apologized specifically to former students of residential schools and to their families and communities. An apology by Parliament would take another decade: it was made on June 11, 2008, the same day my mother passed away in the early morning hours. She had been seriously ill since January and took a turn for the worse on Saturday, June 7. I stayed with her in Winnipeg till the end, missing a historic day in the House.

The catalyst for my initial interest in the issue of Aboriginal rights, as was the case for many of my generation, had been *Northern Frontier, Northern Homeland: The Report of the Mackenzie Valley Pipeline Inquiry* by Justice Thomas Berger, which was released in the spring of 1977. The Berger Inquiry was the federal government's response to the proposal by Canadian Arctic Gas Pipeline Ltd., a consortium of 27 major petroleum, pipeline, and transportation companies, to construct a 4,000-kilometre natural gas pipeline to carry gas from Alaska and the Mackenzie River Delta to southern markets by way of the Mackenzie Valley. Berger's resulting ethical manifesto challenged Canada not just to do justice in the North, but also to change our way of life in the South:

> We have never had to determine what is the most intelligent use to make of our resources. We have never had to consider restraint. Will we continue, driven by technology and egregious patterns of consumption, to deplete our energy resources wherever and whenever we find them?
>
> If we build the pipeline, it will seem strange, years from now, that we refused to do justice to the native people merely to continue to provide ourselves with a range of consumer goods and comforts without even asking Canadians to consider an alternative.

"Years from now" has arrived, and although the pipeline has yet to be built, we are only a bit further down the road of rethinking our consumptive lifestyles. And the reality of climate change wasn't even being discussed in 1977. The first mention of it in Parliament didn't occur until 1983, when it was raised by Simon de Jong, NDP MP for Regina.

It is seldom noted, but Prime Minister Trudeau's appointment of the thoughtful Berger, a former NDP member of Parliament and former leader of the B.C. New Democrats, happened during the famous Liberal minority Parliament of 1972–74 when the NDP under David Lewis held the balance of power. Berger would establish a way of understanding the relationship between Aboriginal and non-Aboriginal Canadians that was diametrically opposed to the assimilationist views characteristic of the Liberal policy up until that time, particularly in the government's White Paper of 1969, a document that reads strangely now, if for no other reason than its use of the term "Indians" rather than the now familiar "Aboriginal" or "First Nations."

The White Paper was seen as advocating an assimilationist viewpoint, because it called for the abolition of the Indian Act in the context of an overall policy framework that talked about ending the separation between Indians and other Canadians, and creating equality between the two groups. Services now provided by the federal government would be turned over to the provinces. And measures to "enable title" would be considered as a way of permitting reserve land to ultimately become private property and be disposable in the marketplace.

The White Paper was a turning point but, ironically, not in the direction it pointed. Instead it was the catalyst for creating within the Indian community a rousing defence of their rights and their relationship with the Crown. *The Unjust Society* by Harold Cardinal, an Aboriginal activist from Alberta, made a significant contribution to the debate following the White Paper. The book's title was a play on Pierre Trudeau's call for a "just society." I read Cardinal's book sometime in the early 1970s and it got me thinking. Later I would read Dee Brown's *Bury My Heart at Wounded Knee: An Indian History of the American West* and still later Vine Deloria Jr.'s *God Is Red: A Native View of Religion*, books that further caused me to question the easy self-righteousness about the past and the present that was characteristic of the Canadian and Christian world view I had grown up in.

The 1969 White Paper is rich in various ironies. It reads in some ways like the things that the Reform Party would say in the 1990s. This is not completely aberrant, in the sense that the Reform Party often sounded like

Trudeau on another issue, the equality of the provinces and opposition to any special status for Quebec, a view that Stephen Harper would abandon in his search for more support in Quebec. The more current irony is that all the court rulings, constitutional developments, and general evolution of the Aboriginal community in Canada, combined with the Harper government's finally agreeing to sign the UN Declaration on the Rights of Indigenous Peoples, have led to a situation where musing about the abolition of the Indian Act is now permissible in many quarters. None other than Shawn Atleo, National Chief of the Assembly of First Nations, has called for serious consideration of such a policy. Of course not everyone has the same idea of what a post–Indian Act reality would look like. How it is done, and what the total policy package should be when it happens, will be a critical debate.

In the summer of 1977, as the student minister at West Hawk Lake United Church in Manitoba's Whiteshell Provincial Park, I led a study group on the recently released Berger Report. At the end of the study we all signed a letter to the federal government advocating a moratorium. The letter read, in part:

> As we understand it, the call for a moratorium on the decision to build a pipeline would provide the time which is required to settle land claims, improve the technology required to protect the environment should a pipeline be built, and enlist the Canadian public in informed and thoughtful discussion about whether it wishes to continue its present energy intensive way of life until it is no longer physically possible to do so, or whether it wishes to begin a serious search for alternatives now.

There was much in the Berger Report that resonated with the biblical commandments to do justice and to be good stewards of creation. Canadian churches had actively presented to the inquiry and pressed for the comprehensive hearings, in southern as well as northern Canada, that made this inquiry so unique. At the end of the day, Berger's recommendations overlapped significantly with the churches' recommendations.

––––––––

As far back as September 1975, the Anglican, Roman Catholic, and United churches had created the Inter-Church Project on Northern Development, which became known as Project North. Very soon the coalition expanded to include the Lutheran Church in America—Canada Section, the Mennonite Central Committee, the Presbyterian Church, the Evangelical Lutherans, and later on the Jesuits, the Council of Christian Reformed Churches, the Quakers, and the Oblate Order.

Having read *Moratorium: Justice, Energy, the North and the Native People* by Hugh McCullum, Karmel Taylor McCullum, and John Olthuis, I was ripe to be recruited, as I was, into the work of Project North. A group of us, in consultation with Hugh McCullum and others from Project North, founded the Manitoba Inter-Church Coalition on Resource Development in the late 1970s, focusing on raising awareness of the proposed Polar Gas Pipeline that was to come down through northern Manitoba. I was the coalition's founding chair.

Work with Project North and its Manitoba offshoot enabled me to get to know many people, many of whom I would continue to stay in touch with for the next 30 years and whose support I would benefit from in various ways. I think in particular of Gerald Vandezande, then executive director of the Committee for Justice and Liberty (which later became Citizens for Public Justice). Vandezande, one of the finest Christian activists I have ever known, was a frequent visitor to my Ottawa office over the years. Locally, I was pleased in the years that followed my Project North work to be supported in my ongoing political life by clergy from other denominations I had first met at that time, people like Lutheran colleagues John Kunkel and Cliff Monk.

In February 1978 Project North sponsored an event at the Indian and Métis Friendship Centre in Winnipeg at which I spoke, along with Hugh McCullum and Stan McKay Jr. McCullum would die in 2008 after a life of prophetic journalism devoted to pointing out injustices that cried out for attention in Canada and around the world. McKay, in his capacity as president of the United Church Conference of Manitoba and Northwestern Ontario, would ordain me to the ministry of the United Church on June 4, 1978, in Ashern, Manitoba. Later he would become the first—and to date the only—Aboriginal Moderator of the United Church from 1992 to 1994.

Connections we had through McKay and with the Aboriginal communities in the north led to a daylong meeting the coalition set up one winter day at Garden Hill First Nation in northern Manitoba. We flew early in the morning by Perimeter Air and returned later the same day. Our connection with Garden Hill was enhanced by the fact that the pastor of the Aboriginal congregation that met at Stella Mission, Annanias Fiddler, was from that First Nation.

We had a good day in Garden Hill, although I was initially very frustrated by how late things got started. That cross-cultural experience laid bare my not-so-residual Presbyterian attachment to punctuality. A week or so after the event, I was contacted by what was then called the Manitoba Indian Brotherhood, headed by Chief Moses Okimaw. I ended up at an executive meeting of the MIB in which the coalition was severely criticized for going into one of their communities without giving them notice or seeking their permission. I listened, and I thought they had a point.

At the same time, I was also aware that we had gone there in connection and co-operation with people from that community. Were we recreating forms of paternalism by going to Garden Hill without contacting the MIB, or did our contacts with church folk in those communities provide us with a legitimate basis for being there? Was the MIB simply protecting their turf, or did they have a larger point to make? When I raised it with members of the coalition at a subsequent meeting, opinion was somewhat divided, but most felt that we had done nothing wrong in dialoguing with our fellow church folk in the north. But somewhere the church's independence had bumped up against the appropriateness of consulting the political leadership of the community.

Over three decades later, in June 2010, I would participate in a round table on Crown/Aboriginal consultations, and have the role of introducing a government presenter. The First Nations responder was Moses Okimaw.

————

In October 1978 I was privileged to attend what turned out to be a historic meeting in Saskatoon, Saskatchewan, where church leaders, Aboriginal leaders, and public interest groups from across the country met to devise a strategy for creating support in southern Canada for Aboriginal rights. It was the first time that many of the Aboriginal leaders had met each other, and the first time that leaders of the Innu from Labrador, then known as Naskapi and Montagnais, were included. Later on, as an MP, I would speak out against the low-level flying over Innu territory by NATO planes in training.

In Saskatoon, I met Georges Erasmus for the first time; his capacity to speak eloquently and intelligently about the issues facing the Dene Nation impressed me very much indeed. Like me, Erasmus was already named as an NDP candidate for the federal election that would come in May 1979. He was running in Western Arctic, and many times I wished he had won and been part of our caucus in Ottawa. Erasmus went on to do great work as the head of the Assembly of First Nations and with the 1996 Royal Commission on Aboriginal Peoples.

When I arrived at the House, coming from work in inner-city ministry and Project North, I was not alone in my concern for Aboriginal issues. These issues were also important to many other new NDP members who were elected that year, or in the election that followed the next year when Joe Clark's short-lived Progressive Conservative minority government fell. Several were from British Columbia: Jim Manly, Jim Fulton, Svend Robinson, and Ian Waddell, who had been legal counsel to the Berger Inquiry. These concerns were also shared by the other new NDP MPs in 1979 from Manitoba, Rod Murphy and Terry Sargeant, and in 1980, Cyril Keeper, MP for Winnipeg–St. James. Keeper was one of the few Aboriginal MPs in the House, but one of two in the NDP caucus, along with Peter Ittinuar, an Inuit MP for Nunatsiaq.

My life in Parliament was to provide three defining moments when commitment to justice for Aboriginal peoples was all-important. The first was on the occasion of the patriation of the Constitution in 1982. In the original proposal put forward by Pierre Trudeau in October 1980 there was no mention of Aboriginal rights. NDP leader Ed Broadbent had endorsed Trudeau's proposal the very evening it was announced without consulting his caucus. He was of the view that we Western MPs would find sufficient an amendment to Trudeau's proposal having to do with provincial ownership of resources. But these jurisdictional issues weren't top of mind for a lot of us.

As I remember it, about half a dozen of us made it quite clear to Broadbent that he would have to go back for more, particularly on Aboriginal rights, if he wanted us to stay on board. This, combined with pressure from the churches and Aboriginal groups, led to a revised proposal that did recognize Aboriginal rights. Yet in the deal that was reached on November 5, 1981, between Trudeau and the provinces, minus Quebec, that language was removed. After a Supreme Court decision in September 1981 that acknowledged a constitutional convention for substantial provincial agreement before significant constitutional change, a finding not to Trudeau's liking, there had been much give and take on the package to get the deal in November. After a great hue and cry, the language of recognition was reinstated, but consciously weakened with the addition of the word *existing*. The final wording of Section 35 spoke of the "Indians, Inuit, and Métis peoples of Canada" as the "aboriginal peoples of Canada" whose "existing aboriginal and treaty rights" were "recognized and affirmed."

In a speech to the House of Commons on December 1, 1981, I had the following to say, in language that anticipated the theme of the United Church's 1986 apology that said, "We confused Western ways and culture with the depth and breadth and length and height of the gospel of Christ."

To a great extent our historic approach to Native people was conditioned by the absolutism of Western Christianity and its missionary zeal for conforming everyone to its way of life. Like the Christian Jews in the Book of Acts who thought that Greeks would have to become circumcised in order to become Christians, Western Christianity thought that the gospel meant that the Indians would have to become something other than themselves.

Of course the patriation debate was about more than Aboriginal rights. It was about the Charter of Rights and Freedoms, and about Quebec, particularly when Quebec refused to sign on to the patriation package because it contained an amending formula that did not give Quebec a veto over further constitutional change. The NDP caucus was divided on these elements of the package. Some voted against it because of the notwithstanding clause that was inserted in the final draft of the Charter, preserving the right of Parliament to overrule the courts in certain circumstances. Personally I liked that clause, although its absence would not have been a deal breaker. The notwithstanding clause was perhaps the only time I remember agreeing with then–Manitoba Tory Premier Sterling Lyon. Fortunately, I did so in the company of Allan Blakeney, then NDP Premier of Saskatchewan, who never abandoned his concern that although the Charter was important to the protection of individual rights, it would have a role in setting public policy that properly belonged to the elected. The debate between Blakeney and Tommy Douglas at the 1981 national convention of the NDP over the patriation package and the Charter was something that those who were there will never forget.

My attitude toward the notwithstanding clause is part of a larger tendency on my part to be wary of excessive judicial activism. I agree that constitutions and charters are living documents, but when judges decide that what Parliament passed did not mean what it clearly did mean when it was passed, or that it means something opposite to the understanding that obtained in Parliament at the time, I think it is legitimate to ask who are the lawmakers and who are not. The Charter was seen to be an uncritical good by most of the left at the time. But the power of Parliament is sometimes surrendered too easily to the courts by the left, and always too easily to the market and corporate free trade agreements by the political right. The property rights that were left out of the Charter have been more than compensated by their elevation to idolatrous levels in the trade agreements, which I will go into later.

On Quebec, the fact that 74 out of 75 Quebec MPs voted for the patriation package should absolve those of us from the rest of Canada from the accusation of wilfully imposing something on Quebec that it did not want. Nevertheless, this was felt to be a real problem, and Prime Minister Mulroney set out to fix it with the much-maligned Meech Lake Accord. The accord, which sought to create a constitution that Quebec would sign on to, was reached in June 1987, and failed in June 1990 when the three years for its adoption expired without the approval of the Manitoba legislature, thanks to the refusal of Elijah Harper, NDP member for Rupertsland, to permit the procedural unanimous consent that was needed to meet the deadline.

I know that Elijah Harper is a hero to many for holding up his eagle feather the day he prevented the vote in the Manitoba legislature. My feelings are more ambiguous, because of what followed from the defeat of the accord, and because he subsequently ran for the federal Liberals in 1993. His later claim that he could not get an NDP federal nomination was just baloney. I was on the NDP election planning committee that beseeched him to run in Winnipeg North Centre, which we had lost in 1988 and which we kept open for him for many, many months.

Meech Lake was not a time when I was at one with the Aboriginal stance on a constitutional issue. I felt that the initial political assessment of the accord by many Aboriginal leaders had been correct, that having a successful Quebec constitutional round would clear the way for a successful Aboriginal round of constitutional talks, in spite of the failure of the post-patriation conferences on Aboriginal rights. This was not to be. More and more was made of the absence of any progress on Aboriginal issues in the Meech Lake Accord, and one by one the politics of the Aboriginal community drove almost everyone into a critical and then an oppositional stance.

The same thing happened in our party. The day after the agreement, Broadbent had walked across the floor to shake Mulroney's hand. By the time of the NDP leadership race in 1989, if you were not prepared to morph on Meech Lake there was no point in running, a trend that Audrey McLaughlin got way ahead of when, in light of the Yukon NDP government's opposition to Meech Lake over the formula for creation of new provinces, Broadbent gave her a special dispensation to oppose the accord as the NDP candidate in the Yukon by-election of August 1987.

The Meech Lake Accord fell victim to concerns about decentralization, national standards for social programs, the distinct society clause, and the Senate proposals, coupled on the left with a visceral dislike of Mulroney over the free trade deal that was also an issue at the time. It was also a victim of internal Liberal politics between the Trudeau-Chrétien position on Quebec and the Turner-Martin position, which was more sympathetic to Quebec's need to be treated as a community or nation within Canada. It is no coincidence that the accord's final weeks coincided with the Chrétien victory over Martin for the Liberal leadership in June 1990.

I could never make up my mind whether anti–Meech Lake politicians like Manitoba Liberal Sharon Carstairs and New Brunswick Liberal Frank McKenna were just opportunists, who played with constitutional matches and started a fire they could not put out, or whether they truly thought the accord was as bad as they made it out to be. To the extent that Manitoba MLA Jim Walding of the NDP contributed to the demise of Meech by voting against his own party's budget, causing the provincial election that allowed Carstairs to defeat the pro–Meech Lake NDP government of Howard Pawley, he played a role in Canadian and not just Manitoba history. So did the people who tried to take the NDP nomination from Walding in 1986, and failed by one vote, thus setting up the 1988 debacle. I often reflected on the significance of that one vote, but to the extent that I thought I might write about it one day, I was beaten to the punch by Ian Stewart, the author of *Just One Vote*.

I can imagine another such book devoted to another significant vote, the vote in the NDP caucus in December 1979 to move a motion of non-confidence that the Liberals could support and thereby create the possibility of defeating the newly elected minority government of Prime Minister Joe Clark. I was one of five who was against the idea, in spite of being assured that the Liberals would not bring down the government when they were leaderless, Trudeau having announced that he was stepping down. We now know that there was contact between the leadership of the Liberals and the NDP on this and that the caucus was not being told the truth about the possibilities. The defeat of the government saw me invited to appear on *The Watson Report* on CBC TV with Liberal Bob Kaplan and Tory Bill Yurko to discuss the vote. I was thrilled to be on such a national program. When it was over I called Brenda from Toronto to say that I was definitely a politician now; I had just publicly defended a decision I did not agree with. Or I had respected the decision of caucus. Canada would be a different place today if the circumstances for Trudeau's return had not been created by that vote on December 13, 1979. We would, for starters, probably have no Charter of Rights and Freedoms, and certainly no Canada Health Act. Which is why, although I did not like the process, I am reluctant to wish that I had carried the day in the caucus debate.

The irony, of course, is that after the closeness of the 1995 Quebec referendum, Chrétien proceeded to do by way of policy and parliamentary resolution much of what the Meech Lake Accord had called for in terms of distinct society, devolution of federal powers, and social programs. My only role in the 1995 referendum was to attend the big pro-Canada rally in Montreal that so greatly irritated the separatists. Despite my attendance at the rally, and all the other ways that Canadians outside Quebec like myself participate in issues affecting Canada and Quebec, my years in Ottawa left me with a feeling that the rest of us are far too often reduced to spectators watching a family fight in Quebec that we have little or no influence over, but which has no end of influence over us.

The way I see it we ended up with some of what was worst about Meech without the benefit of the acceptance of and by Quebec that it had tried to achieve. Instead, out of the failure of Meech, we got the Bloc Québécois, and then out of the failure of the Charlottetown Accord in 1992, which attempted to resolve many of the issues that had crippled Meech, we got the rise of the Reform Party. Reform came together riding a wave of animosity toward Mulroney that, at least in the West, had started in earnest in 1986 when the federal government awarded the CF-18 fighter aircraft contract to Montreal, although Winnipeg had the better bid.

The CF-18 controversy was a classic political dilemma, in which I was torn between region, party, and even conscience to some degree, insofar as the controversy was about the production of fighter aircraft that were arguably not integral to my vision of what our economy should depend on. It was also a tactical challenge. Whenever I asked Winnipeg Tory MPs how the contract talks were going, I was told everything was going all right and not to politicize the issue by raising it in the Commons. When Winnipeg did not get the contract, I was criticized for my silence leading up to the decision. Had I acted otherwise, I would likely have been blamed for spoiling something that was going just fine until I spoke up. Former Manitoba NDP premier Howard Pawley provides an extensive account of the CF-18 controversy in his political memoir *Keep True*.

The Charlottetown Accord, unlike Meech Lake, did contain much in the way of progress for First Nations and Aboriginal self-governance, but it was too loaded with new policy options on a variety of other matters to survive a referendum. One only had to disagree with one policy in the accord in order to vote against it. But the image of Grand Chief Ovide Mercredi at the table with the premiers and the Prime Minister at the Charlottetown negotiations will always be for me an image of what could have been.

The highlight of the Charlottetown Accord disaster for me was the opportunity it unexpectedly provided me with to meet and debate a Manitoba political legend. When I remember that time, I try not to focus on the fact that 69 percent of my constituents voted the opposite of what I was actively encouraging them to do. Instead I remember debating former Manitoba premier Douglas Campbell, who served in the Manitoba legislature for 47 years, retiring in 1969. He was Premier from 1948 to 1958. By 1992, Campbell was 97 years old and had become a member of the Reform Party. He was the person the "No" Committee sent to debate me when Immanuel United Church in my riding sponsored a town hall during the referendum on the accord. No one locally would volunteer. The debate with Campbell was a real treat. In spite of the fact that he was blind, he seemed to know the accord inside and out. But the best part was the civil and gentlemanly way in which he debated, a style I was only too happy to replicate in response. It was one of the best debates I ever participated in. Neither of us persuaded the other, but we did find common ground in our affection for Scotland's Immortal Bard, Robert Burns. Most of my other Charlottetown debates were with anti-Charlottetown Liberals, whose intellectual dishonesty seemed to know no bounds, especially when their leader, Jean Chrétien, was appearing on stages in Winnipeg with me and others in support of the accord.

My second opportunity to follow up on justice for Aboriginal peoples was when I had the pleasure, although it sometimes felt like misery, of voting 141 times against 141 frivolous amendments put forward by Preston Manning's Reform Party in 1999, to protest the ratification by Parliament of the historic Nisga'a Treaty, which made landmark progress on Aboriginal self-government and Aboriginal resource ownership in northern British Columbia.

This protest was definitely a low point for the Reformers. But the future is always open. Chuck Strahl, one of the Reform MPs who acted like the treaty with the Nisga'a (also spelled Nishga) was the end of the world, went on to become the Minister of Aboriginal Affairs in the government of Stephen Harper. In my not inconsiderable collection of political T-shirts, one of my favourites reads "Nishga – 141, Reform – 0."

The third occasion, the debate over the Clarity Act (Bill C-20) in 1999–2000, would be the one in which I had the most personal input. The Clarity Act was the Chrétien government's response to the Supreme Court findings concerning the separation of Quebec from Canada, in terms of both domestic and international law. The Court, responding to a reference put to it by the federal government, argued that the rest of Canada would have an obligation to negotiate separation if Quebecers rendered a clear majority on a clear question, but it left the meaning of *clear majority* and *clear question* up to the politicians. C-20 was an attempt to lay out the process by which that determination would be made and who had a right to participate in the process of defining a clear majority and clear question.

Much to my dismay, the bill did not include the Aboriginal people of Quebec among those who would need to be consulted in determining these two questions. In committee I moved amendments to include the Quebec Cree in the process, but the amendments never came to a vote because the Liberals imposed closure on the committee, demanding that its whole process, witnesses included, be concluded in two weeks.

The NDP had supported the Clarity Act at second reading, mostly on my recommendation as the caucus member with responsibility for constitutional and intergovernmental affairs. But many in caucus and in the party thought that the legislation was an affront to the principle of Quebec's self-determination, and to the commitment of Quebec to fair and democratic due process. A meeting of the party's federal council produced much criticism of the caucus decision, and of me in particular, for supporting C-20. Alexa McDonough, leader of the NDP at the time, quite properly reserved the right of caucus to do as it thought best at third and final reading. When the bill came back to the House for report stage at third reading, I moved the amendments again, though by now with no expectation of their acceptance. The cabinet minister in charge of C-20 was Stéphane Dion, who had entered the House of Commons in 1996 as a result of a by-election in Quebec and was appointed Minister of Intergovernmental Affairs.

My first encounter with Dion had been when he sought a meeting with McDonough; she asked me to accompany her to it. I remember bristling at the way Dion spoke to us. When he spoke about Quebec and the virtues of his own perspective on Canadian federalism, he demonstrated a unique blend of condescension and intellectual arrogance that I was not going to take from someone who had been on the political sidelines when my political neck, and that of my party, had been stuck out time after time in the cause of national unity. After informing him of this rather directly, we got along better. It would not be all that long before we would encounter each other again in a more public context.

In the House at C-20's third reading, I explained that we now felt compelled to vote against the bill, given the government's intransigence on the amendments. The intransigence was a gift in some ways, as it would have permitted us to vote against the bill and thus mollify our critics in the party. But after my speech, one of the best I ever gave in the House, Dion talked with me behind the Speaker's chair. He offered to give me the amendments on the Cree if we would support the bill. I couldn't give any guarantees but I said I would do my best.

We ended up voting for C-20, which passed in March 2000. The Quebec Cree got the amendments they had been asking for, and unfortunately for me, I came to be vilified by the Quebec NDP. In the party's federal leadership race of 2002–03 my role in the Clarity Act would prove to be a burden, not only in Quebec, but also among all those New Democrats who thought that our role should have been to automatically agree with the Quebec National Assembly. In my view, respect for the special story of Quebec should not always mean, short of separation itself, uncritical agreement with whatever the consensus in Quebec happens to be on such issues.

I am proud of the role that I played in securing the rights of the Aboriginal people of Quebec to be consulted about the future of Quebec in Canada. And I do not regret being supportive of legislation that would make it much more difficult for a separatist Quebec government to take Quebec out of Canada without a democratically adequate political process. Suffice to say that Lucien Bouchard, who had gone from being the leader of the Bloc Québécois to the Premier of Quebec, left politics shortly thereafter. In the election of 2011 the NDP swept the province of Quebec with a positive social democratic message, as many voters in that province decided to have some say in what kind of Canada they wanted to live in presently, no matter what the state of the debate about Quebec's future.

In all the constitutional debates, and the divisiveness caused by them, one theme was central to my approach. If we could not agree or reach a compromise for our own sakes, then we needed to do it for the sake of the world. A Canada that fails, when people look to us as an example of where harmony is found in diversity, would be a sin against hope. If we cannot get along with each other, with all that we have going for us, what kind of encouragement or sign would that be to those who struggle in far more difficult circumstances?

An Effective Electorate

What was needed was not a free vote, it was a
full-scale rebellion within the Liberal Party or,
alternatively, the election of a party to government
that would take Canada in a different direction.

The church is not the only institution that is reluctant to make the concrete political choices that, in the context of Nazi Germany, theologian Dietrich Bonhoeffer spoke about. Many social movements or single-issue coalitions, some of which the mainline churches participate in, share a reluctance to move from describing abstract principles to endorsing concrete electoral choices, such as which party to vote for in a particular situation. As an MP, I would often be frustrated with this tendency. An early example came in the 1980s, courtesy of the peace movement.

In the spring of 1982, with the United Nations Second Special Session of the General Assembly devoted to Disarmament (often referred to as UNSSOD-II) approaching in June, a yearning for peace in a disarmed world began to take on new life in the Western world. In Canada, interest was further focused by the debate about a document called *Security and Disarmament: A Minority Report*, issued that same year by six out of 30 members of the House of Commons Standing Committee on External Affairs and National Defence.

With this report began a chapter in Canada's political history that deserves reflection by all who are truly concerned about effecting policy changes. After two years of consciousness raising, peace marches, and other advocacy, the country would be swept by the Progressive Conservatives, the very political party whose prominent spokespeople most poured scorn on the peace movement.

———

The Minority Report called for a global freeze on the testing, production, and deployment of nuclear weapons and their delivery vehicles, a pledge against the first use of nuclear weapons, and denial of permission to the United States to test the cruise missile system in Canada. The low-flying cruise was a development in the nuclear arms race that, by complicating verification, would make the world much more dangerous. The report was signed by three out of the three New Democrats on the committee, two out of 11 Tories, and one out of 16 Liberals. Hardly an all-party consensus!

Yet the rhetoric that grew around the Minority Report and its peace policies suffered from the very beginning from an overuse of concepts like "all-party," "non-partisan," and various other flights of wishful thinking. It is one thing to claim that the issue of peace crosses party lines. It does. But it is a fatal strategic flaw to ignore political reality and contribute to the confusion that the powers and principalities love to keep us in.

In the time leading up to UNSSOD-II in 1982, and then leading up to the Liberals' July 1983 decision to test the cruise missile, organizers of peace rally after peace rally across the country diligently made sure that they had spokespeople from all three political parties, and if possible, from all levels of government. Typically, Paul McRae, the one Liberal who signed the Minority Report, would speak against testing the cruise. Everyone would cheer, and no mention would be made that McRae did not speak for his leader, his caucus, or any other identifiable group of Liberals.

Tory Walter McLean, another signatory to the report, would also speak, with no mention that McLean did not speak for his leader, his caucus, or any numerically or ideologically significant group within the PC party. It was all one big happy family, topped off by a New Democrat like Terry Sargeant or Pauline Jewett, who—though they did speak for their leader, their caucus, and the entire New Democratic Party—could only allude to the differences between the NDP and the other two parties at the risk of appearing "partisan." Too many people went home assured that everyone supported the peace movement, no matter their political stripe. They felt that they were part of a great groundswell that would soon remake Canadian nuclear policy.

Instead, the Liberals would decide to test the cruise missile, a decision they announced in July 1983 after Parliament had adjourned, so there would be no fuss. Not to worry. There was not a murmur of protest from the Official Opposition anyway. Only the NDP protested. In facing a choice to refuse the cruise, thereby refusing to collaborate in the creation of a whole new generation of non-verifiable nuclear weapons, Canada had before it, in the prophet's words, the choice between life and death. ("I have set before you life and death, blessings and curses. Choose life so that you and your descendants may live…" Deuteronomy 30:19.) We chose death.

––––––––––

An NDP motion to refuse the cruise had come to a vote on June 14, 1983, more than a year after the Minority Report was released. The NDP had held off on initiating the motion as long as possible, hoping to build consensus and bring others on board. Still, having waited until it could no longer be put off, we were accused of politicizing and polarizing the issue.

It's hard to know when to take the "don't politicize the issue" argument seriously, and miscalculations can have long-term political consequences. In 1986, for example, I would take such advice from Winnipeg Tory MPs on the CF-18 contract, and a great deal of political hay would be made by those who formed the Reform Party a year later about the NDP's failure to stick up for Western Canada.

In 1983, only one Liberal voted against the cruise. It was not Paul McRae; he hid behind the fact that the motion was procedurally a matter of confidence in the government, a refuge for the timid on opposition motions that would be removed a few years later by recommendation of the McGrath Committee. The only Liberal to vote with the NDP that day was Warren Allmand. Although my regard for Allmand is high, his willingness to vote independently on this and other occasions had the unfortunate consequence—to the quiet delight, I imagine, of the Liberal leadership—of keeping a great many Canadians from giving up on the Liberal party.

Four Tories voted to refuse the cruise: Walter McLean, Doug Roche, Jack Murta, and John Fraser. McLean was a Presbyterian minister, and we would have much occasion to work together, particularly on the External Affairs Committee from 1987 to 1990. Roche, who came to Parliament in 1972 as a Catholic activist, is also someone with whom I shared many perspectives over the years, while he served as an MP, an ambassador for disarmament, and a senator. One of his favourite quotes is also a favourite of mine. It is the words of the famous postwar American diplomat George Kennan, who said, in his book *The Nuclear Delusion*:

> The readiness to use nuclear weapons against other human beings.... and, in doing so, to place in jeopardy the natural structure upon which all civilization rests, as though the safety and perceived interests of our own generation were more important than everything that has taken place or could take place in civilization: this is nothing less than a presumption, a blasphemy, an indignity—an indignity of monstrous dimensions—offered to God!

———

Following the cruise missile vote came Prime Minister Trudeau's peace initiative, in which he personally visited both Eastern- and Western-bloc leaders in the fall of 1983. To his credit, Trudeau had not been panicked by the shooting down of the civilian Korean Airlines flight 007 by the Soviets that September into the same fits of self-righteousness and Manichaean good-versus-evil rhetoric that this tragic event inspired in certain other Western leaders. Instead, he appeared to consider it evidence of the need for *more* attempts at dialogue between the superpowers. Relationships so fragile that they could lead to such events had to be strengthened, not aggravated by the cosmological ramblings characteristic of the American political right. But Trudeau's initiative was also motivated, I believe, by a desire to divert attention from the Liberal unwillingness to act when it came to concrete proposals for breaking the spell of the nuclear arms race madness.

Pierre Trudeau's peace initiative was received with a yawn everywhere else in the world. Trudeau, subsequent peace prizes notwithstanding, did not have the respect he needed to really influence the situation. By downgrading Canada's contribution to NATO over the years and letting our conventional armed forces deteriorate, he had lost the ability to be heard by our allies as a peer. Yet he was not willing to regain their respect the only other way he could: by taking bold action to help stem the rush to the nuclear abyss and firmly abstaining from contributing to technologies of nuclear death. The Prime Minister preferred to be neither hot nor cold, or more accurately, both hot and cold; he would make fine disarmament speeches on the one hand, and test the cruise missile on the other.

Yet understandably, hopeful Canadians grasped at this initiative. Here was a way of redeeming ourselves after our shame on the cruise, a way to believe, once again, that hard political analysis could still be avoided. Canada was a moral agent again, living up to our favourite image of the reconciler, the peacemaker, the nation with the bloodless, clean hands.

Both opposition parties treaded warily when it came to the peace initiative, although they were critical of it for different reasons. Both knew that it was not really being taken seriously. One party was glad of this; the other was sorry. But both parties also knew how mixed up the initiative was with the hopes of the people here at home, and how dangerous it was to criticize it.

The political result for the Liberals, at least temporarily, was satisfactory. Public opinion was favourable, and many Liberals thought that peace might be their ticket to re-election. Trudeau had, in a deft political move, put peace beyond politics in such a way that anyone who criticized him was being inappropriately "political." The NDP was accused of being partisan for trying to include a no-first-use pledge, a nuclear freeze, and a ban on cruise testing in a House of Commons resolution on nuclear disarmament that was otherwise so general as to be almost meaningless.

A political context had been created in which any attempt to substitute the substantive for the platitudinous, or the concrete for the abstract, was either suspect or just plain unwelcome. It was a classic case of what the Hebrew prophets called healing the wound of the people lightly, or crying "'Peace, peace,' when there is no peace" (Jeremiah 6:14).

What the peace movement failed to do, as do many Christian activists on peace and other issues, is to take the nature of political parties in Canada seriously. Candidates were asked to fill out questionnaires asking their position on various issues. Many Liberal and Conservative candidates, whose parties have consistently taken positions not shared by the peace movement, now had their opportunity to differ from their parties. A few would do so sincerely. But many candidates who, the day the 1984 election was called, did not even know what the nuclear freeze was—a radioactive popsicle, maybe?—were suddenly in favour of it. What a pleasant surprise! Canadians concerned about nuclear disarmament could vote for almost anyone now. They did not need to know, and were not helped to know, about any of the events of the last two years, such as which party had voted alone against the cruise.

The energy spent distributing these pious little surveys could have been better spent working for candidates whose political party stood for the things the peace movement stood for. One of the authors of the Minority Report, Terry Sargeant, lost narrowly just outside of Winnipeg, while a great many peace activists wasted away their time giving those who opposed the Minority Report a chance to look good.

Others focused their efforts on pushing for a free vote on disarmament. But what was needed was not a free vote, it was a full-scale rebellion within the Liberal Party or, alternatively, the election of a party to government that would take Canada in a different direction. Even a serious threat of the latter might have produced the former. But instead, those who could have made the threat viable were busy clinging to every hopeful word that came out of the Prime Minister's mouth. Canadians in general, meanwhile, prepared to vote Conservative, presumably for reasons other than their support for the cruise.

Why did Canadians, who in the majority objected to Liberal compliance with American nuclear objectives, vote overwhelmingly for a party that was even more uncritical of those very objectives? Would it have helped if the peace movement had been more politically explicit? Why, apart from naïveté about the Liberals, was there such a reluctance to name New Democrats as the political choice of those who wanted Canada to refuse the cruise, to pledge no first use, and to support a nuclear freeze?

In some cases, tragically, the answer is just plain class-consciousness. There is a class of people in this country who just don't want to have to vote NDP, or even worse, somehow *be* NDP, even though they find themselves agreeing with the NDP's positions. To be a New Democrat is in many respects to be on the outside. Those on the inside find issue groups to be a political halfway house where they can satisfy their conscience without sacrificing their social status. To simplify somewhat, some coalitions thrive on the right side of the tracks. On the wrong side of the tracks, people just join the NDP.

———

A version of what I observed about the politics of the peace movement in the early 1980s would be painfully relived during the years that saw Canada debating first the Canada–U.S. Free Trade Agreement in 1987–88, and then the North American Free Trade Agreement in 1992–93. In the early 1990s, I would find myself in the parliamentary office of an NDP colleague with representatives of the Action Canada Network, an organization formed to oppose the free trade agreements. I watched them listen to a speech by Jean Chrétien, then Leader of the Opposition, sifting through his every word for a basis on which to give some form of approval to the Liberal position on NAFTA. The NDP position, exactly that of the ACN, was taken for granted. The real task seemed somehow to be how to get the Liberals on side, or for some, it appeared to my partisan mind, to so contrive what the Liberals were saying as to imagine that they were taking the ACN line. Why this wishful thinking? Is it personally comforting? Is it done in the vain hope that the Liberals could in the future be held accountable for what they had been imagined to say? Or are some people just loyal Liberals who don't want the coalitions they participate in to come to anti-Liberal conclusions?

At many rallies, NDP speakers spoke with the support of leader, caucus, convention resolutions, and party tradition. Liberal and Conservative speakers at the same rallies were often party mavericks. Yet no distinction was made between the relative credibility of the political parties' messages and no connection to how people should vote, so no real choices were presented. What is the source of this unwillingness to take seriously the reality, the history, and the credibility of political parties on an issue-by-issue basis? And how can voters make choices if only issue analysis, but no political analysis, is provided by social movements?

Such political analysis would not always favour the NDP, of course. But I would rather live with critical analysis than live in a world that avoids it. Distinguishing between the parties seems to be unacceptable; Canadians are treated to a false ecumenism where all politicians are regarded as equally well-meaning—or equally despicable.

The work of coalitions built around social issues can be useful, but it must be capable of a practical political approach when the occasion demands. Coalitions should not be a refuge for those who don't like politics, a safe haven for Liberals to advocate publicly what they dare not push for in their own party, or a context in which a false uniformity, either of common depravity or common zeal for the good, is projected on political parties. The short-term instrumental view that many single-issue groups have of political parties is dangerous to the role of political parties. It leads to too many policy ultimatums and a depreciation of the work that political parties must do to pave the way to electoral success, to unite people behind a comprehensive vision.

The danger is to think that Parliament doesn't matter, that change comes from social movements leading to social consensus leading to social change. When it comes to issues of major redistribution of power or wealth, influencing the parliamentary agenda, which in turn influences the political agenda, is a crucial task. Raising issues in Parliament gives them a legitimacy that they might not otherwise have. And from time to time, the persistence of an opposition party, precisely because it is coming from a party that people just might vote for next time, can make a big difference.

This has been the role of the NDP in Canadian federal politics. But we have to get elected to do it, and we have to get elected in certain numbers. As Stanley Knowles wrote in his 1961 book, *The New Party*, which laid out the vision behind the change from the CCF to the NDP, one of the purposes of those who are dedicated to the well-being of the ordinary people of Canada is to "win enough seats in Parliament and in the Legislatures of the provinces to be able to do the job." No shame there about electoral politics. No doubt there about the importance of the parliamentary realm in the struggle for social change.

There was similarly no doubt on the political right during the late 1980s and '90s. While the unaffiliated left tried to build a social movement and failed politically, Preston Manning built a political movement and changed the face of Canadian politics. A political party that was formed in 1987 was the Official Opposition by 1997, and two mergers later in 2006 formed a government under the leadership of Stephen Harper, one of the original Reformers. I used to kid Reform MPs that they were too anxious to be in power, that they needed the patience and steadfastness of New Democrats. But they were clear about not wanting to be the NDP of the political right, and they weren't.

———

The election of 1993 was a disaster for the NDP. We were reduced to nine seats and lost party status in the House of Commons. I almost lost, myself, coming within a couple of hundred votes of my Liberal challenger, Art Miki. It was an election like no other for me, and not just because it was so close. Miki was a past president of the Japanese Canadian Association, and had worked closely with the NDP over the years in advocating for the apology to, and compensation for, Japanese Canadians who were interned during the Second World War and subsequently relieved of their property. The NDP always had a special passion for this cause—I remember being in Ed Broadbent's office when Miki was there seeking our ongoing help on the matter—going back to the CCF's opposition to the way they were treated at the time. Anyone can look back on such a situation and reflect on the moral inadequacies of their predecessors. It takes something more to be against such things at the time. In the case of the Japanese Canadians, as in so many others, this is the prophetic role that the

CCF/NDP played in Canadian politics. The Liberals, and particularly Trudeau, could never be persuaded to apologize, let alone offer compensation.

Brian Mulroney would be the prime minister who was interested—and succeeded—in doing the right thing for Japanese Canadians. Which is why it seemed so odd that Art Miki would run for the Liberals, and against an NDP incumbent to boot. Mulroney recalls in his memoirs an exchange of notes that took place between us on the floor of the House as to the mystery of Miki's candidacy, given that the Liberals stiffed them for decades, the NDP defended them throughout, from the beginning, and the Tories delivered the apology and compensation package. The story so far untold is the phone call I got one Sunday morning later in the spring of 1993 when Mulroney was still the Prime Minister. The call woke us up. My wife, Brenda, answered the phone beside our bed, and informed me that it was the Prime Minister's Office and would I take a call from him in about five minutes. This being my first prime ministerial call, I said I would and leapt out of bed to get as many synapses firing as I could before his office called again.

Shortly I would hear the familiar voice, beginning with an assurance that he was not calling to offer me a seat in the Senate, so as not to offend my NDP sensitivities. On the contrary, he was sitting on the deck at Harrington Lake, the prime ministerial cottage, with son Nicholas and the dog, "reflecting on the nature of human gratitude." I answered, "Yes…," still wondering what was going on. "So that so-and-so Miki is running for the Liberals. I can't believe it. Just calling to say I hope you kick his ass." After a few other brief comments, the conversation was over and I joked to Brenda that I should have asked him for a substantial donation. In reality, we both took an oath of silence that went unbroken for many years. It was not a political context in which having Brian Mulroney cheering for you was something you wanted anyone to know about.

After our party's devastating showing in that election, it was not long before the living envied the dead, as those of us who did get re-elected became the face of NDP failure rather than of our own ability to have survived it. The worst of it was the Liberals shamelessly abandoning any pretence of being against NAFTA. A few meaningless accords on labour and the environment, and full speed ahead. It was in this context that I attended a conference on renewal of the NDP in Ottawa in August 1994. I participated in the panel on party relations; the panellists were Elaine Bernard, Eugene Kostyra, Maude Barlow, and Peter Leibovitch.

Bernard, a trade unionist who was teaching at Harvard Law School, reminded us that politics is really about deciding what will be handled by individuals and what will be handled by society, citing medicare as an example of how a political agenda spearheaded by the CCF and the NDP moved the financing of health care from an individual to a social responsibility. She characterized the new right as an attempt to push back the boundaries of the social. Kostyra, a trade unionist and former minister in the Manitoba NDP government of Howard Pawley, talked about the need to open the party up to all elements of the progressive left and to work with social movements and coalitions. Leibovitch talked about the current antipolitician fad, arguing that it was all part of a larger antidemocratic strategy. He rightly pointed out that labour and other progressive forces would be seriously weakened if the NDP were to be lost, a discerning observation when one thinks of all the harm that would be done to our social programs in the 1995 budget when the Liberals answered only to the Reform Party in Parliament.

Barlow talked about the role of coalitions, and disputed the idea that coalitions drained people and energy from the party. She argued that politics isn't a zero sum game, and characterized the social movements as the last bastion of "collective" opposition in Canada. The ensuing debate was instructive.

Maude Barlow was chairperson of the non-partisan citizens' organization the Council of Canadians and a founder of the Action Canada Network. I think highly of Barlow's ability to analyze and criticize the corporate agenda; in 1993, she had been the guest speaker at my nomination meeting and her words of commendation were featured in my election pamphlet.

But during that panel discussion in 1994, I challenged her on why Action Canada, of which she was a co-chair, hadn't done more to elect the NDP. Another delegate recalled the example of a big rally against free trade that NDP leader Audrey McLaughlin was not invited to speak at. Barlow countered that it wasn't her job to elect the NDP, that Action Canada couldn't have helped much anyway, and that if our party couldn't persuade people to vote for us then that was our problem. We just weren't very good politicians.

I felt, as others did, that they should have tried and that our problem was their problem, a sentiment that was loudly applauded when I reported it to the plenary on behalf of the panel the next day. Unfortunately for me, the remarks came to be associated with me personally, and I acquired more than a few detractors among the fans and members of such groups.

———

The argument between Maude Barlow and me at the renewal conference goes to the heart of a matter that is yet to be resolved. The failure of the NDP to attract votes in 1993 was not just the NDP's problem, but the problem of all those who believed that a strong vote for an anti-NAFTA party would have been a good thing. Extra-parliamentary groups that operate outside of traditional party structures and develop a following on certain issues have a responsibility, especially when something is being decided at election time that will bind the nation for years to come, to be very explicit, very early, about which political parties are to be supported and which are not. When groups won't do this, or leave it to the last ineffective moment, or endorse only individual MPs but not parties, these groups are part of the problem.

Another version of this syndrome is the habit such groups have of speaking as if all politicians are either ignorant of their position or opposed to it, when pointing out that there are some who agree would be more useful. Otherwise a group like the Council of Canadians becomes a surrogate political party that not only doesn't run for office, but also takes the place of those who do in venues such as nationally televised interviews where the views of real choices could be heard, thus confusing and misleading the voting public.

Barlow tells the story from a different point of view in her book *The Fight of My Life*. Acknowledging a "scathing" criticism I wrote of the Council of Canadians at the time, not unlike that found above, she reminds her readers that she was under attack from Mel Hurtig, her former COC colleague, for not overtly supporting the new National Party that he founded with wealthy Winnipeg businessman Bill Loewen to fight the 1993 election. While I agree with her that the National Party was a disaster—it divided the anti-NAFTA vote even further, and caused the defeat of at least three NDP MPs, exactly the number needed to have kept party status—I disagree on two other points. The bigger division of the vote came from anti-NAFTA spokespeople not being frank about the Liberals. Hurtig at least saw that if you don't like the existing choices, you need to form a party, not just a movement.

In this respect there is some similarity between Hurtig and Paul Hellyer, who formed the Canadian Action Party in 1997 as an alternative to what he saw as the Liberal and Conservative capitulation to the corporate globalization agenda and the weakness of the NDP. Hellyer was a cabinet minister in the Liberal governments of Lester B. Pearson and Pierre Trudeau, ran for the Liberal leadership in 1968, fell out with Trudeau eventually, and ended up running for the Tory leadership in 1976. By the late 1990s, to his credit, he could see that the globalization agenda and the trade agreements were bad for Canada and for democracy, but as politically mobile as he had been in the past, becoming a New Democrat just did not seem an option. What he was prepared to do, after the 2000 election, was argue that the NDP and the Canadian Action Party should merge into "one big party," which inspired him to write a book by that same name. Hellyer met with me a few times about the idea, as NDP House Leader and former trade and globalization critic, but I was not interested. At one level it was a ridiculous proposal. A party with a membership of 70,000 was supposed to welcome merging with a party of several hundred, all so Hellyer and his followers could be spared the fate of having to become New Democrats to live out their opposition to globalization.

Nevertheless, it is regrettable that the energy and intellect of a Hellyer could not be harnessed in an effective way. Like Hurtig, he had the personal resources to even consider forming a party, something that is not true for everyone. I also got the impression that Hellyer, like others who have balked at the NDP, found the trade union connection to be a stumbling block. One of Hellyer's passions was his view that the Bank of Canada should be used more extensively to create money and finance public debt, a view that had a lot of supporters in the NDP, though it was not widely supported in public by the party and its spokespeople. I did support such a view myself, and even had an op-ed piece published on the issue at one point. Paul Hellyer had been elected to Parliament in 1949, two years before I was born. It was a treat to meet and talk with him—would that we could all be so keenly interested and active in the politics of our country at such an age.

A variant of this debate would arise in 2000–2001 with the New Politics Initiative. The NPI was a call to decommission the NDP in favour of an ill-described process by which social movements, principally those associated with opposition to the World Trade Organization, would blend with the NDP to form something entirely new. It was born out of frustration with the party's showing in the federal election of 2000, and out of an exaggerated sense of the depth and longevity of an antiglobalization movement that, though still strong, had actually peaked already with the Seattle protests against the World Trade Organization in 1999. Although the initiative was presented as an opportunity for all to have input into its philosophy and policies, its main proponents acted like it was a foregone conclusion that it would be to the left of the NDP. No opportunity was spared to criticize provincial NDP governments, or to portray the federal NDP as being in the "mushy middle."

It was this claim by my long-time colleague Svend Robinson at the 2001 federal NDP convention in Winnipeg that brought me to the microphone. The debate was on the New Politics Initiative, and it looked like it might actually pass. But the claim that the federal NDP was in the mushy middle—when we had just come through the immediate post-9/11 period, in which the NDP had stood alone against the antiterrorism legislation and advocated a different approach to Afghanistan—was too much for me. As NDP Justice Critic at the time, I had been responsible for the antiterrorism Bill C-36 and knew first-hand just how difficult it had been to be the dissenting voice in the post-9/11 atmosphere.

Reciting at the microphone all the times that the party had stood alone, I believe I rallied the convention to the importance and already existing virtue of the NDP. The federal NDP was highly undeserving of such criticism. Far from being in ideological retreat, the federal party had never embraced Tony Blair or Bill Clinton's Third Way, a fancy name for capitulation to the corporate agenda. Neither did we ever give up on our critique of neo-conservative economics and the accompanying world view that marketizes everything. If anything, we were constantly being criticized for failing to "modernize" in this way. Even our provincial wings, though less radical than the federal party, were mounting battles against the very kind of privatization that Blair was championing in the United Kingdom. The Manitoba NDP, for example, had fought the privatization of the Manitoba Telephone System and remained strongly committed to public ownership of Manitoba Hydro.

The NPI motion failed by a vote of 684 to 401, and the New Democratic Party continues. It was after that speech that many approached me about running for the leadership of the party when Alexa McDonough stepped down. But it was also after that speech that many determined that I wouldn't be their candidate for leader. I had reinforced a false perception created in 1994 that I was somehow hostile in principle to extra-parliamentary politics, which, combined with a sense that I was too defensive about the NDP and not open to change, would contribute to my downfall at the January 2003 leadership convention.

The Medicare Crisis

Any debate about the rising costs of health care will only be real if it acknowledges that...there is a need to challenge the profit strategies of the multinational drug corporations.

Early in my parliamentary life I had a very positive experience of how members in the House could work with others to make things happen in Parliament. From 1980 to 1984, as NDP Health Critic, I worked with the Canadian Health Coalition to bring the Canada Health Act into being.

At that time, there was a great debate in the country about medicare. The medicare crisis, over the threat posed by extra-billing by physicians and user fees by hospitals, would culminate successfully in the passage of the Canada Health Act in April 1984. But if it hadn't been for just the right combination of a committed minister, a persistent NDP, distracted Tories, supportive public opinion, and an extra-parliamentary coalition of active, outspoken Canadians, the debate could well have ended otherwise.

———

The origins of Canadian medicare, first introduced nationally in 1968, cannot be separated from the story of the social gospel and the New Democratic Party. The NDP's predecessor, the Co-operative Commonwealth Federation, believed from its inception that one of a country's most precious possessions is the health of its citizens. It advocated for a public health insurance plan that would provide services to those who needed them without regard to their ability to pay. The party gave political expression to the righteous anger of Canadians who were offended by a society in which serious illness could mean economic ruin or the indignity of dependence on charity. CCF leader Tommy Douglas, whose family couldn't afford an operation to save young Tommy's leg and had to find a doctor who would do it for nothing, never forgot how close the market had come to costing him a limb. Publicly insured health services, prepaid collectively through progressive taxation and available with no direct charge to patients, would recognize health care as a fundamental right, like education, and would be the mark of a more fully human community.

The CCF in Saskatchewan, after being led to victory by Tommy Douglas in 1944, wasted no time in living up to its commitment to establish a provincial hospital insurance plan. Other provinces followed suit in the 1950s, with a federal cost-shared plan finally coming into effect in 1957. Similarly, it was the CCF in Saskatchewan that first brought in provincial medical insurance to cover doctors' fees. And during the Liberal minority government of 1963–68, NDP pressure, led by Douglas, now leader of the federal NDP, contributed greatly to the passage of the legislation in 1966 that would bring Canadian medicare into existence in 1968.

The 1964 report of the Royal Commission on Health Services was another decisive factor. The royal commission, announced by Prime Minister Diefenbaker in 1960, was led by Justice Emmett Hall. Hall competes with Douglas for the title of father of medicare, but ironically, he was a Saskatchewan Tory who had campaigned against Douglas. And the Canadian Medical Association supported the appointment of the royal commission as a way of pre-empting the pressure that Douglas's Saskatchewan experiment was exerting on the federal scene. The CMA hoped for recommendations closer to its own ideas. Instead, the commission's recommendations read like Douglas could have written them himself.

In *Emmett Hall: Establishment Radical*, biographer Dennis Gruending argues that Hall's Catholicism influenced what he would support or not. However, papal teachings were not necessarily consistent—one teaching might exhort opposition to socialism, while another might support comprehensive publicly funded health care insurance. Indeed, in defending his report Hall referred to Pope John XXIII and the way in which the report was based on a recent encyclical that had talked about social principles and the co-operation and participation of society as a whole.

I feel very fortunate to have met Justice Hall and heard him speak on several occasions. In the early 1980s we were on the same plane to Montreal for a medicare conference. I shared a cab with him and others to the hotel. It was a memorable ride, with the cab driver persistently trying to interest us in the seamier possibilities of Montreal night life, oblivious to the fact that he had a distinguished retired chief justice in the car. Hall was smiling in the back seat, and when we got out he gave the driver a tip "for the entertainment."

In 1977—the year I graduated from Emmanuel College in Toronto and returned to Winnipeg, and almost a decade after the introduction of medicare—a major change took place in federal-provincial fiscal arrangements. Initially, to share the cost of the national medicare program, the federal government had matched provincial dollars spent on specified health care costs. By the late 1970s, there was much pressure to change this funding mechanism.

Provincial governments were concerned about a lack of flexibility in what could be cost-shared. Have-not provinces were concerned that they had to spend their own money in order to receive federal dollars, which meant they were getting less on a per capita basis from the federal program than provinces that could spend more. And some provinces objected to federal micromanagement of a sector under provincial jurisdiction.

The federal government, in turn, was concerned that its spending was linked to provincial spending, and had issues about control. It was also, less obviously, looking for ways to limit or even reduce federal spending on medicare.

In 1977 the 50-50 cost-sharing formula was replaced with block contributions, known as Established Programs Financing, calculated on the basis of a base year (1975–76), not on current provincial expenditures. This change, which had been opposed by the NDP, was a decisive factor in producing the ensuing crisis over extra-billing by physicians and user fees imposed by hospitals.

Monique Bégin, appointed federal Minister of National Health and Welfare in September 1977, was just getting her head around the growing crisis when the Liberals were defeated in 1979. The new minister was David Crombie, former mayor of Toronto and truly a progressive Conservative. In September 1979, he asked Justice Hall, who had led the royal commission in the 1960s, to review the state of medicare and report back. But by the time what came to be known as the second Hall report was ready, the short-lived Clark government had fallen, the Liberals were returned to power, and Bégin was the minister again.

During her brief time in opposition, Bégin had made much of what the provinces were doing to medicare, both in allowing extra-billing and user fees, and in using the Established Programs Financing dollars to avoid spending their own share on health care. This latter practice was characterized by some as provincial underspending, and by others as diversion of federal health transfers to non-health-related expenditures. It was now up to Bégin to deal with the provinces.

At the same time as Bégin became minister again, in 1980, I was appointed NDP Health Critic, a role in which I would be ably supported by NDP researcher Karen Stotsky. It would take four years to get what eventually became the Canada Health Act, a piece of federal legislation that amalgamated the previous two acts, on hospitalization and medicare, into one. It contained provisions for dealing with extra-billing and user fees by providing that the federal government would subtract from federal transfers to provinces one dollar for every dollar of extra-billing or user fees permitted by that province.

———

The Canadian Health Coalition, an advocacy group dedicated to protecting Canada's public health system, was founded at the 1979 SOS Medicare conference sponsored by the Canadian Labour Congress and attended by Tommy Douglas, Emmett Hall, and Monique Bégin. The coalition, still ongoing, includes organizations representing seniors, women, churches, nurses, health care workers, and antipoverty activists from across the country. Its members shared the view, ultimately expressed by Justice Hall's 1980 report, that

> if extra-billing is permitted as a right and practised by physicians in their sole discretion, it will, over the years destroy the program, creating in that downward path the two-tier system incompatible with the societal level which Canadians have attained.

Justice Hall's report also observed, in words that eloquently summarize the social and moral basis of medicare:

Canadians understand the full meaning of the *Hospital Insurance and Medical Care Acts*. They said, through these two acts, that we, as a society, are aware that the trauma of illness, the pain of surgery, the slow decline to death, are burdens enough for the human being to bear without the added burden of medical or hospital bills penalizing the patient at the moment of vulnerability. The Canadian people determined that they should band together to pay medical bills and hospital bills when they were well and income earning. Health services were no longer items to be bought off the shelf and paid for at the checkout stand. Nor was their price to be bargained for at the time they are sought. They were a fundamental need, like education, which Canadians could meet collectively and pay for through taxes.

The United Church of Canada was supportive of the 1980 Hall Report, just as it had been of the original commission in 1964, to which it made a presentation in favour of medicare. As James R. Mutchmor, United Church Moderator from 1962 to 1964, indicates in his memoirs, the church presentation followed four General Council meetings that called for a national health insurance system. Some of the doctors in the pews were not happy, but other United Church doctors served on the church committee that drafted the pro-medicare presentation.

The Canadian Labour Congress's representative on the Canadian Health Coalition was the coalition's first chair, Jim MacDonald. MacDonald, a frequent presence on Parliament Hill and a tireless promoter of the coalition, was a trade unionist of Cape Breton origins who, like Father Andy Hogan, NDP MP for Cape Breton from 1972 to 1980 and briefly my colleague in the House, was influenced by the Antigonish Movement.

The Antigonish Movement had its origins during the 1920s at St. Francis Xavier University in Antigonish, Nova Scotia. The movement, which stresses adult education and the formation of co-operatives as a solution to economic adversity, developed a worldwide following. It is generally associated with Father Moses Coady, but it also owed its popularity to the work of Father Jimmy Tompkins. It is an interesting feature of Atlantic Canadian politics that its progressive politics is often grounded in the work of activist Roman Catholic priests. Despite the conservative image of their church, they were living out their own social gospel in their own particular context, as was Dorothy Day, who founded the Catholic Worker Movement in the same era. Another example of the Atlantic Canadian tradition was Father Des McGrath, who was regarded as a co-founder of the Fishermen's Union in Newfoundland. Even now, the current leader of the NDP in Newfoundland and Labrador,

Lorraine Michael, is a former nun and Catholic social activist.

As Health Critic, I was very active in the House of Commons pressing Health Minister Bégin to act on the issues of extra-billing and user fees. I sometimes irritated her by what she would characterize as my lack of pragmatism, but I know that she also welcomed the pressure. One day after a particularly vigorous polemical exchange between the two of us, I was handed a note from her by a parliamentary page. It expressed thanks and encouraged me to not let up, as she needed all the help she could get in persuading her cabinet colleagues to move on the issue. Bégin was in the difficult position of dealing with reluctant colleagues, some of whom wanted to stall on the issue in order to keep it alive for the next election as a card to play against the Tories, and a hostile majority of provinces, with only NDP provincial governments giving her any encouragement.

An opposition critic who was constantly after you to do what you really wanted to do was not a bad thing. But at the same time, Bégin didn't want to enact legislation that was punitive toward the provinces. Extra-billing and user fees had to go. But in her memoir, *Medicare: Canada's Right to Health*, it is clear that she would have preferred the provinces to act on their own to solve the issues. It was only when this was no longer a believable option, and when time was running out on the Trudeau era, that the proper sense of urgency took over, lest medicare be left to the tender mercies of a new Conservative government that would have little appetite for such federally enforced national standards. As it was, the opposition Tories under their new leader, Brian Mulroney, were not falling into the trap of opposing the Canadian Health Act. No enthusiasm, but no opposition either.

I tried to lure Mulroney into a debate on medicare when he was running in 1983 to get a seat in the House of Commons. Long-time Tory MP Elmer MacKay stepped down to create the by-election in the riding of Central Nova, Nova Scotia. I went to his riding and as NDP Health Critic challenged him to a debate. He ignored me. My press conference there was notable only for the awkwardness I felt when a local reporter pointed out to me that by advocating the building of hopper cars in the CN shops in Transcona, I was endangering work at the plant in Trenton, in Central Nova, where such cars were often built. I said something about everybody getting their fair share and could not wait for the next question.

The NDP candidate in that by-election was United Church minister Roy DeMarsh, a long-time leader in the Student Christian Movement and pastor to several Maritime congregations. This would not be the last time that a

United Church minister tried to stand in the way of a future prime minister in a similar situation. In 2002, former Moderator Bill Phipps was the NDP candidate in the Calgary by-election that brought Stephen Harper back to the House of Commons to lead the Canadian Alliance. Mulroney, who was not known for criticizing the faith perspectives of his political opponents, treated DeMarsh much better than the contemptuous way that Harper treated Phipps. The attitude toward Phipps was part of a larger attitude on Harper's part toward the United Church in general that preceded the by-election of 2002.

In a speech just after the 1997 election to an American conservative group called the Council for National Policy, Stephen Harper joked that the NDP was worse than a party of liberal Democrats—the NDP was a "kind of proof that the devil lives and interferes in the lives of men." As to the presence of clergy in the NDP, they are acknowledged in the speech but characterized as believing that the church "made a historic error in adopting Christian theology," whatever that might mean. As the only United Church minister in the NDP caucus at the time, I still find it an odd and obviously unsubstantive and unsubstantiated charge. But it is clear that combining the United Church with the NDP, as Bill Phipps and I both do, is definitely on the Prime Minister's short list of combinations to be avoided. Just as, apparently, are other church and justice-seeking combinations, like the ecumenical justice coalition KAIROS, whose recommended ongoing funding by CIDA in 2010 was, I believe, likely overruled by Harper himself, or in consultation with Immigration Minister Jason Kenney, who had been publicly critical of KAIROS not long before.

Returning to the 1982 Parliament, I've always enjoyed Monique Bégin's account in her memoir of its opening on October 27:

> Bill Blaikie, my NDP counterpart, immediately launched a guerrilla attack to force me to act. I stalled him to gain a little time, but I was backed into a corner. No matter how much and from what angle we looked at the problem, both in the Department and with my own political staff, for the first time I saw no way out...faced with the provinces' cavalier attitude, I decided I was justified in returning to my original goal of ridding Medicare of all surcharges.

The guerrilla warfare in the House would continue for a while yet.

Despite my wrangling with Bégin, I was glad to be included in the Canadian delegation to the World Health Organization meeting in Geneva in 1983. I vividly remember speeches lamenting how just a fraction of what was being spent on the arms trade could make such a difference in addressing clean drinking water, adequate food and medicines, and other unmet human needs. Tragically, this is no doubt just as true today.

The idea of putting conditions on federal heath transfers, as the Canada Health Act would stipulate, was strengthened by another parliamentary process that I participated in, the Special Parliamentary Task Force on Federal-Provincial Fiscal Arrangements in 1981, chaired by Liberal Herb Breau. The other members of the task force were Liberals David Weatherhead, Hal Herbert, and Bernard Loiselle, and Tories Blaine Thacker and Don Blenkarn. Blenkarn, who would later effectively chair the Standing Committee on Finance, was the most colourful of the lot. You were never in any doubt about where he was coming from: no backstabbing, just full frontal assault when the situation called for it. Breau, the very able chair, was from New Brunswick. He brought lobsters to a dinner celebrating the task force's conclusion, recounting that at one time the children of fishermen envied others whose parents could afford to buy baloney for their lunches, when all they had was lobster.

The task force was a golden opportunity for me as a new MP to immerse myself in the nuts and bolts of Canadian federalism, that is, in the fiscal dimension. For a little while at least, I was one of a small group that actually understood what was going on in the arguments between the provinces and the federal government over money. Unfortunately, much of the argument suffered from misrepresentation and arbitrary reversals of position.

For example, when Established Programs Financing was set up, there was an added component called the Revenue Guarantee. The federal government calculated this component as part of what it contributed to the provinces for health; the provinces claimed otherwise, and refused to be criticized for not spending it on health. In 1982, Liberal Finance Minister Allan MacEachen saw advantage in finally agreeing with the provinces and unilaterally subtracted the Revenue Guarantee from the transfer payments, saying that it was not a cut in health funding. The provinces condemned the cut, now claiming it was, after all, part of the health transfers.

At one point, the task force had a private dinner in room 601 of the parliamentary dining room with former premiers from six provinces to discuss federal-provincial issues. For a rookie it was a terrific opportunity to listen to some political veterans, including Duff Roblin of Manitoba, Robert Stanfield of Nova Scotia, Louis Robichaud of New Brunswick, and Robert

Bourassa, then former and also future premier of Quebec. The evening ended with Tommy Douglas, former premier of Saskatchewan, and John Robarts, former premier of Ontario, arguing about medicare. Robarts may have taken Ontario into medicare but he still didn't like it. Another fascinating meeting that I experienced courtesy of the task force on fiscal arrangements was a private meeting with Quebec's Minister of Finance, Jacques Parizeau. Parizeau, who would later be the controversial Premier of Quebec during the 1995 referendum on sovereignty, gave a command performance, but I did not really mind. He knew what he was talking about and presented his view in a way that was easy to understand.

The majority of the special task force agreed with Justice Hall that extra-billing by physicians inhibits reasonable access to services and was contrary to the intent and purpose of medicare. It therefore recommended that any provincial plan that didn't meet the accessibility criteria be ineligible for full federal financial support under the Established Programs Financing. These recommendations helped set the stage for the Canada Health Act, which specified reductions to the federal transfer for provinces that allowed extra-billing and user fees.

When the Canada Health Act was finally passed in spring 1984, it would be the final chapter in a process that had seen the many parts of a successful political process work well together. A minister who truly wanted to do what was needed, a persistent opposition, a well-organized extra-parliamentary coalition, and a Canadian public that valued medicare had teamed up against delinquent provinces, rebellious doctors, and a reluctant federal government to save medicare from the crisis of extra-billing and user fees.

———

The Canada Health Act addressed the problem of preserving the principles of a public health insurance plan. But it did little to change the way that health care was delivered, despite constant encouragement of the Canadian Nurses Association to do so. Dr. Helen Glass, President of the Canadian Nurses Association, and Kathleen Connors, President of the National Federation of Nurses Unions, who figured prominently in putting their views before the special task force, were a great resource during the process. The language of "health care practitioner" was put into the Act at committee, with a view to signalling the need for more of a team approach to health care, but the model remains largely unchanged today.

The extra-billing crisis of the early 1980s was followed by a crisis of funding and federal unwillingness to be a full partner in the growing cost of health care. Unfortunately, the Canada Health Act did absolutely nothing to restore a sense of federal commitment to funding medicare. Trudeau, Mulroney, Chrétien—all of their governments cut back unilaterally on federal transfers to the provinces. Paul Martin restored a great deal of what had been taken away after becoming Prime Minister in 2004, but it had been Martin's budget as Finance Minister in 1995 that finally devastated the provinces. In a move far from the spirit of the recommendation of the Special Task Force on Federal-Provincial Fiscal Arrangements of 1981, the 1995 budget lumped all transfers into one. Health transfers, education transfers, and transfers under the name of the Canada Assistance Program were all collapsed into the Canada Health and Social Transfer.

Today, medicare continues to be under pressure. And it will be as long as the health care bill grows, that is, as long as technological progress continues, drug companies continue to get their way on pricing and intellectual property rights, and baby boomers become elderly and infirm. Though the profit-motivated will continue to claim otherwise, health care costs will not be reined in by the profit motive. But undesirable forms of privatization must be opposed on their own merits. The Canada Health Act is silent about the private or public provision of services; its principle is one of a publicly administered insurance plan, not a publicly administered health care system. When privatization is opposed on the basis that it is contrary to the Act, defenders of various forms of privatization are enabled to say that their idea doesn't violate the Act, as if that it all that needs to be said. The argument is more complicated.

The wait-times issue will need to be dealt with, whether it is waiting lists for tests and important procedures, or waiting ridiculous hours to be seen at emergency wards. Waiting lists can be exploited by the ideologically driven to justify expanding private sector participation in a mixed public-private system. They also create non-ideologically motivated interest in alternative ways of delivering health care. But the danger is that enough privatization, even within the rules and spirit of medicare, will build the infrastructure of a second tier that, when established, will want to set up on its own.

It often comes down to an ideological debate about the roles of the public versus private sectors. It is no coincidence that some of the boldest moves against medicare and toward privatization have come out of Alberta, one of Canada's wealthiest provinces. The alleged financial strains of medicare in a province that doesn't have a provincial sales tax and that, unlike some poorer provinces, charged its citizens health care premiums, rings fiscally hollow but ideologically loud.

It remains a growing problem that ever-increasing percentages of provincial budgets are devoted to health care spending, to the increasing disadvantage of other priorities. The problem of how to pay for increasing health care costs in an environment that is hostile to tax increases of any kind will not go away.

Allan Blakeney had been a leading member of the Saskatchewan government during the introduction of medicare in that province and the doctor's strike that challenged it. I had first met him when, as Saskatchewan's premier, he campaigned for me in the election of 1979. In Blakeney's political memoir, *An Honourable Calling*, he wisely observes that we should spend more on the social determinants of health, like affordable housing, while questioning whether we should continue to spend more and more on health care itself.

But whatever the pressures on medicare, I believe Canadians do not want to return to the day when the market, or one's ability to pay, is the way we ration health care in Canada. Any debate about the rising costs of health care will only be real if it acknowledges that the rising public cost is driven in large part by rising private sector costs like the price of drugs, and that there is a need to challenge the profit strategies of the multinational drug corporations. Otherwise the debate becomes a ruse in which problems that originate in the private sector are blamed on the public sector in order to justify more private sector involvement.

10

Parliamentary Reform

Parliament is not a soap opera. Nor is it a football match and certainly it must not become a kind of ultimate fighting where absolutely anything goes.

In 1984–85, the Special Committee on the Reform of the House of Commons, chaired by veteran Tory MP Jim McGrath, created a body of work that would become a benchmark for all subsequent debate on parliamentary reform. The McGrath Committee envisioned a House of Commons in which members would be more independent, individually and collectively. Long before the Reform Party showed up on the scene in 1993 to trumpet some of the same ideas as its own, the McGrath Committee wanted to correct two problems plaguing the Canadian parliamentary system: the excess of party discipline and the concentration of power in the Prime Minister's Office.

Pierre Trudeau, in one of his more scornful moods, had famously accused MPs of being nobodies once they got 50 yards from the Hill. But the McGrath Committee believed that the real problem—and Trudeau had a lot to do with this—was that MPs are nobodies *on* the Hill. In their constituencies, where they are treated like somebodies, they have to conceal the extent to which they are powerless on the Hill. I was a member of that committee, and as an MP known for my long-standing involvement on this issue, I have often been kidded for managing to relate almost any discussion back to the McGrath Report.

Starting in the early 1980s, right around the time when I was also the NDP Health Critic, I was involved in every successive attempt at parliamentary reform. This continued right through my tenure as NDP House Leader from 1997 to 2003, a position I gave up in February 2003 to become NDP Parliamentary Leader until the general election of June 28, 2004, when Jack Layton won a seat in the House. In May 1982, I was appointed the NDP member on the Special Committee on Standing Orders and Procedure chaired by Liberal Tom Lefebvre. The Lefebvre Committee to some extent grew out of the bell-ringing crisis of earlier that year, where the House had broken down as a result of the Tory reaction to the National Energy Program. The committee held 73 meetings at which we heard from expert witnesses, interested citizens, and our fellow members of Parliament.

Only the first report of the Lefebvre Committee would be adopted; even so, the committee was responsible for significant changes. But reforms, as I would learn over and over, can often result in unintended consequences—or even consequences antithetical to their original intent.

One of the committee's recommendations established a fixed parliamentary calendar. This prevented parliamentary games from pushing sittings long into July, while constituents, unaware of the sacrifices being made on their behalf, assumed MPs were off at the lake.

Evening sittings of the House were abolished, so that when committee meetings were scheduled in the evenings, members would not have to try to be in two places at once. Instead, committees stopped meeting in the evenings as well. The work was telescoped into an even smaller time frame, and those of us without families in Ottawa found the evenings much lonelier than when votes were held at 10 o'clock at night.

Speech length was reduced from 40 minutes to 20, with the addition of a 10-minute question and comment period after each speech to permit debate. Those MPs who started after the question and comment innovation could hardly believe there was a time when no such opportunity existed.

Finally, the rules were changed to make it easier for standing committees to study issues on their own initiative without an instruction from the House— which in a majority Parliament means they could do so without the permission of the government. This remains an important reform, though it also keeps committees perpetually busy, as there is always something else that needs to be studied.

When Brian Mulroney brought in a Tory majority in September 1984, it arrived with a will to carry on the reform process. This was not entirely surprising, as parliamentary reform had been on the agenda of Tory House Leader Walter Baker in Joe Clark's brief parliamentary reign in 1979–80. Baker, who had a genuine interest in the well-being of the institution, was on the Lefebvre Committee but would not live to see the reforms that came after 1984. Tories who were afraid that Mulroney would become less interested as time went on advised us to take advantage of the will while it was still there. This warning had substance, as the same government would later seek to undo some of the committee's early successes, particularly with respect to the role of parliamentary secretaries on committees.

On December 5, 1984, a motion of the House created the Special Committee on the Reform of the House of Commons and asked it to look at, among other things, the role of the private member, the accountability of ministers, the administration of the House, the legislative process, and the power of committees. This committee was chaired by Jim McGrath, a passionate and colourful Newfoundlander who had been in the House since 1957; the other members were past and future Liberal cabinet minister André Ouellet, and four Tories, rookie Quebec MP Lise Bourgault, Albert Cooper from Peace River, Alberta, Jack Ellis from rural Ontario, and Benno Friesen from the Vancouver area.

It was a wonderful feature of that Parliament that the NDP had almost as many seats as the Liberals and therefore equal representation on parliamentary committees. In the House, we had almost half the opposition questions, and with this opportunity to participate and to put our case, the NDP was well up in the polls. No wonder that, when combined with the fact that I was much younger then, I have fond memories of the 1984–88 Parliament, at least until it culminated in the free trade debate.

The first thing the McGrath Committee tackled was the role of the Speaker. We recommended that, to express the House's independence from the government and give the Speaker enhanced status, the Speaker be elected by secret ballot of the members, rather than appointed by the prime minister, with the election being conducted by the Dean of the House of Commons in any given Parliament. Thus it was that I ended up conducting the election of the Speaker after the elections of 2004 and 2006. The McGrath Committee also recommended that it be made easier for the Speaker to throw out a misbehaving member.

Not long after our recommendations were accepted we had a chance to try one of them out. John Bosley, who had been elected as Speaker in 1984, resigned in 1986. Rather than go through a nomination process, all members were regarded as candidates for Speaker unless they formally withdrew their name. But unfamiliarity with the process combined with inattention to ensure that many remained on the ballot who should not have been there, and no de-cluttering procedure—such as removing everyone who did not get a certain percentage on each ballot—had been foreseen. The House voted 11 times over 11 hours until someone won. Needless to say, by the time the next Speaker had to be elected, a de-cluttering provision had been added to the standing orders.

It was widely thought that Quebec Tory MP Marcel Danis was the government's choice, and many could see why. He was bright and bilingual, and many in the NDP caucus were predisposed to vote for him. John Fraser, who eventually won, was not seen initially to be a contender. But the House, I believe, seized an opportunity to right a wrong and send a message to the Prime Minister.

Fraser had been the Minister of Fisheries during the tainted tuna scandal that transpired earlier in the Parliament. Without going into the details, he was handling the controversy over large quantities of tuna that may have spoiled being sold to the public well enough until he contradicted the Prime Minister, which cost him his job. Everyone knew that he had been a victim of internal politics, and Bosley's resignation provided the House with the opportunity to rehabilitate one of its own.

As for the tuna, Fraser was right to suggest that it was not as bad as some were making it out to be. When fish packers came to the Hill during the controversy and gave out cases of tuna to those who would take them, I happily took a case back to the Ottawa apartment I shared with Iain Angus for late-night tuna sandwiches. I'd done a lot of work with Angus prior to his election in Thunder Bay, Ontario, and after he was elected in 1984 we shared an apartment for almost a decade. You have to watch who you help out, I used to kid the caucus—they might come and live with you after.

John Fraser would be Speaker for seven years and is generally regarded as one of the best. We shared a passion for environmental issues and things Scottish, and started the tradition of the Speaker holding an annual Robbie Burns Supper in honour of Scotland's Immortal Bard. Before the Speaker took on the Burns Supper, the tradition had been started in 1981 by a few NDP MPs of Scottish heritage, Ian Deans from Hamilton, Ontario, Ian Waddell from Vancouver, Neil Young from Toronto, and myself. Our guest speaker for the NDP Burns Supper three years running was Tommy Douglas, who gave the Toast to the Immortal Memory. It was as a result of those evenings that I came to appreciate the role that Burns played in shaping Douglas's egalitarian consciousness, and got to know Tommy Douglas in a way that I otherwise would not have.

I learned only recently that Burns also shaped the egalitarian instincts of none other than Abraham Lincoln, who is reported to have kept a book of Burns's work on his night table. My role in those early suppers on the Hill was to pipe the haggis in; later I came to enjoy being the one to deliver the Address to a Haggis, and also to give the Toast. After playing the pipes in the parliamentary restaurant on the occasion of the first Burns Supper, I was delighted to be sought out by legendary Liberal Allan MacEachen, who said that being from Cape Breton he knew a thing or two about piping and he wanted to compliment me on my playing.

Much as I liked John Fraser personally, I didn't always agree with his rulings. On one occasion, I argued that a closure motion used to pass the Free Trade Agreement should be ruled out of order because there had not been sufficient debate on the floor of the House, but he refused. On another, Speaker Fraser ruled acceptable a government motion to go directly to the orders of the day, bypassing the routine proceedings that would have allowed the opposition to hold things up, on the basis that there had been enough debate and the time had come for a vote. If a Speaker can judge that there has been enough debate, why can't a Speaker judge that there has not? Unfortunately, this ruling would set the stage for much abuse of such motions by subsequent governments.

The McGrath Committee's recommendation that the Speaker be able to "name" or throw a member out for breaches of decorum or refusal to withdraw unparliamentary language is a classic example of a reform that did not work as intended. Traditionally the procedure had involved a motion of the House; the convention was that the House, even the party whose member was being disciplined, would support the Speaker. The time and drama involved attracted those drawn to the limelight of martyrdom. The reform was intended to empower the Speaker and make the procedure more efficient and less dramatic, but the new procedure has been used very rarely. It has actually turned out to be more difficult for Speakers, as they must now discipline without the backing of the House and the member's party, and do so in an environment where they may well have re-election as Speaker in the back of their mind.

Speakers, for some time now, have not had at their disposal another of the tools available to their predecessors. By the late 1970s, the habit had developed of giving the Speaker lists each day from the various party whips as to who should be recognized by the Speaker and when. These lists have become inviolable, whereas in the past a Speaker could punish wayward members by just never seeing them rise to get the floor. As some of the most wayward are also the best performers and most likely to win the daily contest for a clip on the evening news, this lack of recognition would anger the party whips. In a more perfect world, of course, their anger would be directed at themselves or at their members instead of at a Speaker who was trying to create a better Parliament.

———

Another area that the McGrath Committee dealt with was the power and makeup of committees. But the recommendations to give committees more power to determine their own agenda were only partially and temporarily implemented.

First the committee wanted to eliminate having the minister's parliamentary secretary on committees, as they tended to curb the independence of government members. Second, it wanted committee members to be appointed for the duration of a session, with the power to appoint their own alternate, instead of the party whip doing it. The goal was to prevent the deployment of parliamentary goon squads to remove government members who dared to think and act independently and replace them with new, uninformed members who were prepared to take the parliamentary secretary's direction on how to vote.

The recommendation to put committee membership beyond immediate party discretion for a fixed period of time never happened. Parliamentary secretaries were removed from committees for a number of years, but a unilateral package imposed on the House in the dying days of the Mulroney era in 1992 would restore them. Liberals were outraged by the package, but soon adapted to the new powers given the government side when they took power the next year.

The McGrath Committee also influenced how the House dealt with private members' business. When I arrived in 1979, private members' bills or motions could only come to a vote by unanimous consent. If a bill or motion made it to the floor of the House it would be debated for an hour, and then drop down to the bottom of the order paper never to be seen again. The possibility of a vote existed only if debate expired before the hour was up and the question could be put, but those opposed to the bill or motion could always make sure there was someone on hand to keep talking, and thus "talk the bill out." One famous exception to this rule got us Canada Day.

The private member's bill that as of 1982 changed Dominion Day to Canada Day, introduced by Liberal Hal Herbert, passed on a Friday afternoon with about six MPs in the House. All present happened to agree, and those MPs who did not must have thought someone else would be around to take care of it. I was driving in Gatineau Park with Brenda and our two children when I heard the announcement on the car radio. I wonder what I would have done if I had been there, as I did not find the arguments against Dominion Day all that convincing. The New Democrat in the House at the time—NDP caucus chair Mark Rose, a former music professor known for his comic abilities as well as his political passion—did.

Responding to a widely held view among MPs, the McGrath Committee sought greater opportunities for private members' business to come to a vote. At its recommendation, out of every 20 items brought forward by private members, six would be selected for a mandatory vote. A special all-party committee chose which six, after hearing arguments from members about their items. Items that were unconstitutional, frivolous, regionally divisive, or already before the House in some way were ruled out. This last criterion turned out to be critical in the debate over whether there would be a straight-up vote on capital punishment that might have passed.

Many backbench Tory MPs were salivating at the prospect of having their favourite political hobby horse come to a vote in Parliament, none more so than the late Bill Domm, a leading advocate of bringing back the death penalty. Very early in the 1984–88 Parliament, he brought forward a private member's bill to reinstate the death penalty. When Domm appeared before the Special Committee on Private Members' Business to argue for bringing it to a vote, I was on the committee. It was one of the times when I truly felt that my presence was uniquely consequential. I was personally against capital punishment, but could not let that be a reason to block it from coming to a vote. My familiarity with the intent of the McGrath reforms, and the authority that I brought to the argument as a member of the McGrath Committee, proved decisive.

Prime Minister Mulroney had promised that that Parliament would hold a free vote on capital punishment. It had been an election promise, to the electorate to be sure, but more importantly to the Tory base. When Domm presented before the committee I made an issue out of whether, by bringing the matter forward in this way, he was saying he did not trust Mulroney. Otherwise, if Mulroney was trustworthy, then the House was going to be provided with an opportunity to vote on it, and his bill was dealing with a matter that, although it was not already before the House, soon would be. Domm was furious, but my argument won the day with the committee.

We eventually did have a vote on capital punishment, but in a context more favourable to its rejection. It was on a motion that accepted capital punishment in principle and then mandated a committee to travel the country to hear testimony about how and in what circumstances it should be reinstated. The prospect of such a grim road show was not an attractive one, even to some who had earlier expressed support for reinstating the death penalty. It would not be the last time that an issue was decided not purely on the issue but on the advisability of revisiting an issue and the process associated with it. The vote came on June 29, 1987, our 14th wedding anniversary. I called Brenda from Ottawa late that night to proclaim the value of my absence, in what might be described as one of the most celebratory anniversary telephone conversations on record.

The motion was voted down, with both the current Tory Prime Minister, Brian Mulroney, and the former Tory prime minster, Joe Clark, voting against it. Stephen Harper would use a similar tactic years later on a 2006 motion to revisit the issue of same-sex marriage, except that he chose to be with the losing side on a motion. In both cases, promises to the political base of the Conservatives were said to have been kept.

––––––––

Regardless of how one felt about the issue, the debate over capital punishment was an exciting one. As MPs wrestled with their own views and the views of their constituents, of their parties, and of their colleagues in the House, the outcome remained unpredictable. It was more occasions for such freedom and unpredictability that the McGrath Committee was looking for when it recommended, not only that more private members' business come to a vote, but also that the language of confidence and its attendant party discipline be restricted to a government's core program.

Since about 2003, as a result of continuous pressure by the Reform Party and the Canadian Alliance, almost all private members' business has become votable, a development I held off as long as I was NDP House Leader. The House now votes constantly on private members' business, and while much passes, much is also defeated that should have been weeded out at the beginning.

Over my years in Parliament, of the many private members' bills and motions I put forward, only one ever passed, and that was in an amended form. It called for a medal to be struck for those who had participated in the Allied raid on Dieppe on August 19, 1942. The need for such recognition had been impressed on me by Canadian Dieppe veterans in general, and in particular by a Winnipeg Dieppe veteran named Harry Long. Long had participated in the Dieppe raid with the Queen's Own Cameron Highlanders of Winnipeg. As it was, I had also taken some piping lessons from Pipe Major Alex Graham, who had played the pipes at Dieppe on the top of a landing craft as it went in to the beach. He was captured that day along with hundreds of others, and spent the rest of the war in a German POW camp, along with Adam Angus, father of my NDP colleague Iain Angus.

Thanks to Tory Defence Minister Gerry Merrithew, I was privileged to play the lament at the Canadian cemetery in Dieppe when I represented the NDP on the 1992 pilgrimage to mark the 75th anniversary of the battle of Vimy Ridge and the 50th anniversary of the Dieppe raid. Brian Mulroney was at the Dieppe ceremony and introduced me to the French Minister of Defence by saying to him, "He's one of yours." The Socialists were in power in France at the time.

In the end, I had to settle for a ribbon instead of a medal in order to get the support of the government. Not all the Dieppe veterans were initially happy, but they wore the ribbon with pride nonetheless. One of the other causes related to veterans that I embraced, along with other NDP MPs, came earlier in my parliamentary life. That was the long-overdue recognition of those who served in the Merchant Marine during the Second World War, a group of Canadians who suffered a casualty rate second to none. Despite this tragic reality, it was not until 1992 that the merchant navy veterans were finally recognized. Some weeks after I retired from federal politics, I was surprised by the delivery of a fine bottle of scotch along with a note thanking me for the support I had given to the cause over the years.

Another group of folks that daily put their lives on the line for all of us are firefighters, in war and in peace. When everyone else is running out of the burning building, they are running in. Working with them occasioned an event in the House of Commons that I remember joyfully. The Canadian section of the United Fire Fighters of America came to Ottawa every year around the same time in April to lobby for changes that were important to their members. One of these was changes to pension rules that would enable firefighters to retire earlier. Every year all the MPs would, as they were individually asked, agree to support such changes, but the next year there would still be no changes made. Finally, one day when the firefighters were present in the House, I got up and angrily asked Finance Minister Paul Martin the obvious question. If all members agreed, year in and year out, and it still was not happening, who else was running the country? The next budget contained the needed changes.

Several of my NDP colleagues would be more successful over the years with private members' business. Rod Murphy, MP for Churchill, Manitoba, initiated what is now a national day of mourning on April 28 for workers killed on the job. Lynn McDonald from Toronto, in one of the first post-McGrath private members' bills, had a bill passed that restricted smoking in federally regulated transportation and workplaces, including Parliament, thus kick-starting a revolution in the way that smoking is dealt with. It is hard to believe now that MPs used to smoke behind the curtains in the House of Commons or in the Standing Committee on Health and Welfare.

In truth, I was not one of the MPs who made maximum use of the opportunity for advocacy, or for publicity, that private members' business can provide. I sponsored a bill calling for a moratorium on the development of nuclear power in 1991, which attracted support from the Campaign for Nuclear Phaseout and some real debate before coming to a vote and being defeated. Three others come to mind that attracted attention.

In 2001 I moved to recognize the five religious symbols—the five Ks of the Sikh religion, including the controversial ceremonial knife the kirpan—and the contribution of the Sikh community to Canada. This motion was not selected as votable despite my arguments that it should be, and a last-minute attempt to make it so at the end of the debate by unanimous consent was obstructed by the Liberals. A similar motion would finally pass five years later, sponsored by the member who seconded my original motion, MP for Winnipeg North Judy Wasylycia-Leis. During my parliamentary life, I enjoyed a good relationship with the Sikh community in my riding and spoke at the local gurdwaras on many occasions. I believe that other religious cultures could possibly learn something from the relaxed way in which Sikh congregations see nothing inappropriate about politicians occasionally coming to speak to them briefly about the issues of concern to their community.

Family campaign picture, 1979. Bill and Brenda Blaikie with 11-month-old Rebecca.

Celebrating victory with
Brenda, May 22, 1979.

First swearing in at the House of Commons, by clerk
Alistair Fraser, June 1979.

With some icons of the CCF/NDP, early 1980s. Clockwise from top left: Bill Blaikie, Tommy Douglas, Stanley Knowles, Grace MacInnis (née Woodsworth).

NDP Burns Night on the Hill, 1982, with Tommy Douglas.

At the Transcona CN shop gate with future Manitoba premier Gary Doer, circa 1993.

Stanley Knowles is welcomed back to the House by the NDP caucus after suffering a stroke, 1981. Front row, left to right: Ian Deans, Stanley Knowles. Second row: Pauline Jewett, Neil Young. Third row: Rod Murphy, Bob Ogle, Bill Blaikie, Terry Sargeant. Back row: Ted Miller, Cyril Keeper, Svend Robinson, Laverne Lewycky.

At the Transcona CN shop gate with Stanley Knowles, 1979.

McGrath Committee on parliamentary reform, 1985. Left to right: Jack Ellis, André Ouellet, Albert Cooper, Jim McGrath (chair), Benno Friesen, Bill Blaikie. Seated: Lise Bourgault.

Some members of the Special Committee on Acid Rain with special envoys, 1986. Left to right: Charles Caccia, Gary Gurbin, U.S. envoy Drew Lewis, Bill Blaikie, Stan Darling (chair), Canadian envoy Bill Davis.

The NDP caucus rises in question period to support a strong response to the government, circa 1998. Left to right: John Solomon, Nelson Riis, Chris Axworthy, Bill Blaikie, Lorne Nystrom, Libby Davies. Seated: Alexa McDonough.

Meeting church activists on Parliament Hill advocating jubilee debt relief for the world's poorest nations, 1999.

Free Trade Area of the Americas (FTAA) protest in Quebec City, 2001. Left to right: John Paul Harney, Bill Blaikie, Lorne Nystrom, Yvon Godin, Dick Proctor.

In the Speaker's chair, as Acting Speaker in Peter Milliken's absence, 2007.

With Monique Bégin at the World Health Organization in Geneva, 1983.

Special Committee on the Peace Process in Central America with Nicaraguan president, 1988. Left to right: Bud Bird, Lloyd Axworthy, President Daniel Ortega, Bill Blaikie, John Bosley (chair).

In Taiwan as an election observer with former United Church Moderator Bruce McLeod, 1992.

Shaking hands with Prime Minister Mulroney after playing the lament at the Canadian War Cemetery, Dieppe, on the 50th anniversary of the Dieppe raid, 1992. With United Church chaplain David Estey.

With former Manitoba premier Duff Roblin at 60th anniversary of D-Day, Juno Beach, 2004.

Meeting Nelson Mandela in the Speaker's chambers, with Leader of the Opposition Jean Chrétien, 1991.

Family, 1992. Clockwise from top left: Jessica, Bill, Brenda, Daniel, Rebecca, Tessa.

Turning the sod at Transcona Place (seniors' housing project) with father, Bob Blaikie, and mother, Kay Blaikie, 1994.

In 2002 the House debated a motion of mine calling for imprisoned Aboriginal activist Leonard Peltier to be returned to Canada from the United States, on the basis that he had been unfairly extradited in 1976 after dubious evidence implicated him in the murder of two FBI agents during a conflict on the South Dakota Pine Ridge Reservation near Wounded Knee. The motion did not pass, but I received a letter from Peltier thanking me for trying.

Another motion of mine that was debated but not passed was one calling for the banning of talking on a hand-held cellphone while driving a vehicle. I was a guest on many radio talk shows in which drivers called in on their cellphones to vociferously disagree with me. Fortunately, no one was hurt in the process. I was several years ahead of the curve—pun intended.

A new trend that worries me with respect to private members' business is the growing habit of deliberately characterizing bills and motions as partisan motions that, if passed, would accrue credit to the party rather than to the individual MP. The NDP has done this a fair bit in recent Parliaments, and I have even noted it being done retroactively, whereby past motions of mine have been referred to as NDP initiatives. They were not. They were the private initiatives of an NDP MP, a distinction that needs to be maintained if the nature and integrity of private members' business is not to be compromised for partisan strategic objectives.

———

In the debate on capital punishment, several other debates were going on at the same time: about the role of an MP, about what constitutes a moral issue, and about the proper role of the church in politics.

The debate about the role of an MP would be strongest at the peak of the Reform Party's presence in Parliament, after the election of 1993, when Reformers used to get up and say that they were voting such-and-such a way unless their constituents instructed them to do otherwise. In addition to seeing MPs as delegates of the majority view in their ridings, the Reform Party also advocated referendums on controversial issues like abortion and capital punishment.

To begin with, it would be near impossible for MPs to establish their voters' views on all the issues that come before them. Even round-the-clock perpetual polling would not suffice, as the public mind often changes as the debate proceeds. The absurdity of a system wherein members might vote one way one week and another the next should be self-evident. To employ a biblical analogy, the poll taken of the crowd on Palm Sunday when Jesus entered Jerusalem would be different from the poll taken when the crowd was calling for the release of Barabbas and the crucifixion of Jesus.

In the capital punishment debate, many MPs were very focused on what their constituents thought, and the argument cut both ways, depending on what polls they were looking at or, perhaps, looking for. I always took the view that I was not just a delegate, that there were certain things I believed either personally or in concert with the New Democratic Party that were known when I was elected, and that my fidelity was to these positions. This fidelity could only be broken for good reasons, public opinion not being a sufficient reason unto itself.

When I was elected in 1979, I did a phone interview from a noisy victory party at the Union Centre in Winnipeg with Peter Warren, a local radio talk show host. Warren asked me, now that I was elected, whether I would respect the opinion of my constituents and vote for capital punishment. My answer was that I had just been elected by people who knew where I stood on the matter and that I looked forward to voting against capital punishment if it came up. As I would put it when I spoke to these issues in Parliament on June 25, 1987:

> Allow me, Mr. Speaker, to address the question about whether I should vote according to my own view or according to what the majority view in my riding might be, particularly if it is true that a majority might favour capital punishment.... I have run three times—in 1979, in 1980, and in 1984—each time against someone who wanted the return of capital punishment and who tried to make a big deal out of it. Each time I made it perfectly clear where I stood on capital punishment. I therefore believe that I can vote against capital punishment with a clear political as well as moral conscience....
> I subscribe to the traditional Tory view of the responsibility of a member of Parliament put forward by Edmund Burke in 1774, that a member of Parliament owes constituents the exercise of his or her judgment and must be held accountable for that judgment at election time. He said: "Your representative owes you, not his industry alone, but his judgement, and he betrays instead of serving you if he sacrifices it to your opinion."... A final word. This is a free vote. A free vote does not mean that we all receive the freedom to become Pontius Pilate. It does not mean that we all receive the freedom to do simply what the crowd wants, to ask the question what is truth and let the mob answer.

It is in respect to deferring to the crowd like Pontius Pilate that I always had trouble with the Reform Party philosophy, at least insofar as it came in a political package that was often associated with a certain kind of Christian politics. The Reform penchant for putting everything to a referendum, especially those issues that were either regarded as moral issues or rights issues, was diametrically opposed to a politics of principle, Christian or otherwise. I was never sure whether this was just a political trick or misplaced confidence in the outcome of such referendums.

Both sides saw capital punishment as a moral issue. But there was disagreement on what else might be a moral issue, or for that matter, what else might occasion the kind of moral outrage that so often found expression in pro–capital punishment speeches. One Tory MP conceded on the one hand that capital punishment was the kind of issue, a moral issue, that the church had a right to say something about. On the other hand, he was really irritated with his own church, the United Church, for having views on such matters as refugee laws, immigration, and free trade, and suggested that on these issues, the leadership of the church is completely out of touch with its congregations.

Perhaps the church's disagreement with the government on these issues was part of the problem for him, but his criticism of the church was a classic statement of a widely held view. I see it differently. The essence of the social gospel tradition is that economic issues, and immigration issues, are also moral issues. The idolatry of the marketplace that free trade represents is a profound *theological* issue, as well as a justice issue, for many Christians.

One issue you will never hear Liberals and Conservatives talk about is the ongoing subordination of our democratic institutions to global trade, investment, and financial agreements that constrain democratic debate within increasingly narrow parameters. This subordination leads many Canadians to conclude, not entirely irrationally, that it doesn't matter who gets elected because all governments must abide by the same agreements. As the parameters of debate systematically exclude ideas that challenge corporate power and the market ethic, it could certainly be argued that democratic reforms that do not address this larger context are only revitalizing increasingly irrelevant institutions.

The populist political right's combination of support for trade deals like the North American Free Trade Agreement with support for "grassroots" democratic reform is arguably a clever political strategy. Trade deals that strip democratically elected governments of their sovereignty and entrench a radical market ethic that tolerates no ideological or political diversity, no matter how democratically arrived at, make it more and more difficult for governments to respond to the needs and aspirations of citizens. No amount of Senate reform will deal with this, yet when citizens question the efficacy of their democratic institutions, the right then presents its democratic reforms as the antidote to the malaise created by the very agreements it supports so uncritically. It is ironic that those who are so quick to defend Parliament from any usurping of its power by the judicial activism of the courts have been so docile about the abdication of Parliament's policy-making powers to international trade lawyers and tribunals.

––––––––

After the 2004 election, when Jack Layton first won a seat in the House of Commons, I moved from being Parliamentary Leader to NDP Defence Critic. That Parliament was led by Prime Minister Paul Martin, who, contrary to many years of expectations, did not produce a winning combination after succeeding Jean Chrétien. Instead, he brought in the first minority Parliament since 1979, and it was a learning experience for many, including me.

I had gotten so used to having my proposals ignored or voted down that I was surprised when in this new context, if the other opposition parties agreed with you, you actually had the majority on some issues, and it became possible to pass a motion against the will of the government. The government, however, was able to selectively ignore many such motions. Though abhorred as a contempt of Parliament by Stephen Harper as Leader of the Opposition, this selectivity was eagerly adopted when he became Prime Minister of a minority Parliament himself in 2006. Indeed, it could be argued that Prime Minister Harper has few if any equals in the contempt for Parliament stakes, having misused the power of prorogation in 2008, and having had his government found in contempt of Parliament just prior to its defeat on a motion condemning it for this very reason on March 25, 2011.

The new dynamic of the minority Parliament was particularly significant in parliamentary committees. There is no executive power that can act separately from the committee itself, and the majority, however configured, can actually run the committee. In October 2004, the HMCS *Chicoutimi*, the last of four diesel-electric submarines that the Chrétien government had bought from the United Kingdom, was on its way to Canada when a fire broke out on board.

One submariner, Chris Saunders, died of his injuries in the fire; two others were sent to hospital. There was much speculation about the cause of the fire, and even more about the terms of the purchase.

I called for an inquiry into the deal, and moved at the Standing Committee on National Defence to have the committee conduct the inquiry. The motion passed. For the next six months, the committee was immersed in trying to get at the details of the deal that had brought the subs to Canada. We concluded, among other things, that politics had played a role in the submarines' condition.

The decision to purchase the subs had been made in 1995, but they were not actually bought until 1998, and the years in dry dock did not improve their condition. The purchase was put off because it was thought that it would look bad to be spending so much money on submarines at a time when the Liberals were slashing social spending. The committee also found that the financial terms of the deal had been misrepresented to the Canadian public.

The standing committee worked largely in a non-partisan way under Liberal chair Pat O'Brien, who would eventually fall out with his party over his opposition to same-sex marriage. I found myself working well with Bloc Québécois MP Claude Bachand; when the topic was something other than federalism, Bloc MPs could be quite reasonable. But the role of the Parliamentary Secretary to the Minister of Defence, Keith Martin, reminded me of why the McGrath Committee had so long ago recommended that parliamentary secretaries be kept off committees when, much to my irritation, he unwaveringly hewed to the government line. Having said this, Martin, originally elected as a Reform MP from Vancouver Island, was the kind of MP who was known for his civility and a genuine desire to make Parliament a better place. Despairing of the possibilities, he decided not to run in 2011.

In 2008, when I chose not to seek re-election after nine Parliaments, I had mixed feelings about not running again. But I had no regrets about staying out of an election that seemed to be just an extension of the juvenile exchanges between the Liberals and Conservatives that plagued the floor of the House of Commons in the Parliament that was dissolved on September 7, 2008. I knew that I would not miss the constant sense of disappointment that debate in the House of Commons does not live up to what Canadians have a right to expect of their representatives, and a corresponding disappointment that the parliamentary process does not do justice to the power that Canadians think they are investing in their elected MPs.

In my first years in Parliament, I had caught the end of an era when everyone would run down to the House because Pierre Trudeau or one of the other leaders was going to speak. Some of the excitement had to do with the big-ticket issues, especially the constitutional debates.

I also remember leaders—John Turner and Joe Clark come to mind—who went out of their way to show respect for collegiality in the House of Commons. They saw the House as a venue for bringing people together. When Joe Clark was Minister of Foreign Affairs, he used the House as the venue for announcements and ministerial statements. I wish more ministers would emulate his example.

Parliament is not a soap opera. Nor is it a football match and certainly it must not become a kind of ultimate fighting where absolutely anything goes. What is needed is a sense of forgiveness. For too many years our Parliament was driven by a sense of revenge, of exaggeration and mutual recrimination. Surely, at some point one has to forgive and move on, although it is perhaps easier to break the cycle of revenge in a majority situation. This is the hope that I cherish for the Parliament elected on May 2, 2011. If the NDP can provide a more policy-oriented and positive Official Opposition, and if the Conservatives can put aside their attack dog tactics, Canadians may yet learn to feel better about their parliamentary democracy.

It's not about the calibre of people attracted to run for Parliament. Like every other collection of Canadians, they are a mixed bag. It's more a case of good people falling into a toxic culture. The triumph of character assassination, simulated indignation, and trivial pursuit over substantial debate is a tragedy. Constructive, rational criticism from the opposition is seldom answered in the same spirit, and is too often ignored by the media. Likewise, honest answers from the government are only exploited. Add to this the failure of successive prime ministers to even try to set the proper tone in the House, and you have a recipe for the disrepute that Parliament has fallen into.

The way out of this culture is not clear, but a willingness on the part of both the Official Opposition and the government to discipline themselves and their members will be crucial. My fear is that at some subliminal level, even though their members find it distasteful, the focus on scandal serves the purposes of parties whose policies aren't often very far apart, and who thus must seek out their differences in dark corners.

The role of Parliament has also been diminished by one of its own creations—the Canadian Charter of Rights and Freedoms. This development is not necessarily negative, but it is a fact that many more things are now decided by the courts. Also, some things that appear to be decided by Parliament are now done in response to decisions that have already been made in the courts.

First Ministers have an increasingly prominent role. The last major reorganization of medicare took place at the First Ministers' Conference that Prime Minister Paul Martin chaired, whereas in earlier years, it was Parliament that addressed these problems.

Public opinion polling and focus groups overshadow members of Parliament in keeping the party leadership in touch with what the people are thinking. Another problem, in terms of public perception, is the cult of efficiency that characterizes all delay as somehow unproductive. As I said in a debate on parliamentary reform on April 10, 1991:

> Delay is one of the features and functions of parliamentary democracy. This is something that the public does not always understand. Oppositions, when they try to delay things, are not always just sort of huffing and puffing and blowing off steam. They are providing crucial political time for the public to mobilize against something which they may or may not regard as something they want to oppose. Oppositions provide that time.

Civility and collegiality are key to successful parliamentary institutions, and there has been an erosion of both compared to the era when I arrived. Some of the reasons are purely technological. I did not have a TV in my office in 1979; now one no longer has to go to the House of Commons to listen. How much damage has this convenience done to collegiality?

Cellphones and Blackberries have made us more isolated. I used to get to know a range of other members when we shared a cab together from the airport. Now, if you ride in a cab or wait in a lobby with a colleague, you just listen to them talk to someone else on their cell. And the parliamentary dining room, a victim of antipolitician rhetoric that saw it as an unacceptable perk, is no longer the gathering place it used to be, where members could meet other members and their families or guests. The Reform Party made a career out of attacking the partially subsidized meals in the parliamentary restaurant. But they had no objection to the fully subsidized lunches served in the privacy of the parliamentary lobbies.

When it comes to parliamentary decorum, another perennial parliamentary issue, I have always been proud of the role of the NDP in the House of

Commons. Sure, we've had the odd louder-than-appropriate voice and the occasional unparliamentary incident. But my memory of life in the NDP corner will primarily be one of trying to raise important issues while the Liberals and Conservatives, aided by the fatal attraction of the media, preferred to spend their time debating which of them was the least corrupt. It's not that corruption doesn't matter, but if in the future we cannot drink the water or breathe the air, it will not matter who gave what favour to whom or what was a conflict of interest.

In the NDP we were always torn between the issue of the day, often an interminable debate about some real or alleged scandal, and what we thought was really important. Ignore the issue of the day consistently, and people think you aren't doing your job because they don't see you on TV. Spend too much time on it and you start to hear from New Democrats that they didn't send us to Parliament to muckrake like the other parties. I remember being particularly frustrated by all the attention given to the antics of the "Rat Pack" in the 1984–88 Parliament—Liberals like Sheila Copps, John Nunziata, and Brian Tobin—while in my view we were concentrating on the issues that were truly important. The fact is that a good question period strategy demands a certain nimbleness on the part of those who are on the list that day. When I was leading off, I prided myself on being able to discern the story of the day as it was developing in the questions asked before the NDP's turn, and being able to sometimes quickly abandon the agreed-upon plan for an unscripted opportunity to get in on the story on the news that night. Those who depended on written notes could not be that flexible.

Through my involvement with the Lefebvre and McGrath committees, I became known as someone who took an interest in the institution as such, a perception that would both help and handicap me in years to come. Some portrayed my commitment to Parliament as an impediment to effective partisan politics, a view with which I strongly disagree.

CHAPTER

11

Our Environmental Deficit

Worst of all, beyond not dealing with the
fiscal deficit as it said it would, worship of
the market has put off dealing with the real deficit,
that of the environment.

Nowadays, when just about everyone's on the environmental bandwagon, it's difficult to tell the authentic from the inauthentic, the policy commitment from the public relations strategy. In this task of discernment the churches, environmental groups, and environmentally conscious citizens will have an important role to play.

In my three years as NDP Environment Critic—I was appointed in 1984 by NDP leader Ed Broadbent after the election that made Brian Mulroney Prime Minister of the first majority Conservative government in over 20 years— I would come to appreciate the accuracy of environmentalist Barry Commoner's prescient words. In 1971, decades before *sustainable development* became a common watchword, Commoner wrote in *The Closing Circle* that the world was

> being carried to the brink of ecological disaster not by a singular fault, which some clever scheme can correct, but by the phalanx of powerful economic, political and social forces that constitute the march of history. Anyone who proposes to cure the environmental crisis undertakes thereby to change the course of history.... That we must act is now clear. The question which we face is how.

So intense was the environment portfolio that it would be a relief to move to external affairs in 1987, where, though I would face many grave issues, not least the possibility of nuclear war, the passing of each day in and of itself did not necessarily make the matter worse. With the environment, the problems are cumulative and will take a long time to resolve; even if we could have started yesterday, there was always a feeling that nothing was happening at anywhere near the required pace. Later, the inaction of the Chrétien era that followed the Mulroney years would make Mulroney look activist by comparison, but only by comparison.

My predecessor as NDP Environment Critic was Jim Fulton, MP for Skeena, British Columbia. He would become our Environment Critic again in 1987 and stay in that job until he decided not to seek re-election in 1993. His knowledge of and commitment to the environment were second to none, and he went on to serve as Executive Director of the David Suzuki Foundation. Jim lost a battle with colon cancer in 2008, at the age of 58. The environment lost a champion, and I lost a colleague and friend with whom I had stayed in touch after his departure from Parliament. Whenever he came to Ottawa he would call and see if I was available to meet for dinner.

I visited him in Vancouver in early 2008. Our last conversation was over the phone when I called him from my Ottawa office the night before I was to give it up. I told him that Manitoba Premier Gary Doer had asked me to consider seeking the nomination in the provincial constituency of Elmwood, where a vacancy had been created when the MLA for Elmwood resigned to run for the federal NDP in my old riding. Fulton was excited about the idea, and speculated on all that might be possible if I became the Minister of the Environment.

Fulton achieved a certain notoriety and certainly a special place in the anecdotal history of Parliament, when he pulled a large salmon out of his pants one question period when he had the floor, and proceeded to slap it down on a minister's desk to make a point about disappearing salmon habitat. This incident was often cited as an example of Parliament's deterioration. But while I wouldn't encourage this kind of behaviour, I feel it is important to distinguish acts of protest motivated by genuine concern from the lack of decorum represented by unwarranted personal attacks and the constant shouting down of the other that rightly brings Parliament and politics into disrepute.

Fulton also figured prominently in several incidents from my time as Environment Critic. The first has to do with a PCB spill that occurred just outside Kenora, Ontario, on Sunday, April 14, 1985. A truck carrying transformers out west for storage had overturned and 400 litres of oil, containing 56 percent PCBs, spilled on the Trans-Canada Highway near Dogtooth Lake. For the first part of the following week, New Democrats asked constructive questions of the Minister of the Environment, Suzanne Blais-Grenier, or in her absence, of the Minister of Transportation, Don Mazankowski. Our questions were not carried on the extensive TV coverage that the event received, and we were getting calls criticizing us for not caring about the issue and for not raising the matter in the House of Commons.

On the Thursday, at our daily question period strategy session, it was decided that Fulton and I would team up to create a little theatre around the issue, by intemperately denouncing the way the government was handling the situation. We were helped by new information that had come to light: a family following the truck had been treated inadequately, and the transformers had not been reported to be full when they left Quebec for their destination. That night we were on the national news, and the next day the calls were positive. Job well done, or so it appeared. I thought we had been doing a good job on the days when we were not being reported. But it's a good example of what is wrong with the way politics is covered. Being civil and constructive is too often a recipe for obscurity. If a parliamentary tree falls in the forest and it is not reported, it didn't fall.

Just before the PCB spill, on March 17, the nation witnessed the Shamrock Summit in Quebec City between Prime Minister Mulroney and President Reagan. Though their rendition of "When Irish Eyes Are Smiling" was a hit, the outcome of the meeting was a disappointment. The American position had been that more research on acid rain was needed; the Canadian position, that the time had come for action. At the meeting it was agreed to appoint special envoys who would report in a year's time, and to undertake more research. In the meantime—as Quebec maple syrup producers, for example, were tapping significantly fewer trees and expressing concern about the future of their industry—Canada would continue to suffer the effects of acid rain.

Leading up to the summit, my role had been to press the Canadian government for action in order to come to the table with cleaner hands and a stronger moral stance to bargain from. A major federal-provincial agreement on acid rain reduction in 1985 was entered into as part of the Canadian strategy, not only to reduce acid rain per se, but also so that the Americans could not accuse us of hypocrisy or inaction. The NDP and our environmental allies also advocated making Canada's auto emission regulations at least as strong as the American ones, which eventually did occur a year later.

The special Canadian envoy appointed at the Shamrock Summit was Bill Davis, who had recently retired as premier of Ontario; the American envoy was Drew Lewis. Mulroney portrayed these appointments as the beginning of a process and an improvement over the impasse that he had inherited. But the special envoys' report in January 1986 was a disappointment. Even the Tory-dominated Special Committee on Acid Rain criticized its recommendations, which centred on a five-year period of yet more research into cleaner, more efficient coal-burning technologies. It was not until March 1991 that the Canada–U.S. Air Quality Agreement would be signed, not with Reagan but with George Bush the first.

The government had set up the Special Parliamentary Committee on Acid Rain in June 1985. It was chaired by Progressive Conservative MP Stan Darling, who represented Parry Sound–Muskoka, Ontario, an area greatly affected by acid rain. I was the NDP member on the committee, which also included Charles Caccia of the Liberals. We held many hearings and meetings, including a trip to Washington to meet with our American colleagues, and worked closely with the Canadian Coalition on Acid Rain, headed by Adele Hurley and Michael Perley.

My work on acid rain led to the only time I know of when I was quoted in The New York Times. On April 26, 1987, I was quoted as saying: "There is a widespread perception that Americans really don't give a damn if we have any forests, any fish, or any lakes. The sense of an incredible selfishness on the part of the U.S. government is going to have a fundamental effect on the way that Canadians think about the United States." This quote also made it into the 1991 edition of Colombo's Dictionary of Canadian Quotations.

Suzanne Blais-Grenier would have a short-lived career as Environment Minister. She was immediately put in a difficult position with Tory cutbacks to important environmental programs like the herring gull egg program, designed to monitor pollutants in the Great Lakes. At a crucial time when Canada was urging the United States to take the acid rain problem more seriously, such cuts undermined the government's environmental credibility.

Blais-Grenier's successor was Tom McMillan, appointed in August 1985. McMillan proved to be much more adept with the issues and with Parliament. It was during his time as minister that a most unusual thing happened, which has already been told by Elizabeth May in the chapter she contributed to

Endangered Spaces: The Future for Canada's Wilderness. May was an assistant to Tom McMillan at that time. The Green Party wasn't even a glint in her eye then, at least as far as anyone knew.

On May 14, 1987, the House was debating a non-votable NDP Opposition Day motion moved by Jim Fulton, calling for the creation of a national park on South Moresby Island, a space that many activists, like the late Colleen McCrory and Haida Chief Miles Richardson, had been working to save from logging. The motion was not expected to be even voted on, let alone passed. The minister was supportive, but it was well known that there were Tory backbenchers who didn't like the idea.

But there came a point just before lunch when it seemed to me that everyone who was in the House at that particular time was in favour of the motion. Rising on a point of order, I suggested to the Speaker, John Fraser, himself an environmentalist, that he ask the House for unanimous consent to not only deem the NDP motion votable, but also deem it adopted as of the end of the day and the time prescribed for debate. The minister nodded in agreement. Brian Tobin agreed for the Liberals, and when the pro-logging Tories showed up in the afternoon they were shocked to find out that the motion was already a done deal.

When I spoke to the motion that afternoon, I believe it was the only time I spoke to a motion that had already been passed. The next day the minister was able to negotiate with British Columbia, with the benefit of a parliamentary motion to back him up. South Moresby, including Lyell Island, was saved shortly thereafter.

———————

As Environment Critic I was also active on issues of pollution of the Niagara River and in the Great Lakes, ozone layer depletion, investment in sewage treatment modernization, protection of the porcupine caribou herd from American oil and gas exploration, the preservation of the Khutzeymateen Valley, British Columbia, for grizzly bears, the expansion of national parks, the need for a ban on drift net fishing, the regulation of herbicides, the need for a national water policy, the Environmental Protection Act, and the future of nuclear energy.

The federal NDP's concern about the lack of an informed debate on nuclear energy led to countrywide hearings on the subject that were conducted by NDP Energy Critic Ian Waddell and me. The Tories had not kept a promise to hold such an inquiry, so we held one ourselves. I was particularly interested in the question of what to do with high-level radioactive waste created by nuclear reactors, and concerned about plans for deep geologic disposal of such wastes at a site near Lac du Bonnet, Manitoba. Atomic Energy of Canada, in nearby Pinawa, Manitoba, had constructed an underground research laboratory to test the feasibility of the idea.

In the early 1980s, I worked with a group called the Committee of Concerned Citizens, one of whose leaders, Walt Robbins, wrote a book on the disposal controversy called *Getting the Shaft*. In it he refers to me as the only politician to take up their cause without prompting. He recounts that back when I had asked Prime Minister Trudeau about public hearings on the matter, Trudeau deflected the question by saying that he would be happy to discuss the issue with Allan Blakeney, the NDP Premier of Saskatchewan, where most of the uranium came from.

Uranium mining in Saskatchewan was an issue of some controversy in the NDP. The NDP Premier of Manitoba, Howard Pawley, had the legislature pass a law banning the storage of nuclear waste in Manitoba. For my part I did not hesitate to be severely critical of the mining, given the environmental concerns and the connection between uranium mining and the nuclear arms race. I raised issues on behalf of northern Saskatchewan communities like Wollaston Lake, and was glad over the years to work with critics of the nuclear industry including Dr. Gordon Edwards and Dr. Rosalie Bertell. In September 1986 I spoke at a conference on nuclear waste at the University of Winnipeg, where I hastened to point out that the NDP was the only political party in which there was actually a debate about such issues. The other parties were largely uncritical of the industry, and did not want to discuss the matter.

I would have occasion to test my critique of the Blakeney government's uranium policy sometime after his government's defeat in 1982, when Allan Blakeney and I were both speaking at a conference on medicare at Memorial University in St. John's, Newfoundland. The conference adjourned early in the evening, but it was in the early hours of the next morning back at the hotel that we finished a wide-ranging discussion of politics, aided by a bottle of scotch that somehow turned up. Although we had to agree to disagree about uranium, he showed himself to be one of the most civil and intellectually impressive people ever to have graced a premier's office.

Water exports were also a focus of mine in the 1980s. As Environment Critic, I sponsored a private member's motion, which reached debate, condemning the Great Recycling and Northern Development (GRAND) Canal Project. The

GRAND Canal was a hare-brained scheme associated with Robert Bourassa, then between his two terms as Quebec premier, and Simon Reisman, later the Canadian negotiator of the Free Trade Agreement. It proposed to dam James Bay, making it into a freshwater reservoir, and then pump it back down south through a pipeline powered by several nuclear reactors to the American market. Newfoundland engineer Thomas Kierans, who was responsible for its design, was still advocating for the project in 2010.

My concern about water exports would be greatly magnified later by the glaring inadequacies of the free trade agreements when it came to water. The debate about water and the free trade agreements was still very much alive when on February 9, 1999, I moved an NDP Opposition Day motion calling on the government to ban the bulk export of water. The day began with a joint press conference between Maude Barlow of the Council of Canadians and myself for the NDP. I was happy to be working with Barlow again, after our well-publicized disagreement in 1993 over the role of social movements in electoral politics. In true Liberal fashion, the governing party voted for the motion but discarded it the very next day, in a way that reinforced our concern about the exemption for water that they claimed to have obtained in NAFTA. The day after supporting a national ban, the Liberals said it had to be done on a province-by-province basis, not on a national basis that might trigger certain unexplained trade obligations.

Until that day, I didn't know whether the Liberals had been deceiving themselves or Canadians about the alleged exemption for water. To break the argument down is no easy task, but it goes something like this. Water is protected in its natural state, but not when it is commercialized. Therefore if you don't trade water it is protected, but if you do it is not protected. How comforting is that? It is only when water is being traded that the alleged exemption could have any meaning, but apparently then it's not applicable.

The day will come when the Americans will come knocking on our door for water, and we are not ready for that debate, in part because, like medicare, it is such a sensitive topic that no one wants to go near it. I may have contributed to this stifling of debate myself in 2001 when as NDP House Leader I successfully obstructed the creation of a special committee on water to be chaired by Toronto Liberal MP Dennis Mills, after learning that in a 1991 pamphlet he had seemed to advocate water exports.

The proposed mandate of the committee was curious in that it referred to "the challenge of achieving freshwater security at home and internationally, including with regard to the North American Free Trade Agreement." I saw it as a set-up. I could still hear former Liberal trade minister Sergio Marchi's voice ringing in my ears when he had said with great gusto that water would be the oil of the 21st century. God forbid.

In 2010, I would attend, as Manitoba's Minister of Conservation, a meeting organized by Premier Greg Selinger to bring together the best advice possible on matters of the economy and Manitoba's future. The keynote speaker, Colin Robertson, a retired Canadian diplomat who served many years in the United States dealing with trade matters, made the point that soon we would have to deal with the water issue, as it is on the American agenda, and that we had better be ready for it. We should be ready all right, but ready to do what?

My fear over the years that elements of the Canadian corporate elite would like to create a market for Canadian water were not allayed, when in March 2011 former prime minister Jean Chrétien publicly mused about "sharing" Canadian water and the need for a "mature debate" about the issue. Former prime minister Brian Mulroney has called for a mature debate about medicare. Beware those who call for a mature debate. Too often the call is designed to implicitly disadvantage a particular approach—such as preserving the principles of medicare or opposing the bulk export of water— as somehow immature.

Blame for the modern world's exploitation of nature is often placed at the feet of Christianity. The notion of human dominion over nature that has led to our present situation, the argument goes, is derived from the creation story in Genesis. This is no doubt partially true. Many modern attitudes can be traced to the selective expansion of a particular biblical theme.

In the creation story, for example, we read that God created those things over which humans are said to have dominion, before the creation of the first person. And they are called good, even before human life is added to them, which suggests that non-human creation has value in the eyes of the creator independent of its use to human life. That this way of reading the creation story has not been emphasized is the fault of its interpreters, not so much of the story.

Likewise, it is quite out of context to notice only the dominion of humanity in Christian theology without noticing the dominion of God and God's intentions for the dominion of humanity. Humans are uniquely able to understand and explain the rest of creation, and the power that this role gives to humanity over the rest of creation is certainly a form of dominion. But should this dominion ever have rightly been interpreted as a licence to treat the world as a mere instrument of human goals? While a human dominion over nature is supported in the biblical teachings, this dominion is more appropriately understood as a form of stewardship rather than of exploitation. Human life is responsible not only for itself, but as the image bearer of the same God who created the rest of creation and called it good, it is responsible for the well-being of non-human creation as well.

Human responsibility implies a separation of human life from nature. This view is sometimes contrasted with one in which we begin again to see ourselves as a part of nature, as a part of a larger whole with which we must live in harmony both to survive and to be more fully human. These should not be seen as opposing views. It is true that human vanity, aided and abetted by advances in technology, has led us to imagine that by dint of scientific and technological achievement in everything from medicine to pesticides, we could put ourselves beyond a place where we would need to conform to given natural realities. This has been a mistake. But it would also be a mistake to imagine that somehow we can throw off our own nature and abdicate our humanity by simply leaving nature to itself. Even organic farmers need to weed their gardens.

A way of looking at the environment is needed that sees humanity as included, albeit in a special way, in the realm of nature, and in which the idea of stewardship, insofar as it is grounded in the Christian tradition, takes its meaning from what we learn about the true human in Christ, the servant-king. Our dominion is a form of service, to all creation and to our fellow human beings. Here, I suggest, are the beginnings of a view adequate to the current ecological crisis.

But service implies sacrifice, responsibility, duty, prudence, morality— particularly intergenerational morality—and learning to accept limits. These traits, formerly seen as marks of character, may seem anachronistic in an age of rights, expectations, self-fulfillment, and individual choice. Yet the values of service may be the values upon which an ethic of survival will have to be built. Whether these values can be sufficiently nurtured in the context of 21st-century capitalism—liberal, conservative, or even social democratic—is the question.

Only the most diehard ideologues of the right would be unwilling to admit that there is a certain challenge built into a capitalist economy when it comes to being a responsible steward of creation. The logic of competition is to exploit a particular aspect of nature before someone else does. The logic of corporate monopoly, having cornered the market, is to create, through advertising and other marketing strategies, needs for your product that may not be genuine needs. People as well as nature are reduced to the status of things. We live in a society that worships the person who can create a product that nobody knew they needed and sell it by the millions.

The gifts of creation—clean air, water, fertile soil, and abundant oceans and forests—have been regarded as free goods whose replacement value we have not had to figure into the real cost of our economic activities. Ironically, many of those who worry most about someone getting a free lunch have had a free private banquet at the table of our common heritage and our common future for years.

Those of us who were raising environmental and energy issues in the House and outside of it in the 1970s and '80s, issues that have only recently been taken seriously enough, should be forgiven if, in this day when everyone says they are "green," we feel somewhat like the older son in the New Testament parable of the prodigal son. We may well be tempted to resent the recently converted, instead of celebrating the fact that others are now waking up to the correct point of view.

———

Jim Fulton and I were part of a new generation of MPs elected in 1979 that brought a keen sense of environmental issues to the NDP table. Most of us were quite young, in our twenties and early thirties. A *Maclean's* article about the new caucus, titled "Kiddies Corner," featured comments about Jim Fulton, Bob Rae, Svend Robinson, and me. Our generation had been sensitized, if not traumatized, by things like the 1972 Club of Rome report that predicted all manner of future problems if the planet did not solve the interrelated realities of pollution, population growth, and resource depletion. The Club of Rome didn't get all the details right, but its pessimism may turn out to have been well founded. Problems like the greenhouse gas effect and climate change were still to come, although not far off. I believe the first mention in the House of Commons of the greenhouse gas effect came in 1983 in the form of a statement made by Simon de Jong, also an NDP MP of the class of '79.

As Bill McKibben argues in his most recent book, *Eaarth: Making a Life on a Tough New Planet*, there was a chance that we could have acted in time, a window that was closed when Ronald Reagan defeated Jimmy Carter in 1980.

Instead of thinking about how we could break the momentum, the world was led by someone who thought taking our foot off the gas, both literally and metaphorically, was somehow un-American or part of an anticapitalist plot. Years later right-wing politicians would still think this way, including Prime Minister Harper, who at one time seemed to think—hopefully not anymore—of the Kyoto Protocol for reducing greenhouse gas emissions as a socialist plot.

Today, with politicians of all stripes declaring themselves "green," the innocence of the doves welcoming all to the eco-table must be matched by the wisdom of serpents, the wisdom to discern who is there for what reason. The politicians that are there only because of what the polls are telling them. The businesses that are there because of what their marketing specialists and image makers are telling them. Those who are there to save the environment and those who are there to save the system. Or even those among the public who have been moved to awareness by something in their own backyard, while for years they were indifferent about what happened in the backyards of others. Those, to go back to Commoner's words, who want to change the course of history, and those who want to salvage the established course of history.

For not all is what it seems. *Sustainable development* is already a greatly debased coinage. Far too often, all that is really meant is sustainable exploitation. And yet, it is only out of this complex web of motives and agendas that, with appropriate leadership, solutions will be found.

The term *sustainable development* was introduced by the UN's World Commission on Environment and Development. Its 1987 report, *Our Common Future*, is known as the Brundtland Report, after Gro Harlem Brundtland, the commission's chair and the first female Prime Minister of Norway—an oil-producing nation that stands in stark contrast to Canada when it comes to planning for the future and the end of oil. The Brundtland Report described sustainable development as meeting the needs of the present without compromising the ability of future generations to meet their needs. This report led to the 1992 Earth Summit in Rio de Janeiro, chaired by Maurice Strong, a Manitoban and global citizen with whom I have travelled on several occasions. The Rio summit produced the 1992 Convention on Climate Change, which in turn would lead to the Kyoto Protocol in 1997.

I had occasion to put Prime Minister Mulroney to the test given his effusive praise of the Brundtland Report, which recommended that all major policy decisions be subjected to environmental analysis. In the fall of 1989 it was announced that there would be major cuts to passenger rail service. I asked Mulroney in the House if the decision had been subject to any analysis of the environmental consequences of forcing people to drive or take the bus when they would otherwise take the train. It was clear that no such analysis had taken place, just like there has never been any government-sponsored analysis of the effect of rail line abandonment and the increased use of trucks to haul grain to market. I was particularly upset about the removal of a service from Winnipeg to the lake and cottage country east of Winnipeg and into Ontario. The cut there was a microcosm of what was happening all across the country. Instead of a train with hundreds of campers on it, the Trans-Canada had hundreds of cars and SUVs added to it as people headed for newly created or expanded roads to get to their lake or an adjoining one, where they had to keep a boat and motor. Anyone keeping a set of books that took into account the total environmental footprint of such a decision could hardly regard it as sustainable.

A consuming and polluting civilization must be called upon to really change its ways, not just proceed to the final eco-disaster with a clear conscience because the blue recycling box has been faithfully filled and green products faithfully purchased. This is not to be cynical, it is simply to put these gestures in proper perspective. Unless they are part of a more fundamental change in how and what we produce and consume, we may simply be shuffling the deck chairs on the *Titanic*.

A unique set of planetary factors calls for a transcendence of traditional political paradigms, on the left and on the right. Environmental concerns played no small part in undermining the confidence of the people of the Soviet Union in the communist system. I attended a conference on the arctic environment in Moscow in January 1989, along with Liberal Environment Critic Charles Caccia, Tory Pauline Browes, and Senator Philippe Gigantès, where I had the pleasure of briefly meeting American civil rights activist Jesse Jackson in the hotel where we were staying. Thanks to the openness created at the time by glasnost and perestroika, we were treated to horrifying accounts of the irresponsible environmental degradation that a command economy can create when it's teamed up with an arms race and other forms of geopolitical competition. The scale of the pollution of the Soviet Arctic, and the Baltic Sea, by an unaccountable, undemocratic regime made the capitalist West look good on the environment, if only in contrast. Even without the Chernobyl nuclear disaster, but certainly in response to it as well, the Soviets realized that they were steadily poisoning themselves and their country.

In a talk I gave after I got back from that trip, at Garneau United Church in Edmonton, I said:

> The danger for the global environment, and for the West, spiritually, is that in this era in which it is common to talk about the end of the Cold War and/or the end of communism, we will forget what we have come to know about the limits and problems and, indeed, the grave moral flaws of capitalism.

We did forget, and subsequently embarked on two decades of self-righteous triumphalist free market fundamentalism that put off dealing with all the ways that the market can stand in the way of saving the planet.

Nevertheless, it seemed to me that the citizens of the centrally planned command economies of the communist bloc had gotten all the environmental downsides of industrial civilization, and more, with little compensation by way of the consumer commodities that have made Western industrial society so much more comfortable. These comforts in themselves are also often environmentally harmful. As economist John Kenneth Galbraith observed at the time, the East's failure to live up to the consumption standards set by the West's consumer society—standards they could see on satellite TV—played an important part in hastening economic reform in Eastern Europe. But if progress means that eventually the whole world will live like we do, the question becomes one of whether the global ecosphere can take it. If this question was pertinent in 1989, it is all the more so two decades later as countries like China and India modernize their economies and their consumption habits.

Some might argue that it is not the developed countries that are currently causing the most extreme forms of damage to the global environment, like cutting down rainforests to produce pasture and timber. But many of the unfortunate practices of developing countries cannot be separated from the larger questions of poverty, and what it drives individuals and families to do, and of debt, and what it drives countries to do in search of exports and hard currency, regardless of the environmental consequences. And poverty and debt cannot be separated from the international economic order, the values behind it and the powers that uphold it because it serves their interests. This is an economic order created by the West, or the North if one uses the North-South paradigm, and through the harsh rules we impose on others we have arranged to receive from them much more than we give back in development aid. The global economy is a far cry from the new, just, participatory, and sustainable international economic order that the churches were calling for in the 1980s, before the corporate model of globalization co-opted the internationalist lingo for its own purposes.

———

Production for profit, and the attendant marketing techniques to sell that production, can encourage the premature depletion of valuable non-renewable resources, pollution of the environment, and an inherently short-term view that is inimical to good environmental planning. Antipollution measures are simply not profitable, unless they are subsidized by the taxpayer. It is particularly irritating when the technology required to improve the environment is available but goes unused—as with the electric car—because corporate morality, or lack of it, dictates otherwise.

Until very recently, we were in an ideological landscape in which those who were critical of the marketplace and its values took a real political beating. In the 1980s, the capitalist revival spearheaded by Ronald Reagan and Margaret Thatcher, and imitated here in Canada—characterized by deregulation, privatization, tax breaks for the rich, cutbacks in social spending, and finally the free trade agreements, regionally and globally—exhibited an idolatry of the marketplace that seemed to know no bounds.

This last fling of unrepentant market worship has multiplied the poor among us and allowed the infrastructure of our civilization to deteriorate. Worst of all, beyond not dealing with the fiscal deficit as it said it would, worship of the market has put off dealing with the real deficit, that of the environment. This is the deficit that we may not be able to pay off. It accumulates in a potentially lethal geometric pattern that could make the interest on the fiscal debt look harmless by comparison.

Dealing with the environmental deficit will require more and better planning, regulation, and intervention on behalf of the future. Who are the real realists—those who believe we can carry on like this, or those who think we will have to change our ways or die? This change will be painful for everyone, the powerless and the powerful—perhaps more so for the powerful who will have more to give up.

Governments will have to appeal to the common good, not just to the interests of certain groups or sectors. People will respond if they are asked to make sacrifices for something worthwhile, for their own environment and the environment of their grandchildren. Politicians must resist the temptation to sound like there are no hard decisions to be taken. People know otherwise.

They know that things can't continue as they are, so when they are presented with a choice between a "hard choices" right-wing agenda, and a "no hard choices" agenda by the left, they often vote for that which has the ring of truth to it. Unfortunately, the right's hard choices are most often designed to serve not the common good, but private economic interests.

Democratic socialists and social democrats have participated over the years in the general lack of regard that modern society has had for the environment and for future generations. But, progressively expanding our egalitarian imagination to include the people of the future, we may yet be able to help the world make the critical choice that J. Philip Wogaman describes in *The Great Economic Debate*. The world must choose between putting drastic limits on our production and consumption for the sake of an unlimited future, or limiting our future for the sake of unlimited present economic activity. This is the truly hard-choice agenda, an agenda that the right wing is incapable of putting before the people without challenging its own assumptions, except perhaps in some hour of eco-catastrophe, when survival may come in the form of an authoritarianism that demands sacrifices only of the powerless.

New support systems will be needed for those who lose their jobs because of changes made for environmental reasons. New jobs will also be created by environmental policies, but not always, and certainly not always for those who lose their jobs for environmental reasons. Yet why do we accept as a necessary tragedy that every day people lose their jobs because of the financial bottom line, but rebel at the thought that jobs might be lost because of the bottom line of survival? Why are credit ratings, quarterly profit margins, and other economic "realities" that cause layoffs hard facts that have to be accepted, while a different way of thinking applies to jobs lost because of environmental regulations?

Being faithful to creation is no easy task. It is a constant struggle against the temptations of righteousness on the one hand and despair on the other, each of which can be a form of giving up on the prospect of larger changes. It is a struggle against the temptation to lament the way things could have been if better decisions had been taken earlier. A struggle to keep presenting relevant hard choices, and where history provides, making the hard social, economic, and ecological choices that will be needed to save the human prospect.

In thinking of the urgency of the environmental challenges we face, I've found this story instructive. Because the nature of environmental harm often accumulates exponentially, it is revealing to employ the mathematical analogy of a lily pond that, starting with only one lily pad but doubling every day, will be fully covered with lily pads in 28 days. The first day there is one lily pad, then the one becomes two, the two become four, then eight. On the last day before the end of the 28-day process, how much of the pond is covered? Exactly half. At a glance, the coverage may not seem that substantial. But in that one remaining day, all is completed, or finished, as the case may be.

David Suzuki, the well-known environmental activist, likes to make the same point by telling the story of a test tube that will be filled by exponentially growing bacteria. On the third-last day, the test tube is only one-quarter full, and those who know how the bacteria behave are outnumbered by those who take false comfort from how empty the test tube still is. Suzuki was a guest speaker at the federal NDP convention in 1985, where he was introduced by Jim Fulton, my colleague on the environment portfolio, and thanked by me. In the 1993 election, I was honoured to be able to use a quote from Suzuki in one of my pamphlets, complimenting my work on environmental issues.

12

Hope in the Post-Cold War Era

Between condemning the party's policy on NATO,
and condemning any move to rethink the policy
as a betrayal of NDP principles,
the media had a heyday.

The NDP's internationalist approach to foreign policy has been a matter of lively debate. Just as the NDP has taken a critical view of Canada's dominant political and economic model, the party has been unafraid to critique the conventional wisdom of Canadian foreign policy and decisions made in the heat of a crisis.

But a prophetic stance, though it may be praised in hindsight, is not always designed for maximum political appeal in the present. Biblical prophets were often accused of disloyalty for daring to question whether their king, or their side, was in the right. Likewise, in the international realm, the NDP has been willing to challenge simplistic dichotomies that pit good guys against bad guys, and particularly any suggestion that the planet was worth sacrificing in a nuclear war to save Western capitalism. This approach was sometimes a matter of lively debate—among Canadians, and within the party itself.

Ed Broadbent appointed me External Affairs Critic in 1987, a position I would hold until fall 1990, when internal party politics under new leader Audrey McLaughlin, who was elected leader in early December 1989, saw me move on to become Tax Critic just in time for the debate over the GST. McLaughlin had promised the external affairs position to one of her early supporters in caucus, but after some discussion of the matter immediately after the convention it was decided that I would stay on for a while.

I was able to pack a lot into three years in this role. I would be responsible for responding to issues like the first intifada in the West Bank and Gaza, apartheid in South Africa and the push to free Nelson Mandela, the peace process in Central America, and the end of the Cold War. Also, as one of the two NDP members on the Standing Committee on External Affairs and International Trade, I would have special responsibilities in our party's opposition to the Canada–U.S. Free Trade Agreement.

Pauline Jewett, my high-profile predecessor, had been in the role since 1979. A former president of Simon Fraser University and, briefly, a former Liberal MP, Jewett had left the Liberal Party over Pierre Trudeau's imposition during the October Crisis of 1970 of the War Measures Act, which the NDP under Tommy Douglas opposed. Jewett once got into political hot water when she suggested that she understood why opponents of apartheid, like the African National Congress, might think that violence was a justified response. No doubt some of those who vilified her at the time were the same people who lined up to have their picture taken with Nelson Mandela, leader of the ANC, when he visited Canada after his release from prison in 1990. I was glad to shake his hand, too, but I had always thought him a hero.

Intellectually fearless and good on her feet, Jewett would be a hard act to follow. But I was thrilled at the prospect, and glad to leave my environmental post for this assignment. Jewett did not seek re-election in 1988 and was replaced by her assistant Dawn Black, who with Iain Angus would co-chair my leadership campaign in 2002–03. Black will be remembered by many as the MP whose private member's bill created the Day of Remembrance every December 6, the anniversary of the 1989 École Polytechnique massacre in Montreal.

———

The end of the Cold War, as a result of the events that transpired from 1989 to 1991 when the Soviet Union came apart, marked the end of close to a century of strife, including two world wars, in which the world was repeatedly torn apart by the shifting rival military alliances of the great industrial powers. During such an age, it undoubtedly often seemed necessary to seek security in military alliances. But it was always an illusion to imagine that security was exclusively to be found in military strength and military alliance.

The NDP, and its predecessor, the CCF, were among those internationalists who argued that it was important to think of security as something broader and deeper. The CCF had supported the view that danger was found not only in military threats, but also in the tensions created by economic exploitation and inequality, by the international arms trade, and by great powers manipulating smaller states in their strategic rivalries. The NDP built on the CCF critique in the 1960s by adding the nuclear arms race to the list of security threats. By the 1980s global poverty, environmental degradation, and widespread human rights violations were also seen by New Democrats as essential elements of any risk assessment.

Canada's Stake in Common Security, a major foreign policy paper in the CCF-NDP tradition, was prepared in 1988 by the International Affairs Committee of the NDP, which I co-chaired as External Affairs Critic. It was adopted by the NDP that same year. More attention than usual was being paid to NDP ideas on foreign policy, as the party was very high in the polls, and had won three out of three by-elections in the summer of 1987. Our prospects had never looked so good, and the attention showered on me by some when they thought I might be the next minister of external affairs stands in stark contrast to the treatment I would experience a few years later from the same people, when the NDP lost party status in 1993.

In my previous experience on party committees, I often lamented the lack of a person charged with and able to make an objective attempt to draft a document that accurately reflected the committee's decisions. So I initiated having a writer sit in on the committee's deliberations to help us draft a representative and readable report. We hired Clyde Sanger, a well-respected independent foreign affairs journalist, who many years later would coin the description of Prime Minister Paul Martin as "Mr. Dithers" in a column he wrote on Canada for *The Economist.*

The committee's report articulated the framework of NDP foreign policy, and was influenced greatly by the 1982 Independent Commission on Disarmament and Security Issues, chaired by Olof Palme, a former prime minister of Sweden who was assassinated in 1986. The commission, which produced a report entitled *Common Security: A Programme for Disarmament,* was composed of eminent persons from 16 countries. In summary, it embraced the principle of common security, which holds that countries can only find security in co-operation with their competitors instead of against them, as was the case with the traditional collective security of military alliances.

According to the Palme Report:

It is...of paramount importance to replace the doctrine of mutual deterrence. Our alternative is common security. There can be no hope of victory in a nuclear war, the two sides would be united in suffering and destruction. They can survive only together. They must achieve security not against the adversary but together with him. International security must rest on a commitment to joint survival rather than on a threat of mutual destruction.

The NDP's 1988 paper is dated in its details now, but its essence remains relevant. A policy of global common security is crucial to human survival in the post–Cold War era. We must not put to rest the bipolar world of the Cold War only to slip back into a multipolar world of competing regions or ideologies. Nor should we regress to the anarchy of the international system before the First World War, or assent to a unipolar scenario that would allow the Americans, or any other country for that matter, to assume the role of global policeman.

At the end of the Cold War, Canadians had high expectations for the possibilities of this new approach. Many hoped that with the end of the horrifyingly surreal definition of international security as a nuclear balance of terror, opportunities would open up for authentic common security. Such security would continue to have a military dimension; systems of mutual independent surveillance, global arms reductions treaties, and military information sharing—all integrated into a new global security architecture, preferably under the auspices of a reformed and revitalized United Nations—would have to be developed and maintained. But at the same time, governments could spend more on international development, poverty reduction, and environmental protection. They could engage constructively in the democratic advancement of developing societies as a way of achieving genuine international security, rather than propping up "friendly" authoritarian regimes as happened so often during the Cold War.

The world has taken a few welcome steps back from the brink of nuclear holocaust, but nuclear weapons remain the single greatest threat to the future of the planet. On another threat that affects millions of innocents daily, especially in war-ravaged countries—antipersonnel land mines—hope did eventually manifest itself. This plague was lessened to some degree by the mine ban treaty signed in 1997, a process which the NDP actively supported. My fellow Winnipeg MP Lloyd Axworthy played a key role in bringing it about when he was Canada's Minister of Foreign Affairs, and he was nominated for the Nobel Peace Prize for his efforts.

The NDP wanted to harness the post–Cold War hope to build a global architecture of common security. Unfortunately, leading up to the election of 1988, our attempt to emphasize the need for new thinking on security always seemed to boil down to a debate about the NDP position on NATO.

The North Atlantic Treaty Organization had come into being in 1949, in the early stages of the Cold War, amid a widely held perception that Western Europe, threatened by Soviet actions in Eastern and Central Europe, needed the military assistance of the United States and Canada. The CCF supported the creation of NATO and Canada's membership in it from its inception and throughout the 1950s. But over the course of the next decade, many members of the NDP became critical of American foreign policy and of NATO's policy regarding first use of nuclear weapons, which years later, in 1996, the World Court would declare illegal.

As the nuclear arms race progressed in the 1960s to a point where many saw NATO's nuclear strategy as more of a threat to the planet than a source of security, members of the NDP questioned the wisdom of Canada's membership in NATO. In this same period, the United States escalated its involvement in the Vietnam War, with little or no consultation with its NATO allies, and openly supported vicious military dictatorships in Latin America and other parts of the world. Thus, the NDP adopted a policy in 1969, at the height of the Vietnam War and with the nuclear arms race at full throttle, to seek Canada's withdrawal from NATO. As federal NDP leader at the time, Tommy Douglas had been outspokenly critical of American policy in Vietnam.

In spring 1982, I attended the session of the North Atlantic Assembly, the parliamentary arm of NATO, in Madeira, an island in the Atlantic that is part of Portugal. I had the opportunity as part of the Canadian parliamentary delegation to speak to the plenary session, and chose to set out the basis of the NDP's critical stance toward NATO. An American-led NATO, because of its nuclear policies and American support of military dictatorships, was no longer true to its original democratic ideals. And participation in NATO prevented Canada from pursuing an independent foreign policy of its own. This inability would be amply demonstrated the following year, when Prime Minister Trudeau, despite overwhelming public opposition, and probably his own, cited NATO obligations for Canadian participation in testing the cruise missile. Criticism of NATO in Canada and elsewhere was, as I said at the meeting in Madeira, an authentic human response to the threat to human survival posed by the nuclear arms race, and to the lack of integrity in the West's rhetoric about democracy and justice. "Indignation about Poland

and Afghanistan," I said, "without indignation about Chile or El Salvador is transparently empty to increasing numbers of people in all countries and in all walks of life."

Internal party debate in the 1980s, which culminated in the *Canada's Stake in Common Security* policy paper, was many-layered. Leading New Democrats who were active in the Socialist International, the worldwide organization of labour, social democratic, and democratic socialist political parties, were encouraged by their European counterparts to rethink the NDP position on NATO. The Socialist International was led at the time by Willy Brandt, hardly an unprogressive voice that could be easily dismissed. Brandt had been chancellor of West Germany from 1969 to 1974, and was a promoter of Ostpolitik, which sought better relations with Poland, East Germany, and the Soviet Union. In 1980 he chaired a commission on North-South relations that issued what came to be known as the Brandt Report.

The NDP was often further to the left than the European and British socialists who controlled the Socialist International. Some might say that this was because we were neither in government nor likely to be, and could therefore be more idealistic. The debate about who the real realists are will no doubt continue, but sometimes it merits observing that what looks like idealism is in fact the only realistic hope for a better future.

The first of two meetings of the Socialist International that I attended was in 1989 in Stockholm. I went with party leader Ed Broadbent, party president Johanna den Hertog, Shirley Carr, president of the Canadian Labour Congress, Yukon Premier Tony Penikett, and Dick Proctor, then federal secretary of the NDP and later a Saskatchewan MP. In 1996 I would attend the Socialist International in New York with Alexa McDonough, who by then had become leader of the NDP.

At the Stockholm meeting, I tried unsuccessfully to amend a draft document that purported to describe the origins of the democratic socialist movement with no mention of religion. Attempts to include the historical fact that many have come to their left-wing politics through faith got nowhere. Broadbent informed me that the Spanish delegation—because of the identification of the Roman Catholic Church with fascism in Spain during and after the Spanish Civil War in the 1930s—would have no part of such wording. Not everyone has The United Church of Canada in mind when the role of the church comes up for discussion.

In our party's debate over NATO leading up to the election of 1988, some wondered whether NDP policy on NATO was realistic, not just in terms of electoral acceptability, but more importantly in terms of what an NDP government could hope to do in the course of an otherwise challenging mandate. Though Canadian withdrawal from NATO was never a centrepiece of the peace movement's agenda, it became clear that both inside and outside the party, many people saw the maintenance of the NDP's NATO policy— whether or not it was worth upholding or in need of modification—as a test of whether the party would stand by its principles. Between condemning the party's policy on NATO, and condemning any move to rethink the policy as a betrayal of NDP principles, the media had a heyday.

It was a little-known fact that for his entire time as leader, Ed Broadbent was personally very critical of the party policy on NATO and wanted to change it. It was not the only time that I observed political leaders caught between their own better judgment and the judgment of party activists. Broadbent's discomfort with the NATO policy would, when the issue came up, hamper his performance in the leaders' debate during the 1988 election.

In the end, caught between the politics of the position and the politics of changing the position, a compromise was arrived at. *Canada's Stake in Common Security* said that an NDP government would withdraw from NATO only in its second term, after spending the first term trying to change those NATO policies it opposed.

––––––––

Our party's work in 1987–88 on defence and foreign policy attracted support from outside the usual NDP universe. Of particular interest was our 1988 candidate in Kingston, Ontario, retired Canadian Army General Leonard V. Johnson. A former commandant of Canada's National Defence College and the author of *A General for Peace*, Johnson was the NDP candidate in a race that eventually went to Liberal Peter Milliken. Milliken went on to be the longest-serving Speaker of the House of Commons, from 2000 to 2011, before retiring as an MP.

I had occasion to campaign with General Johnson, and often wonder about the contribution he might have made to the NDP and to the national debate about certain issues. In his book Johnson records that Admiral Robert Falls, the Canadian chair of the NATO Military Committee who would later become president of the Centre for Arms Control and Disarmament, was known as an independent thinker who questioned the need for so much nuclear overkill. Falls's heresies weren't appreciated by his international military staff or, no doubt, by his American colleagues.

I had had the pleasure of meeting Admiral Falls at a reception held at Strategic Headquarters Allied Powers Europe (SHAPE) in 1982, when I participated in a parliamentary study tour of NATO, the Organisation for Economic Co-operation and Development, and what was then called the European Common Market, now the greatly expanded European Union. I recall the admiral confiding to me, in a whisper, that he was as afraid of the American willingness to go to war as he was of the Soviets.

That study tour gained some notoriety, not for what we learned, but for the way all the Tories on the trip, notorious Newfoundlander John Crosbie included, stole away in the middle of the last night to catch an earlier flight as part of a strategy to surprise the Liberal government on a parliamentary vote the next day. As it turned out, they still didn't have the numbers to defeat the government, but parliamentary travel took a hit for the next while after that.

David Dingwall, then a newly elected Liberal MP, was on that 1982 trip and I got to know him a bit. Years later in 1994 when he was the minister in charge of housing, a conversation that had taken place on the trip would prove critical. My father had been instrumental, in his work with the Transcona branch of the Royal Canadian Legion, in getting a senior citizens' apartment block built and was to cut the ribbon along with a representative of the federal government, which had helped to finance the project. My father asked if I could be that person, and the housing bureaucracy turned him down. I remembered the conversation I'd had with Dingwall about our fathers. I got through to him, explained the situation, and within the hour the bureaucrats were phoning my father to say how nice it would be if I could be available to cut the ribbon with him.

On that trip, I also vividly remember pressing to visit a Canadian war cemetery while we were overseas. Eventually we visited the Second World War Cemetery at Adagem, Belgium. As I was walking, looking at the graves, row on row, and noticing French and English Canadians buried side by side, it suddenly struck me that all the Quebec MPs had stayed on the bus. This experience of the two solitudes left me angry and confused. I am less angry as the years go by, but still puzzled.

My first opportunity to visit a Canadian war cemetery had been in 1971. I was cycling from Calais, France, to Amsterdam with my friend from Transcona, Brent Gushowaty, when one day we noticed a very impressive gate with Canadian flags coming up ahead of us. We got off our bikes to check it out and discovered the Canadian cemetery at Bergen-op-Zoom in the Netherlands. We walked up and down the rows of headstones, and were struck by the similarity in age between those who were buried there and ourselves. We were both just months short of our 20th birthdays, and felt fortunate indeed to have an experience of Europe that was so different from that of our fathers' generation; both of our fathers had served with the Canadian armed forces in the Second World War. After Adagem in 1982, I would visit Canadian cemeteries in France in 1992 at Vimy Ridge and Dieppe, and in 2004 at Benys-sur-Mer. Each time, as I grew older, the sacrifice of so many young lives and all that might have been for them became poignantly clearer in my mind.

With the Cold War drawing to a close in 1989, New Democrats engaged briefly in a new internal debate about NATO policy. NATO was clearly going to play a central role in establishing the political and military architecture of Europe in the post–Cold War era. And Canada, as a major participant in the two European wars of this century, had a stake in the future shape of European institutions.

On this basis, it was argued by some New Democrats, including myself in a 1992 article in a party magazine called *The Alternative*, that an NDP government would want to be in on such a process, and that the policy of withdrawal from NATO should be rethought from a post–Cold War point of view, without prejudice to whether the policy had been right for a previous historical set of circumstances. I also found persuasive the argument that Canada would be better served by not running the risk of being institutionally intimate only with the Americans, and losing the broader relationship that NATO made possible. The policy, however, remained unchanged.

As I had in the 1980s, in the 1990s and beyond I would remain active in the NATO Parliamentary Association, and attend several annual meetings in capitals of NATO countries. My participation was criticized as hypocritical in a 1991 book called *A Capital Scandal*, but I was keeping informed about an institution that was very important to Canada, whether the NDP wanted out or not.

By the time of the book I had already been publicly involved in a critical analysis of the merits of the NDP policy. I was also amused to read of our "loud" opposition to NATO, when I cannot think of even one occasion when the NDP actually asked the government to withdraw from it. And after all the criticism that the NDP took for occasionally questioning the utility of keeping Canadian troops in Europe, it was the Mulroney government that would decide in the early 1990s to unilaterally end this long-standing presence.

I raised concerns about what I thought was unfair comment with one of the authors, John Warren, whom I knew and respected as a former host of House of Commons broadcasting. He offered to try and correct the record somehow, but I told him not to worry about it. In the end, I am not sure how well-read the book was; no one has ever raised the matter with me.

At the time there was much criticism of parliamentary travel, some of it fair, most of it not. Only a few years later, Reform MPs would come to Ottawa vowing to avoid international travel and criticizing others for participating in it. I was never sure whether it was just a political tactic, or some deep-seated commitment to being ignorant of the world and what could be learned by seeing other places and meeting other people. After a few years they changed their minds, as they did on a number of other issues, and Reform, Canadian Alliance, and now Conservative MPs are just as keen on international meetings as anyone else.

————

In the late 1990s, the war in Kosovo would bring issues about NATO to the fore again. Kosovo was an "out of area" intervention of the type that had been debated in the abstract at NATO meetings throughout the decade. I was skeptical about the wisdom of such an expansion of NATO's role, particularly as an alternative to the role of the United Nations. I was additionally skeptical of arguments from American delegates that a weak UN necessitated a strong NATO, as the United States actually preferred a weak UN and for many years hadn't paid its annual dues. After bringing this to the attention of a plenary session of a NATO Parliamentary Association on one occasion, I received a scolding from American delegates in the lobby, while delegates from other countries quietly indicated that I had made a good point. This seems to be my role at so many meetings, to say what other people are thinking and wonder afterwards why, if they agreed with me, they didn't say so at the time.

The NATO intervention in Kosovo made for some strange politics. I myself had been affected by the presentation at a 1998 NATO parliamentary meeting in Barcelona of an Albanian woman from Kosovo, who tearfully pleaded for an intervention to stop the anticipated wholesale slaughter of Kosovar Albanians. Thus I was ready, but still surprised, to find that our External Affairs Critic at the time, Svend Robinson—who was not known for agreeing with the Americans or for supporting NATO—was advocating support of the NATO action. Yet that was the nature of the debate over Kosovo; it did not break itself out in the usual pattern. I recall, for example, Václav Havel, leader of the velvet revolution against communist rule in what is now the Czech Republic, surprising many with his support for the intervention in Kosovo. I had the opportunity to hear Havel, and meet him, when he spoke to the House of Commons in April 1999.

For Havel the intervention in Kosovo was first and foremost a question of human rights, not of his country's national interest. For him and many others, the Kosovo situation was an opportunity for the world to shed the doctrine of the inviolability of states, particularly of states that were victimizing elements of their own population. This was a sincerely held view on the part of many and is related to the doctrine adopted by the United Nations a few years later in 2005 called the Responsibility to Protect, or R2P, a doctrine that seeks to legitimize interventions within states rather than just between states. However sympathetic one might be to such a doctrine, and I am, it is hard not to notice that it is a doctrine invoked and implemented usually only when it complements the older doctrine of acting in the national geopolitical self-interest.

A prominent front-bench Liberal assured me that, based on a previous confrontation with Serbian President Milosevic in Bosnia, the bombing would last only a few days before Milosevic came to the table. We were also assured that only military targets would be bombed and that the action would stop the mass exodus of Albanians from Kosovo. None of this proved to be true, and it was not long before the NDP began to be critical of the mission.

One of the things that caught my attention at the time was the nature of the Rambouillet accord, a peace proposal drafted by NATO in 1999 at Château de Rambouillet in France that laid out a number of demands to be met by the Serbian president. Slobodan Milosevic's refusal to sign it had been a reason for the war, although many argue that it was a proposal designed for rejection.

What was interesting to me about the accord was a provision, related to a larger debate about democracy, calling for the institution of free market principles and the privatization of publicly owned assets. It was a good example of what I regard as a mistaken or ideologically driven insistence on a certain way of organizing the economy in order to be declared democratic.

This is a way of seeing the world that infuses the World Trade Organization, except when it comes to China, but that is for another chapter.

To privatize or not to privatize is a decision that should be left up to democratic processes to decide. Privatization of public assets and resources is not a necessary feature of democracy. In fact, it can lead to less democratic control over entities that were once public, as we've seen in such domestic examples as the privatization of the Manitoba Telephone System and Canadian National Railways, which now serve primarily the financial interests of shareholders rather than the public interest. Speaking of privatization, I once had the pleasure of hearing former Conservative British prime minister Harold Macmillan speak in the House of Lords, chastising the Conservative Thatcher government for its privatization policies, which he characterized as selling off the family jewels for short-term gain.

———

Later, as NDP Defence Critic, I would accompany Liberal Defence Minister Bill Graham in February 2005 to the annual Munich conference on security policy. The conference focused on the future of NATO and the nature of European military capacity. While in Munich I visited the site of the Nazis' failed Beer Hall Putsch of 1923 that led to Adolf Hitler's imprisonment, during which he wrote *Mein Kampf*. The Americans at the conference, I noted, including Secretary of Defense Donald Rumsfeld and Senator Hillary Clinton, were careful to not be seen as telling the Europeans what to do. I had a chance to speak with Senator Clinton; we exchanged concerns about the religious and political right in America. Although I was grateful to have the opportunity to meet such a famous U.S. politician, I have to say that I sensed in her the same lack of active interest in the Canadian experience that I have found in so many other American notables, from all sides of the political spectrum.

What I remember most about NATO meetings was the constant frustration, indeed irritation, at the debate being constantly framed as one between the different perspectives of Europe and the United States, with nary a mention of Canada. Sometimes the Canadian position was much closer to the European one than anyone would have bothered to discover, and it often fell to me to speak up on various matters. Ironically, at a variety of international parliamentary gatherings I found that it was the New Democrat who had to take to the microphone to defend or explain the Canadian position, sometimes when I didn't necessarily agree with it.

The debate about NATO continues. Much will depend on what happens in Afghanistan, and whether NATO is seen to succeed in its Afghan mission. Whatever the outcome, I hope it acknowledges the unique role that Canada can and perhaps should play in NATO, without an expansion of NATO that could unnecessarily recreate the Cold War, and in a way that does not neglect the need to revitalize and reform the United Nations. Better still, Canadian leadership in NATO on the abolition of nuclear weapons would be a real service to the future of the planet. That could be the needed follow-up to the agreement reached between Russia and the United States in April 2010 to slash a third of their nuclear weapons. One-third down and two to go. But the proliferation of nuclear weapons to so many other countries has rendered the old idea of superpower agreements hopelessly inadequate to safeguard the planet. Despite widespread complacency, the world is probably in as much, or more, danger of a nuclear conflict as it has ever been.

13

A Willingness to Turn the Page

The politics of Northern Ireland, or Ulster, as it is also known, had created the circumstances of my birth.

The good news of the Christian gospel is the forgiveness of sins. However this good news is theologically understood or explained, the practical good news is the freedom of an open future and the ability to begin anew. I was able to observe a similar spirit or kindred freedom in a number of countries with long-standing conflicts that I had the opportunity to briefly experience as a visiting Canadian MP. A willingness to turn the page is hard to come by, but people who are up to the challenge can make all the difference for themselves, and for the world.

In the fall of 1989 I was part of a small ad hoc committee struck by External Affairs Minister Joe Clark to visit Namibia and assess its pre-election context. The country was preparing for independence and its first elections that year, and Canada was part of the United Nations Transition Assistance Group (UNTAG). Namibia had been a German colony until the end of the First World War, when it came under British control and subsequently South African control, complete with apartheid. The election would be the culmination of a nationalist political and guerrilla campaign led by Sam Nujoma, and Namibia would formally become independent on March 21, 1990.

Our delegation of four was led by Tory Walter McLean, a Presbyterian minister with a long history of involvement in international issues, particularly on the development side. He had first come to my attention in the early 1980s as one of the few Tory MPs concerned about the nuclear arms race. It is no coincidence that the most progressive Progressive Conservatives in those days often had an explicit connection to the church, people like McLean and David MacDonald, a United Church minister who was twice a Tory MP. Later, Christians of another persuasion would take the progressive out of conservatism altogether.

Together with Liberal Bob Speller and Quebec Tory MP Marie Gibeau, we flew to Namibia from New York on Zambian Airways, McLean's way of supporting the African economy. We were accompanied by Bob Miller from the Parliamentary Centre, an organization in Ottawa that does work for parliamentary committees. Miller was a resource to several parliamentary trips that I was on, and could always be counted on for reliable information and thoughtful analysis.

A largely empty jumbo jet took us safely to Lusaka, the capital of Zambia, and then on to Botswana, where we had to take a different plane to Windhoek, the capital of Namibia. Windhoek was tense with the possibility of political violence; the night before we left a prominent White pro-independence lawyer would be assassinated. We met with many Namibians who were excited about their new future. At one meeting, I recall being surprised by the informed questions I got about the NDP's fortunes, as many of those present had studied in Canada. The Canadian student diaspora in the world too often goes unrecognized, and its possibilities for Canada's relations with other countries are too little appreciated.

Our trip took us to the northern Namibian town of Rundu, where we had to fly low to avoid heat-seeking missiles, signs of the civil war in the adjacent Angolan territory. In Rundu we visited the barracks where the UN peacekeeping force was stationed, and were briefed by officers from FINBATT, the Finnish Battalion on duty there. The final briefing for McLean and me with the commanding officer took place, with the periodic delivery of various nibblies and cold beer, in a sauna constructed beside a small pool that one could enter for relief, an amusingly stereotypical Finnish environment superimposed into the Namibian setting. Speller and Gibeau were visiting another part of Namibia at the time. Otherwise, a mixed-gender briefing in the sauna might have been more problematic.

Walter McLean was a great communicator. Watching him at a political rally that we attended as observers of the South West Africa People's Organization shaking hands, introducing himself, and handing out Canadian flag pins, I was tempted to shout, "Walter, they don't vote in your riding." On Sunday, he arranged for us to attend church—an African Lutheran service courtesy of the German colonial heritage. Both of us ended up preaching unplanned extemporaneous sermons to the enthusiastic congregation.

On the way home from Namibia we spent a day in Zambia, and met with President Kaunda over breakfast at the presidential palace. Formerly the mansion of the British governor, its backyard was a nine-hole golf course. Kenneth Kaunda, whose father was a Church of Scotland minister and missionary, had obviously read his briefing book. Before breakfast, he asked if Reverend Blaikie would please say grace. Kaunda was president of Zambia from 1964 to 1991, when a return to multi-party elections would lead to his defeat.

At a reception at the Canadian embassy in the capital, Lusaka, I met the legendary White anti-apartheid activist Joe Slovo. He was in exile in Zambia, but would sooner than we thought return to South Africa to serve in the government of Nelson Mandela. Slovo's wife, Ruth First, had been assassinated for her anti-apartheid activities, and he himself was short a few fingers from opening a letter bomb.

Gibeau and I needed to leave a day earlier than the rest, and were driven together from Lusaka to Harare, Zimbabwe, for the flight home. As the eight-hour drive ended along the banks of the Zambezi River on a Friday afternoon, people were leaving the city, towing big boats with big motors on them, heading out for the weekend. I noticed they were all White Zimbabweans.

In the late 1980s, the Baltic Canadian community was carefully monitoring the fate of their home countries of Latvia, Lithuania, and Estonia, all of which were chafing under Soviet rule. Canada recognized Soviet rule in the Baltic states on a de facto basis, but not on a de jure basis. In other words, in theory we did not recognize Soviet sovereignty over the Baltic states, but in practice there really was no other choice. Thanks to reforms initiated by Mikhail

Gorbachev, the Soviet President, the prospect of a free and fair election became possible in Lithuania, though it needed to be carefully observed.

I was asked to participate in a delegation of politicians that the Baltic Canadian community sponsored to observe the first free election held in Lithuania in February 1990. The delegation included Bob Rae, then leader of the opposition NDP in Ontario, Richard Johnston, who had run against Rae for the provincial leadership, and Sam Cureatz, an Ontario Tory MPP.

We were allowed into the Soviet Union, while an American delegation, which had made too much of the geopolitical dimension of its mission, cooled its heels in Germany. The Canadian embassy was not thrilled about us being there, because if anything controversial happened to us it would be a challenge. And we were somewhat concerned that so many Lithuanians thought we had come "to stop the Soviet tanks." But in the end, there would be no tanks, and Sajudis, the Lithuanian independence party led by music professor Vytautas Landsbergis and supported by the Baltic Canadians, would win the election.

In Vilnius, the capital city, I was billeted with Josas Oleksas, a surgeon and social democrat who supported Lithuanian independence. Oleksas's parents had been sent to Siberia for some years by Stalin. His family graciously accepted me as a guest in their very modest apartment. On my last night in Lithuania, I had a long conversation with my host about the wisdom of declaring independence right away. I was worried about their personal safety and the future of the struggle for independence if they moved too quickly. He was worried about losing momentum and about seizing the historical moment. His instincts were the right ones, as it turned out.

I also attended town hall debates on the north coast, near Klaipeda, where I was amazed by the civility that political opponents showed for each other, given the depth of the historical animosity and violence that had characterized their previous relationship. I complimented the participants on their civility, and wondered aloud whether Canadians take democracy so much for granted that we too easily let our politics be dominated by the trivial and the cynical.

The morning after the Lithuanian election we flew Aeroflot, the poorly reputed Soviet airline, from Vilnius to Moscow. Shortly after takeoff there was some sort of explosion, flames were reported on one side of the fuselage, and we began to lose altitude. Amid announcements all made in Russian, the flight attendants seemed quite concerned. With Sam Cureatz asleep beside me, I was faced with a dilemma: Should I wake him, or let him sleep? I opted for a conscious death on his part and woke my seatmate to tell him what was going on. "What the hell am I supposed to do?" he exclaimed, with a mix of sarcasm and worry.

As it happened, the fire went out, and we levelled out just above the trees and circled for an hour to burn up fuel before landing right back in Vilnius. I remember kissing the ground when we got off the plane, and bumming a smoke from a Lithuanian security guard. Sometime later we made it to Moscow, where we put a great dent in the liquor cabinet of the Canadian embassy before departing for Paris and a celebratory dinner there.

Shortly after the election, Lithuania dared to follow through with a declaration of independence, a reality unthinkable only a few years before. The newly independent country's story would not be trouble-free, and it looked endangered a year later when Soviet troops seemed poised to intervene in the country. I worked with External Affairs Minister Joe Clark and other MPs who had been in Lithuania to pass a motion urging President Gorbachev to let Lithuania be. He did, but it probably contributed to his downfall; he was overthrown that same year.

Some years later, my Lithuanian host Josas Oleksas would visit me in Ottawa, having spent some time as Minister of Health in the new government. As is often the case with independence movements, success had meant that they were now free to disagree about other things. When he came to Ottawa, Oleksas was out of power and a leader of the social democrats in Lithuania.

––––––––

In Namibia and Lithuania, I observed a willingness to move on, to not let the past imprison the future. I observed the same thing in December 1992 in Taiwan, as part of a Canadian delegation sponsored by the Taiwanese Canadian community, the Presbyterian Church in Canada, and the Presbyterian Church in Taiwan to observe the first free elections in that country. This trip to Taiwan was different from the trips that many MPs had taken as guests of the government during the years of Kuomintang rule. It was NDP policy not to go on such trips because of our disapproval of the repressive KMT regime. But the custom of trips to Taiwan survived the regime's demise, and Taiwan is now well visited by Canadian MPs of all stripes.

Taiwan had been ruled by the KMT since the Chinese revolution of 1949, when Chiang Kai-shek fled Mao Zedong's Communist army to what was then known as Formosa. Chiang Kai-shek's party had never permitted free elections to the Legislative Yuan, but 1992 was different. Hopes were high for the opposition Democratic People's Party, which would eventually, though not in that election, become the government.

I had become involved with the Taiwanese Canadian community's struggle for democracy when I raised concerns in Parliament about a Taiwanese Canadian, Y-S Columbus Leo. In December 1989 he had been arrested, beaten, and detained for going to Taiwan, despite being blacklisted, to participate in the free election of 7 percent of the Taiwanese legislature. The other 93 percent of the seats were held by members who still claimed to represent seats in mainland China, from where the KMT had long since fled in defeat. At the end of 1992 all the "old thieves," or lifetime members, retired, and an election was held for all of the seats in the legislature. The first free election of the president followed in 1996. Y-S Columbus Leo was ultimately released thanks to the efforts of all those who advocated on his behalf, and much to the relief of his wife, Pi-Ling.

The 1992 delegation to Taiwan included Bruce McLeod, who had been Moderator of the United Church from 1972 to 1974 and whom I had heard preach at Bloor Street United in Toronto when I was a student at Emmanuel College. It also included Taiwanese Canadians Albert Lin, Steve Chen, and Shane Lee, Liberal MPs Jim Peterson and Mary Clancy, and York University professor Michael Stainton. Stainton was a student of Taiwanese history, and I was surprised to learn that the Chinese are not indigenous to Taiwan. The indigenous people of the island are an Aboriginal Malayan people who now live primarily in the mountains of Taiwan.

At some of the huge election rallies we attended in Taiwan, I tried to hand out Canadian flag pins to the Taiwanese children. I say tried, because at six foot six and with the beard, most of the kids fled in terror from the alien monster that was trying to befriend them. I'm sure Walter McLean could have pulled it off.

While we were there, Jim Peterson got carried away at a press conference and declared that if the Liberals won the next election, they would recognize Taiwan over the wishes of China, which still regards Taiwan as part of China. Word got back to Canada, and the next day he was skating, despite the warm weather in Taiwan. The Chrétien Liberals would be the last people on earth to challenge China in that way. In fact, Taiwan is still seeking such recognition, and it is a shame that first geopolitical concerns, and now economic concerns, will likely prevent Taiwan from getting this recognition in the foreseeable future.

When it came to Northern Ireland, the political situation was not only of interest in my role as External Affairs Critic, it was a matter of personal and familial interest. The politics of Northern Ireland, or Ulster, as it is also known, had created the circumstances of my birth. My Irish grandmother, Mary Taylor (nee Kane), only agreed to come to Canada to get my grandfather, Alex Taylor, an excitable Orangeman in his early twenties, out of harm's way in the aftermath of the civil war that ended in 1922. They had been married at Toberkeigh Presbyterian Church in Ballycastle in 1920 and then lived in Belfast; in 1923 they emigrated to Canada with Alex Jr. The following year my mother, Kathleen, was born in Transcona. My Grandpa Taylor never joined the Orange Lodge in Canada and never returned to Ireland. But in 1958 he was reunited in Montreal with his older sister, Margaret, whom he had not seen since she left for New York City in 1908 when he was nine years old. My grandmother eventually returned to Northern Ireland in 1969, 46 years after her departure.

 I tell this story because it led my family and me into a greater appreciation of the Catholic Church. Aunt Margaret had married an Irish Catholic in New York, and one of her sons had gone into the priesthood. In 1966 that son, cousin Steve, or Father Emmanuel Sullivan, came to visit us in Transcona, and there began an important relationship that continues for me to this day. Father Sullivan, an ecumenist, was the Catholic observer on the British Council of Churches for many years, and authored two books, one of them on the thought of Cardinal John Henry Newman, the famous 19th-century Anglican who converted to Catholicism. Steve was pleased to report to me in 2010 that Pope Benedict XVI had consulted his book in preparation for his historic visit to the United Kingdom for Newman's beatification.

In 1970, while playing in the Edinburgh Tattoo with the pipes and drums of the Queen's Own Cameron Highlanders of Winnipeg, as part of a larger Canadian army band sent for the occasion, I visited my newly connected relatives in Northern Ireland for a few days. I spent my first evening there at Stormont Castle, the home of the Northern Irish parliament, listening to the fiery Protestant leader Ian Paisley speak at great length. The next day I was taken on a tour of County Antrim, where I met 42 relatives in one day. I was anxious to get back to Ireland, and in the spring of 1971, after taking a year off from university and working at CN, my friend Brent Gushowaty and I cycled the North Antrim Coast, on to Donegal, and then to Sligo, where we visited the grave of William Butler Yeats. From the moment I experienced the troubles first-hand by witnessing the presence of British troops in border towns like Strabane, I took an interest in the peace process, or lack thereof, in Ulster.

As an MP I would be able to keep in touch with the situation in a unique way. Ulster politicians came to Ottawa, including Unionist leader David Trimble and Sinn Fein leader Gerry Adams, and I was able to meet with them in a meaningful way. I met with Trimble at Earnscliffe, the home of the British High Commissioner to Canada, where over the years I enjoyed many fine evenings with other visitors from the United Kingdom. The meeting with Adams was a lunch in the New Zealand Room of the parliamentary restaurant. It was hosted by three Irish Catholic Liberal MPs, who warned Adams, somewhat in jest, that I was a Protestant clergyman. He replied that not all of them were bad.

I was also able to visit Northern Ireland in the context of the Canada–U.K. Parliamentary Association. In addition to the formal parliamentary opportunities, in 1999 I participated in the annual Canada–U.K. colloquium, which took place that year in Newcastle, County Down, on the topic of federalism and devolution of powers, as 1999 was the year that Scotland and Wales got their own parliaments. I was invited to the colloquium again in 2007, in Warwick, United Kingdom, on the topic of social cohesion. As part of an intensifying debate about what it means to be British, there was much discussion about looking to Canada for ways of dealing with the multicultural diversity that is now also characteristic of the United Kingdom.

Twice in Northern Ireland, I stayed at the Europa Hotel in downtown Belfast, famed as the most bombed hotel in all of Europe. I first stayed there for one night in 1985, during negotiations leading up to that year's Anglo-Irish consultative agreement on Northern Ireland. The agreement was seen as betrayal by Ulster loyalists and worthless by most Irish nationalists, and the Europa was on high alert. It was surrounded by barbed wire, and could be entered only through a guardhouse where you were searched before entry.

The Canadian delegates had left our spouses in London, and Brenda was worried that I might be in danger. Ironically, when we got to Belfast, we learned that the main negotiations were going on in the very hotel in London that our spouses were staying in. They were probably in more potential danger than we were, though they had the consolation of spotting TV star Patrick Duffy, a fellow hotel guest, from time to time in the lobby.

The 1985 meetings in Belfast were informative but depressing, as we learned just how hard it was to even get people together in the same room. The next time I stayed at the Europa was in 2005, several years into the Good

Friday peace process that began in 1999. The wire and the guardhouse were gone, a major renovation had been done, and except for the presence of the Crown Bar—one of the oldest pubs in Belfast—across the street, I hardly recognized the place.

The meetings in 2005 were much more upbeat, although challenges remained, particularly with respect to building a non-partisan police force in Northern Ireland that would reflect the community's diversity. We were repeatedly told of the important role played by a Canadian, General John de Chastelain, a former ambassador to Washington. As head of the Independent International Commission on Decommissioning, de Chastelain was overseeing the critical process of seeing to it that the Irish Republican Army was disarmed and meaningfully separated from its weapons.

I had first met de Chastelain in 1989 when I was External Affairs Critic and he was Chief of the Defence Staff, at a dinner party hosted by the West German ambassador. I was seated beside the general, and the other guests were puzzled that the New Democrat and the general got on so well. It turned out we both played the bagpipes, and knew many of the same people in the piping community. In the years that followed, we would enjoy the odd pint together with a group of pipers that I knew from playing with the Air Command Pipes and Drums of Ottawa.

Similarly, at a NATO Parliamentary Association meeting in Edinburgh in 1998 I would confound the NDP stereotypes of my colleagues by taking an empty front-row seat beside U.S. General Wesley Clark, Supreme Allied Commander of Europe. He was a friend of a friend of mine in Transcona, Willie Parasiuk. Parasiuk and Clark had been Rhodes Scholars together at Oxford, and I had first met Clark when he stopped off in Transcona in 1979 on his way to a top NORAD posting in Colorado. In the same vein, I also enjoyed chatting with the Queen's piper at a NATO reception at Buckingham Palace in the 1990s—it turned out we had played together in the Edinburgh Tattoo of 1970. When my colleagues asked who I was talking to, I got a kick out of replying that he was the Queen's piper and that we used to play in the same band.

Another prominent Canadian in Northern Ireland was Sir George Bain, President of Queen's University in Belfast from 1998 to 2004. I was delighted to meet him in Belfast in 2005, as he had grown up in East Kildonan, a part of Winnipeg that was in my riding. I had long known of him through mutual Manitoba friends. Bain had gone to Oxford in the early 1960s, stayed in the United Kingdom, and in 2001 was knighted for his public policy service to the government of Tony Blair. Given the high regard in which he was held by visiting Canadian MPs, I took great delight in informing them that he had been the first president of the Manitoba New Democratic Party when it was formed in 1961.

A highlight of the 2005 trip was a hockey game in Belfast. The Belfast Giants, which included a number of Canadian players, were the first team in Northern Ireland to be organized on a non-sectarian basis. When they scored that evening against England, both Catholics and Protestants cheered for the same team. In a similar spirit of reconciliation, in Dublin on that same trip, Tory Jason Kenney and I put aside our political differences to enjoy a concert by The Fureys, a famous Irish band. Kenney's obvious sympathy for Irish nationalism provided ample opportunity to rib him about the curious affinity between the former head of the rabidly right-wing Canadian Taxpayers Federation, and the Marxist Sinn Fein.

Ian Paisley and Gerry Adams finally sat down together in 2006 and resolved to live together in peace and hold an election in the spring of 2007. It was truly a great moment for Northern Ireland, and a hopeful moment for the world. It also meant that I could finally get Brenda to consider a visit there; we went in the summer of 2007.

———————

As an MP I would visit two other places that still await the spirit of reconciliation, or an inspirational exhaustion with violence and division—Cyprus and Israel. I went to Israel in 1981 as a guest of the Histadrut, the Israeli Federation of Labour, and to Cyprus in 1986 as part of a Canadian delegation sponsored by the Greek-Cypriot community in Canada.

My "tour guide" in Israel was Yitzak Shelef, who would later be the Israeli ambassador to Canada in the early 1990s. I was thrilled at the opportunity to be in Israel, both as one interested in the politics of the Middle East and as one familiar with the biblical story. To see the Jordan River and the Sea of Galilee, to visit the ruins at Capernaum, all this and more was wonderful from a personal religious point of view. When I ordered St. Peter's fish off the menu at the restaurant in Tiberius, I finally saw a fish that actually looked like the ones in the Sunday school pictures I remembered. The sight of people water-skiing on the Sea of Galilee, though, initially seemed like some sort of sacrilege to me. Politically, although the situation currently differs substantially in some respects, the visit to Israel was an education that continues to be of value.

The challenge of the Israeli-Palestinian conflict for outsiders is to find ground on which one can be legitimately critical of a particular Israeli policy without contributing to whatever antisemitism, new or old, is to be found in some criticism of Israel, while at the same time not being intimidated by the possibility that whatever criticism is offered may be tactically dismissed as antisemitism by those who would prefer not to deal with the substance of the argument. The attitude of "you are either uncritically with us or you are against us" is unfortunate, and is found in abundance on the Palestinian side as well. I remember only too well the nasty mail I got when during a debate in the House I denounced those who would recruit young people to be suicide bombers.

The Cyprus delegation included Toronto Tory MP Andrew Witer, former MP and British Columbia NDP attorney general Alex MacDonald, Liberal MP Don Johnston from Montreal, and, recently retired from politics, Jean Chrétien, who had lost the Liberal leadership race to John Turner in 1984. Johnston had also been a candidate in that race, and it was still very much on their minds. I spent a fair bit of time with the two of them after-hours on that trip, and learned a lot about the inner politics of the Liberals at that time. Too bad I didn't keep notes. The one lasting impression I had, which was borne out in 1990 when he became Liberal leader, was that we had not seen the last of Jean Chrétien.

The trip to Cyprus established a friendly relationship with Chrétien that I valued over the years, and that enabled us to talk from time to time in a way that might not otherwise have been possible. Sometime in the last few years of his tenure as Prime Minister he invited me to 24 Sussex Drive for lunch. I think it happened at the suggestion of Winnipeg Liberal MP John Harvard, to whom I had observed, or perhaps even complained, that after two decades in Ottawa I had still never been to 24 Sussex, whereas I had been inside 10 Downing Street, the residence of the British prime minister. At a 1993 reception at 10 Downing held for a visiting Canadian Commonwealth Parliamentary Association delegation that I was a part of were gathered in the same room four British prime ministers: the incumbent, John Major, Margaret Thatcher, Ted Heath, and Jim Callaghan, the last Labour prime minister at that time. My conversation with Lady Thatcher, urged on me by a U.K. Tory MP whom I knew, was brief.

I did not go to lunch at 24 Sussex Drive, and I still have never been inside the place. Chrétien later kidded me that I was scared to be possibly seen with him, as it was during the time when my name was coming up as a possible candidate for the NDP leadership. His political instincts were not far off the mark. On the other hand, Brenda has been in 24 Sussex. In 1979 when I was first elected, Maureen McTeer, Joe Clark's wife, had a reception for all the parliamentary wives.

Brenda's other prime ministerial memory of that time is of a conversation at Rideau Hall, at the Parliamentary Ball held to celebrate the opening of the new Parliament. Brenda and I were chatting with Governor General Ed Schreyer and his wife, Lily Schreyer, when Pierre Trudeau joined the conversation. Trudeau was the Leader of the Opposition at the time. He took an interest in Brenda and told her that he was very glad to see young people like me being elected to the House of Commons, even if they were from the wrong party. Brenda responded by saying that some thought it might be him that was in the wrong party. Trudeau was at his charming best when he graciously retorted that it was possible and that perhaps she might be able to convince him. Her encounter with the legend will always be one of her favourite political stories.

On the other hand, I did once make it into the Prime Minister's Office. Immediately after Stephen Harper's election on January 23, 2006, New Democrats were worried about the fate of the $4.6 billion in social spending that had been added to the 2005 budget, as a result of an NDP amendment that Paul Martin accepted as the price for NDP support of the Liberal budget. The money was to be found in the cancellation of a portion of the corporate tax cuts that had been part of the budget. Even so, the budget deal that was made in April only passed in June as a result of the vote of former Reform MP and then independent MP Chuck Cadman, who was terminally ill.

Cadman was an unlikely Reformer, with his blue jeans, ponytail, and passion for playing rock and roll, but he had embraced the law-and-order agenda of the political right after his son was murdered. I got to know him a bit when he and his wife, Dona Cadman, and I were on the same parliamentary delegation to the Channel Islands of Guernsey and Alderney in the spring of 2003. In his youth he had played once with what became the famous Winnipeg band The Guess Who.

The worry was that Harper, who had condemned the NDP amendment, would seek to sabotage its implementation, particularly of any funds that had not flowed yet. For reasons I cannot remember, Jack Layton was not available and it was decided that I would meet with Harper to try to dissuade him of any such idea. The argument would be twofold, that those other levels of government that were already planning to receive and spend the money on things like affordable housing and post-secondary education would not be pleased with him, and that doing so would be getting off to a really bad start with the NDP at the beginning of a new and unpredictable minority Parliament. NDP House Leader Libby Davies came with me to the meeting in the Langevin Block, a legendary edifice I had only seen from the outside before. Our strategy was to let me do the talking, but I was glad to have Davies with me. I am happy to report that my one and only direct meeting with a prime minister was successful. My record was not endangered by subsequent opportunities for failure.

CHAPTER 14

The Gulf Wars and Parliamentary Diplomacy

I was privileged to meet many people who
were courageously fighting for social justice in
environments far more hostile than any
the Canadian left has experienced.

My time in Parliament spanned two wars in the Persian Gulf, a period of intense political intrigue in Central America, the collapse of the Soviet Union, and the integration of China into the global economy, not to mention many other events and developments that I did not have a personal engagement with as an MP. What I did have the opportunity to engage was plenty enough.

In the summer of 1990 I tried as NDP External Affairs Critic to keep open the possibility that, if there was a consensus at the United Nations, the NDP might support military action to free Kuwait from the Iraqi army of Saddam Hussein. I knew that the geopolitics of oil were as operative as any idealism about protecting states from invasion. But still, I saw such a consensus action as a potential start to a new era for the UN.

In a statement that I issued on August 10, 1990, I cautioned that "what is going on in the Gulf is of our own making by virtue of the arms trade, which has gone on for years, indeed for decades, including the sale of arms to Iraq, to Iran and to other Middle East countries.... We are beginning to reap what we have sown." Similarly, I suggested that we were reaping what we had sown "by our excessive dependence on fossil fuels, and on oil in particular," and expressed hope that the Western world would wake up to this dependence and begin charting new energy policies.

Iraq had annexed Kuwait on August 2, 1990. The immediate response from the United Nations Security Council was a call for economic sanctions and then an embargo against Iraq that began on August 6. The next day Operation Desert Shield was launched by the United States to protect Saudi Arabia from Iraqi invasion. At that point, if there was to be military action beyond the embargo, the UN and Canada were far from clear on a framework for such action. As NDP External Affairs Critic, I argued against a NATO-led action and against an American-led multinational force without UN approval. But I did not argue against a UN force. Rather than let the United States play the role of global policeman, I wanted Canada to seize the post–Cold War moment, and have the world act as the world.

There were those on the left who argued that the invasion of Kuwait was no different than the 1982 invasion of Lebanon by Israel. I rejected that kind of inaccurate moral equivalency. The Kuwaitis were not harbouring anything akin to the Palestinian Liberation Organization that was launching attacks into Iraqi territory, nor were they questioning Iraq's right to exist. Nevertheless, during the parliamentary debate on the war, I moved an NDP amendment calling for an international peace conference on all outstanding Middle East issues. It didn't pass. One could rightly see that, for example, the issue of the occupied Palestinian territories needed—and still needs—to be dealt with. But whether the proposal was actually what was needed at that time was certainly debatable. I had forgotten that I had even moved such a motion until I discovered it in Hansard doing research for this book.

In analyzing the invasion of Kuwait, I preferred to raise more accurate comparisons, like the Indonesian invasion of East Timor, which at that point was not getting the attention it deserved. As an early member of Parliamentarians for East Timor, I was hopeful that a properly energized post–Cold War UN might take an active interest in East Timor's liberation. It eventually did; East Timor, which was invaded by Indonesia shortly after gaining independence from Portugal in 1975, would regain its independence through a UN-sponsored process in 1999.

Saddam Hussein was given until January 15, 1991, to comply with UN resolutions, or all necessary means were authorized by the UN to make him do so. A debate in the House of Commons commenced on the day of the deadline, and while it was going on, Operation Desert Storm was launched by the U.S.-led coalition, of which Canada was a part, on January 17. To his credit, Prime Minister Mulroney had called Parliament back early to deal with the situation and to seek parliamentary approval of the decision to participate in the coalition. The House of Commons voted on January 22, with only the NDP voting as a party against the motion, along with Liberals Warren Allmand, Marlene Catterall, Marcel Prudhomme, and Christine Stewart, Bloc Québécois MPs Gilles Duceppe and Louis Plamondon, and Tory Alex Kindy.

The Liberals, who began the debate arguing for more time to let sanctions work and calling for Canadian withdrawal if the embargo were escalated into an act of war, had been criticized by the Tories for not supporting the UN. By the end of the debate, the war had begun, the Liberals supported the government, and they were criticizing us for not supporting the UN. Too often the United Nations is used selectively by politicians as a club with which to beat their opponents. Similar flexibility abounded on the issue of sanctions. People who had argued that voluntary sanctions against apartheid South Africa needed years and years to work were willing within months to abandon mandatory sanctions against Iraq for military solutions.

There was, however, a theme to the Liberal critique of the NDP, that we were against military action on principle, even if the UN was for it, and shirking our responsibilities as citizens of the world. This theme would come up again on February 24, 2003, when the NDP pressed Prime Minister Chrétien about whether Canada would participate in the invasion of Iraq, or the second Gulf War. Responding to NDP leader Alexa McDonough, Jean Chrétien opined that the NDP thought everything could be solved by a "good singsong." I was tempted to organize a singsong on the Hill the next day; protest singers like Pete Seeger might have something to say about the power of music. In the end, Chrétien chose to sing rather than fight—and we did not send our troops.

In January 1991 NDP leader Audrey McLaughlin spoke eloquently about the resort to war as failure, which of course it always is. For some in the party our vote against the motion was a matter of pride. For me it was a cause of some ambivalence. I voted with the caucus, but I was bothered that our position seemed motivated more by a mixture of pacifism and anti-Americanism than by a rigorous analysis of the issues. On this issue, there was disagreement on the left; for example, Neil Kinnock, leader of the U.K. Labour Party, and one seen as being on that party's left, disagreed with the NDP position.

I want to credit Prime Minister Mulroney for his willingness, in contrast to the Liberal tradition, to involve Parliament on such issues. Under the Liberals, Canada was the only NATO country not to have its Parliament vote on the expansion of NATO in 1999 to include former Warsaw Pact countries. And again in 2003, Prime Minister Chrétien was adamant that Parliament could debate the invasion of Iraq, but the decision would be an executive one. The opposition was welcome to move a motion of non-confidence, but of course that would rule out any freedom of thought on the Liberal benches. It's too bad, really. I'm sure the Canadian Alliance under Stephen Harper would have loved to have voted against a motion that called for Canada not to participate. And Liberals would probably have found the record of that vote to be useful later. A few years later, in a return to parliamentary votes on such issues, but also with an eye to exploiting internal Liberal divisions on the issue, Prime Minister Harper would involve the House in voting on the Canadian mission in Afghanistan. Unfortunately he seemed to abandon this need for Parliament in 2010 when the Liberals agreed with him about extending the mission in a non-combative form after 2011. No mischief to be had. No vote.

The NDP had opposed the first Gulf War even though it had UN approval, and was arguably a good, old-fashioned, unambiguous invasion of one country by another. Yet we initially supported the late 1990s war in Kosovo, even though it didn't have UN approval and was only a NATO action. In 2003 we were opposed to an invasion of Iraq, and were not put to the test insofar as the UN was concerned because the second UN resolution on Iraq that even the Liberals finally required was not forthcoming. We aren't the only party to be all over the map like this, as I pointed out earlier, and consistency can be a refuge for those who do not want to do the challenging work of addressing the particulars of the dilemma before them. But I sometimes felt that the way we tended to position ourselves as uniquely supportive of the United Nations was compromised by the fact that when push came to shove, we only supported the UN when our party activists agreed with it. I felt that after a UN decision was taken, even if we did not agree, there should be at least some critical understanding extended to a government that was abiding by a UN decision.

The second Gulf War, or the invasion of Iraq, was a different matter for me from the first. I was never tempted to support the invasion, as along with many others, I did not find the arguments for the alleged link between Saddam Hussein and al Qaeda to be persuasive, nor the alarmism over the weapons of mass destruction that were allegedly being stockpiled in Iraq. With respect to the latter, it would have been better to let the UN weapons inspector Hans Blix exhaust the process, but that might have eliminated a helpful pretext for a war that George W. Bush seemed committed to beyond any argument to the contrary. The one truly amazing thing is that not only did they not find any weapons of mass destruction, they actually admitted it. This for me was a sign of hope in a strange sort of way. There appeared to be a limit to deception. After all, it could have been arranged for the appropriate weapons to be found. Yet they were not.

As Parliamentary Leader of the NDP from January 2003 to June 2004, I led off the daily question period for the party, meaning I had the privilege of waking up in the morning and considering what question I would ask the Prime Minister today, a rare privilege that I enjoyed immensely while it was mine to enjoy. In the lead-up to the invasion in 2003, I asked Jean Chrétien a number of questions about Canada's intentions. So convoluted and evasive were his answers that when he finally announced that Canada would not participate, he could have announced the opposite and still not have contradicted anything he had said.

Though I suspect Chrétien's decision on Iraq had more to do with Quebec politics than has been admitted, it was the right one. Unfortunately, I believe that it set the stage for Canada to assuage the disappointed Americans by making more of a commitment in Afghanistan than we otherwise might have. One such example would be the decision by Prime Minister Martin in the summer of 2005 to accept a war-fighting role in Kandahar that departed from the nature of Canadian involvement to that date. Paul Martin's decision was also likely influenced by a desire to make up for Canada's decision earlier in 2005 not to participate in the American plan for Ballistic Missile Defense (BMD).

The Liberals had promised a vote on BMD, but it never happened. The argument went that there was no decision for Parliament to vote on, but in my view it would have been the right thing to do, and instructive, to vote to approve a decision not to do something that was so actively being sought by the Americans. Many Liberal MPs were probably glad to avoid a vote, as they would have found themselves voting against something they had been gearing up to support until Martin changed his mind. The NDP agreed with the decision to opt out of Ballistic Missile Defense, an issue I had more than one lively discussion about with U.S. Ambassador Paul Cellucci at luncheon meetings sponsored by the Canada–U.S. Parliamentary Association. He could not understand why Canada would refuse to be a part of something so significant and remain on the outside, so to speak. Opponents of BMD did not want Canada to be on the inside of something they regarded as a dangerous development in the ongoing struggle to rid the world of nuclear weapons. President George W. Bush probably did not help the American position when shortly after his re-election in 2004 he came to Canada and openly advocated Canadian participation in BMD. Nevertheless, I believe that through subsequent amendments to the NORAD agreement in 2006, the Americans got, on a practical basis, what they really needed from Canada.

————

I would visit the Soviet Union three times, counting the trip to observe Lithuania's 1990 election, and once more after it had become Russia again. My first visit had been for the eye-opening conference on the arctic environment in January 1989. In 1990, after returning from Lithuania, I went with the External Affairs Committee on a trip to Moscow, Leningrad, Kiev, and West Germany. The trip was the culmination of a study of the situation in Eastern Europe we had conducted that fall and winter, a study that would be a classic case of the limits of expertise. Expert after expert told the committee that the Soviet Union was in no danger of coming apart. Within a year or so, it had done just that.

Nor was the imminence of such historic events apparent to the committee, with the exception perhaps of what was to happen in Germany. On May 1, 1990, we experienced in Berlin a huge street party that stretched from one side of the Brandenburg Gate to the other, as East and West Berliners celebrated the impending removal of the Berlin Wall. It was a great privilege to be present for such a moment and, as people tried to hurry the process by breaking off pieces of the doomed wall, to come away with several souvenir pieces of it. Ten year earlier, at a meeting of the Interparliamentary Union in East Berlin, a trip that included a tour of the still-visible ruins from the Allied bombing of Dresden that had killed so many Germans, and also a visit to Wittenberg, the home of Reformation leader Martin Luther, I'd had to pass through the notorious Checkpoint Charlie at the border between East and West Berlin. Now citizens of East and West Germany were freely passing back and forth, and the reunification of Germany was under way.

In 1990, at a meeting with some East Germans, one of those present, upon hearing my name, thanked me for writing on his behalf when he was in prison, and told me how much it had meant to him. He was a Christian peace activist who had been jailed for his activities. I did not remember the letter, but I know that I did faithfully respond to requests for such letters by Amnesty International, the churches, or whoever else was calling attention to the plight of those who were being persecuted for their beliefs. It was a lesson in the disproportionate importance of a letter. To me it was written and over with. To the imprisoned it was a comfort long remembered and appreciated, to know they were not alone and that someone on the outside cared and was trying to influence their captors. I would keep up my letter-writing, now with an added feeling of its importance.

Other memories of that committee's trip range from the tragic to the ridiculous. I will never forget the garden of mass graves in Leningrad (now St. Petersburg again), with the statue of Mother Russia overlooking the grim reminder of the mass starvation and death caused by the city's siege during the Second World War, and the wedding couples having their pictures taken at a place that obviously had such meaning for their community. On the ridiculous side, I recall a huge restaurant in one of our hotels with dozens of items on the menu. After much time wasted ordering and being informed after a delay that they were out of that particular item, it turned out that only two of the dishes listed on the extravagant menu were actually available.

Walter McLean, with whom I had been in Namibia the year before, was also on the Standing Committee on External Affairs, and took part in the 1990 trip. In Moscow he arranged for the two of us to attend a Baptist service, which was dominated by American preachers who promised to meet their listeners in the sky when God's final trumpet call summoned the faithful. As I reflected in an article I wrote for *The United Church Observer* after our return, the underground church was about to receive a rude awakening. Communism was the kind of foe that the faithful could understand and resist without ambiguity. Capitalism, ostensibly a friend, since it came with religious freedom, would prove to be a tougher foe in some ways, as Soviet dissident novelist Aleksandr Solzhenitsyn would find to his despair after his return to post-communist Russia.

Shortly after the committee returned from our trip to Eastern Europe and the Soviet Union, I had a chance to meet the Soviet President, Mikhail Gorbachev, and Mrs. Raisa Gorbachev when they came to Canada in late May 1990. Earlier in the year I had the opportunity to meet, and to question before the External Affairs Committee, Soviet Foreign Minister Eduard Shevardnadze, whom I found to be very frank, reflective, and impressive. After the breakup of the Soviet Union, he would become president of a newly independent Georgia. In the fall of 2003, when I returned to Russia as part of the state visit of Governor General Adrienne Clarkson, I had occasion to visit the famous Novodevichy cemetery in Moscow, where I stopped just down the way from the grave of former Soviet president Nikita Kruschchev, at the grave of Raisa Gorbachev, who had died in 1999.

The 2003 trip with the Governor General turned out to be controversial.

I had received an invitation that summer to be one of the parliamentarians on the delegation, but by the time we departed, criticism of the size, cost, and nature of the delegation—which included many Canadian artists—was at a fever pitch. The Bloc Québécois and Canadian Alliance MPs pulled out. Since the delegation was going to be meeting with Russian MPs, I felt that it would be strange not to have any Canadian MPs along and decided not to be intimidated by all the howling, including from some New Democrats. I did not then know Clarkson, but I had enjoyed books written by her husband, John Ralston Saul. I had met him during hearings on the Free Trade Agreement, when he told the External Affairs Committee about the terrible treatment of workers in the Maquiladora Corridor, a free trade zone in Mexico.

The trip was a memorable one indeed, as it provided my only opportunity to spend time with the likes of authors Michael Ondaatje and Yann Martel, filmmaker Denys Arcand, and broadcaster Mark Starowicz, to name a few. Adrienne Clarkson and I shared a walk—with bodyguards who had to be dissuaded from throwing people out of our way—down the Nevsky Prospect in St. Petersburg to the apartment where the great Russian author Fyodor Dostoevsky lived when he wrote *The Brothers Karamazov*. Another highlight was a meeting at the Kremlin with President Vladimir Putin, during which he commented on how surprised he was that Canada had not joined in the 2003 invasion of Iraq. At the dinner that followed, there were enough layers of cutlery and different glasses per place setting to service a family of five.

In the northern town of Salekhard, at the mouth of the river Ob, we enjoyed a feast and Aboriginal singing and dancing at an Aboriginal village. There is an incredible cultural similarity between the people we visited and the Inuit, although their languages are quite different. The presentation was wonderful, but it seemed staged for the occasion. Liberal MP Peter Adams and I snuck away at one point to see what lay beyond what we were being shown, and found plenty of evidence of the same harsh conditions associated with the North in Canada.

And then there was a voyage by helicopter across the tundra to a former forced-labour camp in the Siberian gulag. Its bunkhouse and guard towers were decaying, but as we viewed the remains of that terrible era, the images of the suffering that had gone on in the mid-20th century there were alive and well. The piece of barbed wire that I brought from the gulag is kept with the piece of the wall that I had picked up in Berlin, symbols of a tyranny that the world is well rid of.

As NDP External Affairs Critic, I was privileged to meet many people who were courageously fighting for social justice in environments far more hostile than any the Canadian left has experienced. I was particularly moved by the courage of those who put their lives on the line opposing brutal U.S.-supported right-wing dictatorships in Central America. The regime backed by the Americans in El Salvador was particularly brutal, even demonic, in its capacity for inflicting death and torture on its own people. The martyrdom of Archbishop Oscar Romero, who was assassinated while performing mass on March 24, 1980, in his church in El Salvador, is a symbol of all those who made such sacrifices. Romero was assassinated by a follower of Roberto D'Aubuisson of the ARENA Party, whose new leader, Alfredo Cristiani, I would meet in El Salvador in 1988.

I was appointed that year to the Special Committee on the Peace Process in Central America, chaired by John Bosley, former Speaker of the House. The other members were Lloyd Axworthy, the Liberal Critic for External Affairs, and Progressive Conservative Bud Bird; Bob Miller of the Parliamentary Centre was our chief researcher and writer. The committee spent two weeks visiting all five Central American countries, meeting people from all sides of the various conflicts taking place at that time. We met with presidents, opposition leaders, guerrilla leaders, church leaders, human rights activists, journalists, and others. Sometimes the people we were meeting feared for their safety and we had to meet them clandestinely or outside of their own country.

The committee spent an evening with Daniel Ortega, the leader of the Sandinistas, whose overthrow of the American-backed Somoza regime in Nicaragua in 1979 had sparked renewed American paranoia about Central America. He was accompanied that evening by his Foreign Minister, Father Miguel D'Escoto, whom I had met before when he testified in Canada before the External Affairs Committee. D'Escoto was one of many Roman Catholic priests who took a stand against the injustices of the regimes that allegedly defended freedom and democracy in Central America. A Maryknoll priest, he was suspended by the Vatican for his political activities, along with two other priests, brothers Ernesto and Fernando Cardenal.

The committee also spent an evening at the Canadian embassy in Costa Rica with a leader of the Contras, an American-backed rebel group trying to overthrow the Sandinistas. Not letting ideology get in the way of a good smoke, the Contra leader happily smoked Cuban cigars throughout the evening. Many times in Central America, particularly in El Salvador, Guatemala, and Honduras, I was conscious that either as a social democrat or as a church activist, I was the kind of person who, if I lived in those countries, might have been already killed or marked for such a fate because of my politics.

The committee's final report for External Affairs Minister Joe Clark would recommend how Canada could support the peace process that had been proposed by Costa Rican President Oscar Arias, whom we had met at his home in the capital, San Jose.

When this trip is remembered by those who were on it, the story is often told about our meetings in Washington, D.C., on the way home. While we were in Central America, I had had a few arguments with American officials, which John Bosley often stepped in to moderate. But during our trip Bosley had become so irritated with the American role in that region, and with their complete lack of self-critical capacity, that it was he who got into a heated exchange with an American politician in Washington. This time, to the amusement of my colleagues, I was the one who intervened to moderate the dispute.

The Sandinistas would lose the Nicaraguan election in 1990, and the region started to slip off the geopolitical map, as the Americans got their way by hook or by crook. I had come to know the Nicaraguan ambassador to Canada, Sergio Lacayo, and I suggested to him that despite the obvious U.S. interference in the upcoming 1990 election, perhaps the greatest gift the Sandinistas could give their fellow Nicaraguans would be the historical precedent of a government voluntarily giving up power. Which is what they did.

Many years later, Daniel Ortega would be re-elected as President of Nicaragua in 2006, and Miguel D'Escoto would be chosen by Latin American and Caribbean countries to serve from September 2008 to September 2009 as President of the United Nations General Assembly.

———

I had first begun to think seriously about China as a student at the Toronto School of Theology, in a course entitled Love and Justice in the Thought of Mao Tse-Tung taught by Dr. Ray Whitehead, then chair of the Canada-China Program of the Canadian Council of Churches. He would later serve a term as Dean of Theology at the University of Winnipeg, and in retirement taught with his wife, Rhea Whitehead, at Nanjing Union Theological Seminary in China.

Given the extent of missionary work that went on in China prior to the revolution in 1949, there had been much division in the church over how to perceive the revolution. A person of great controversy in that debate was James Endicott, a United Church minister and missionary in China who ended up being supportive of Mao and was disciplined by the church for his troubles. Endicott came to the class on Mao one evening. Though quite elderly by then, he was still very sharp, and it was a treat to hear from someone who had been so involved at such a critical time in history.

My first experience of China in person was a brief visit to Hong Kong. In April 1984, I was part of a large Canadian delegation invited to India by the Speaker of the Lok Sabha, India's lower house. On our way to New Delhi we first flew to Hong Kong, then still a British colony; it would revert to China's jurisdiction in 1997. Time was tight, and I was disappointed not to be able to visit the memorial to the Canadians—including many Winnipeg Grenadiers— who had died defending the colony in 1941. It has been my privilege to know a number of Hong Kong veterans, and to advocate for compensation on their behalf as an MP, something that came to pass on December 11, 1998, when 350 of the original 1,300 were still alive.

On our way home from India, we circumnavigated the globe, flying to Toronto by way of London, where a reception was held for us by the Canadian High Commissioner to the United Kingdom, Don Jamieson. Jamieson, a cabinet minister in an earlier Trudeau government and a broadcaster by trade, was from Newfoundland, where I had once been on his brother Basil's open line radio show in 1979. After the reception, over a drink with Jamieson and two other Newfoundlanders, MP John Crosbie and Senator Bill Doody, I listened, fascinated, as the three of them reminisced about Newfoundland politics and the legend of their province's first and long-serving premier, Joey Smallwood.

The trip to India was highlighted by a good meeting with Prime Minister Indira Gandhi. By the time it was my turn to ask a question, most of the usual political issues had been covered. So, as she had known Mahatma Gandhi very well, I asked what she thought of the recently released movie *Gandhi*. Gandhi, no relation to Indira, had been a mentor of her father, Jawaharlal Nehru, who became the first prime minister of an independent India. She recalled that she used to argue with Mahatma Gandhi when she was a teenager. As for the movie, she quite rightly pointed to the artistic need to emphasize the role that Gandhi played, when he was actually part of a much larger movement toward independence. That was April 1984. In June Indian troops inflamed the Sikh community by attacking the Golden Temple in Amritsar in the Punjab in pursuit of a militant by the name of Jarnail Singh Bhindranwale. Later that year, in October, Prime Minister Gandhi was assassinated by her Sikh bodyguards.

Having been to Hong Kong and Taiwan, I was glad to be able to finally get to mainland China in November 1998, as part of the first Canadian delegation of the newly formed Canada-China Legislative Association. Our visit overlapped with the meeting of the Canada-China Business Council in Beijing, which Prime Minister Chrétien was attending. An extraordinary will to please China characterized the Chrétien era, and a lot of business interests shared a similar approach. At the business council meeting, I found Canada's obsequiousness embarrassing, as with but a passing reference to human rights, the real business of setting up investment opportunities was attended to.

Our delegation had travelled to China commercially, but we were able to bum a ride home on the prime ministerial airbus. On this long flight, I was surprised to see no special compartment for the Prime Minister, just an ordinary business-class seat with no special luxuries. The way home from China would be clouded with sadness, particularly for some of the Liberals, including the Prime Minister and Senator Jack Austin, the leader of the delegation, who were long-time friends of Pierre Trudeau. In China we had learned that Trudeau's youngest son, Michel, had been killed in an avalanche. My thoughts, too, were with Pierre and Margaret Trudeau, as I recalled the pain that our family had gone through when my brother Bobby, who like Michel was the youngest of three brothers, was taken from us at age 20 by a traffic accident.

The Canada-China Legislative Association has its origins in an agreement that Jean Chrétien made with Chinese leaders to set up an association between Canada's Parliament and China that would be the equivalent of the Canada–U.S. Parliamentary Association, an association of members of Parliament, members of Congress, and senators that meets yearly to discuss bilateral concerns and issues of contention between the two countries.

The problem with Chrétien's commitment was twofold. First, he had committed Parliament to something without talking to parliamentarians. Second, more significantly, there was no Chinese parliament. At least that was a problem for me. As NDP House Leader I was invited to meetings on how to fulfill the Prime Minister's commitment. When I pointed out that, unlike our Parliament, China's had no opposition, and questioned the appropriateness of creating something called the Canada-China Parliamentary Association, I felt as welcome as the proverbial skunk at a garden party. The investment opportunities in China were great, and this would be an important step in the further improvement of Canada-China relations. Moreover, I was told, the Chinese would never settle for anything different from what the United States had.

I would not agree to anything that had the word *parliament* in it, and suggested the word *legislative*, on the grounds that the National People's Congress in China does legislate, even if it cannot properly be called a parliament. A few meetings were held; I had to be sure to be at all of them. In the end my intransigence paid off and the Chinese agreed, despite predictions to the contrary, to form the Canada-China Legislative Association.

When it comes to China, there has been plenty of inconsistency, or even hypocrisy, to go around, on both the left and the right. At one time—before President Deng Xiaoping opened China's economy in 1978 and began to create China's own unique brand of state capitalism, when it still retained a possibility that it was a grand experiment that would realize some dream, and long before the cameras captured the tanks descending on peaceful protesters in Tiananmen Square in June 1989—it was the left that said the West needed to judge China less harshly. The political right, and even the centre, was more focused on the internal oppression that was going on in China, and the godless undemocratic communism of it all.

When things changed and you could make money exploiting China's cheap labour market, the lack of democracy and the human rights abuses were suddenly judged less harshly. After all, it was only going to be through more trade with the democracies that China would come to be more like those democracies. Around the same time, the left suddenly lost its blind spot on China, and became concerned about the oppression of Tibet, about human rights, and about the effect that competition with China was having on wages in parts of the world where, unlike in China, free trade unions exist. When I was vice-chair of the Canada-China Legislative Association, I was also active in the Parliamentary Friends of Tibet, and was delighted to meet the Dalai Lama on one occasion when he visited Ottawa in 2004.

The other way in which I was engaged in the China file was as NDP Trade Critic, raising concerns about admitting China to the World Trade Organization. Though the reality of China in the global economy defies simplistic ideological responses, that reality should not cause us to abandon critical moral reasoning altogether, about the lack of human and democratic rights in China, and about the tremendous disadvantage that working Canadians suffer when they have to compete with that environment. China has the worst of all possible combinations from a competitive point of view, that is, an authoritarian state collaborating with a global capitalism that is only too happy to drive down wages by exploiting cheap Chinese labour. This is not the level playing field sung about in hymns to free trade. It is a stacked deck.

15

Free Trade—A Chosen Powerlessness

Instead of moving slaves and indentured labourers to capital projects in the New World, now capital moves to jurisdictions with indentured labourers, child labourers, and labour markets that deny basic labour rights.

Toward the end of the 20th century, large multinational corporations experienced an increasing freedom to move goods, services, and investment capital around the world. Unhindered by the regulations of democratically elected state governments, this freedom became the defining characteristic of the international order. It was enshrined in the Canada–U.S. Free Trade Agreement (FTA) and the North American Free Trade Agreement (NAFTA), and later by the creation of the World Trade Organization (WTO) and attempted agreements like the Multilateral Agreement on Investment and the Free Trade Area of the Americas.

The implications for individual Canadians are immense. Just as our working lives and jobs have been thrown open to the forces of globalization, our elected governments have less and less power to influence how the economy will affect Canadian society.

The scandal is that this powerlessness was by and large self-inflicted. It was chosen out of ideological preference disguised in the language of free trade, or worse, out of a reluctance to name and challenge what was actually going on. I had two opportunities to focus on these issues, from 1987 to 1990 as one of two NDP members on the Standing Committee on External Affairs and International Trade, and from 1995 to 2000 as the NDP Trade Critic.

————

The implications of corporate globalization are ominous not just for workers, but for the entire planet. Unrestrained market forces are antagonistic to sustainability and equality, and blind to human rights and democratic development. The main challenge in global governance today is to establish a level playing field between democratic institutions of community—be they national or subnational, like provinces and cities—and the powerful global corporations that dominate international trade.

The emergence of the global economy is often portrayed as the inevitable result of the technologies of the information age. But globalization is not a recent development dependent on computer technology. It has been an integral part of the world economy since European ships first crossed the Atlantic in the 15th century. In that earlier phase of globalization, capital was more or less fixed in the form of mines and plantations, and it was labour that was mobile. For centuries, slaves from Africa and indentured labourers from Asia were moved by the multinationals of the day to wherever they were needed.

Today, capital in all its forms moves around the world with ease. The computers and fibre optic cables of the international financial markets handle a trillion dollars daily. Those capital flows are far greater than the actual volume of trade of goods and services. Multinationals can now source their manufacturing, research and development, marketing, and financial services in separate locations around the world. Instead of moving slaves and indentured labourers to capital projects in the New World, now capital moves to jurisdictions with indentured labourers, child labourers, and labour markets that deny basic labour rights.

Globalization is not, therefore, simply a process determined by technological novelties. It is about the relationship between the most powerful and the most vulnerable on the planet. It is about the responsibilities and obligations we can rightly expect from powerful economic actors and about our political choices, as Canadian citizens and as members of the international community. Just as democratic movements emerged to abolish slavery, in spite of the profits that powerful groups were making from it, the challenge today is to assert democratic values in defence of human rights and responsible economic practices. We must find a way to achieve globally what national social democratic parties and labour movements once achieved nationally within the context of the nation-state. Unfortunately, the current architecture of international trade agreements severely limits the democratic possibilities.

The mechanisms used to handcuff democratically elected governments have been international trade agreements. Far from being just about tariffs and the dumping of underpriced goods from one country to another, they are the legal infrastructure of a trading order in which large swaths of legitimate democratic activity have been handed over to unaccountable tribunals of trade lawyers enforcing agreements designed to give multinationals maximum freedom from public accountability and public regulation. Taken together, these agreements amount to the equivalent of a constitution with an entrenched corporate bill of rights.

There was a time when international trade liberalization was seen as an ally of democratic development. The original General Agreement on Tariffs and Trade was explicitly allied to the democratic project. GATT was designed after the Second World War to avoid the collapse of the international economy into protectionist blocs, which in the 1930s had contributed to the Depression and the rise of Nazism in Germany. Before that, the 19th-century campaign for free trade was similarly allied with the democratic movement, targeting the political power of the landed elite who used their dominance of government to uphold self-interested tariffs on agricultural goods.

In the 1980s and '90s, this sometime alliance between free trade and democracy was shattered. With the Canada–U.S. Free Trade Agreement, then the North American Free Trade Agreement, and then the World Trade Organization, the free trade agenda moved beyond the GATT process of tariff reduction into challenging the legitimacy of what are termed non-tariff barriers. Non-tariff barriers are policies that originate in social, environmental, or health concerns and that lead to preventing the import of a particular product.

The new trade order seriously limits national sovereignty in areas vital to the public interest. This is not a continuation of the GATT process, but a sea change that threatens the reach of even well-established democracies within their own jurisdictions. An array of public policies that properly belong to the democratic state are now subject to the undemocratic decision-making of unaccountable trade bureaucrats.

Canada, for example, used to have one of the most effective drug patent regimes in the world, moderating the prices of new drugs and preventing monopolistic practices by allowing generic manufacturers to produce new drugs under compulsory licence from the patent holder. This was a reasonable compromise between the pharmaceutical industry's interest in getting a fair return on its investments in research and development, and the public interest in reasonable drug prices.

In 1993, during the negotiation of the North American Free Trade Agreement, and in anticipation of its final content, the Mulroney government abolished compulsory licensing under Bill C-91, allowing drug multinationals to monopolistically benefit from their patents for a full 20 years. These terms were then written into NAFTA and ultimately into the rules of the World Trade Organization. The Liberals, though they had been opposed to C-91 in opposition, refused when they came to power in 1993 to take action on drug prices. They had the nerve to cite NAFTA as the reason for their inaction, when of course it was the Liberals who passed on an opportunity to try to change NAFTA when they were elected that fall. It was the same infuriating line of argument that they also employed when it came to water exports.

Canadians saw a similar infringement of their sovereignty on questions of culture. When the Conservatives were negotiating the Free Trade Agreement and NAFTA, and when the Liberals were negotiating the creation of the World Trade Organization, Canadians were assured that culture was to be exempted from the trade rules. Yet the WTO then issued a ruling against Canadian tax regulations favouring Canadian magazines.

When such cases are taken to the WTO or to NAFTA panels, they are dealt with in secret, by a closed shop of "experts" who helped design the system, against whose decisions there are no external appeals. The Harper government has been unable to persuade farmers or a minority Parliament to dismantle the Canadian Wheat Board as the single desk selling wheat, but some expect that the WTO may yet dismantle it for them. Or with the majority given the Conservatives in 2011, I fear they may now be able to realize the destruction of this important, but ideologically unacceptable, Canadian institution.

The multinationals have thus insulated themselves from democracy. The agreements create democracy-free zones that ensure that multinationals do not have to come into contact with elected representatives, labour leaders, environmental groups, or other representatives of the community interest, including churches and other faith-based groups.

The rules that are not enforced are as significant as the ones that are. Member states of the WTO are bound by no rules to obey even basic labour rights. Regulations enforcing international agreements on the environment may be overruled as non-tariff barriers to trade. On human rights, the WTO is mute. The countries whose economies use child labour, indentured labour, or conscripted labour face no consequences under its trade rules.

China, in order to achieve WTO membership, had to prove that it would respect the intellectual property rights of multinationals that do not want their CDs copied illegally, but did not have to demonstrate respect for the labour rights of the workers who manufacture those CDs. And though the WTO claims to be powerless to do anything about a repressive regime selling products produced with child labour, Canadian Elaine Bernard, the Harvard trade unionist who had been on the 1994 NDP panel on party relations, noted in a 1999 article in the *Washington Post* that if these same children in sweatshops produce pirated CDs or fake designer T-shirts, the WTO can "spring into action with a series of powerful levers to protect corporate 'intellectual property rights.' So it's really not a question of free trade versus protectionism, but of who and what is free, and who and what is protected."

When I sat on the Standing Committee on External Affairs and International Trade, which held hearings from coast to coast on the Free Trade Agreement, my NDP colleague was Trade Critic Steven Langdon, who had been elected MP for Essex–Windsor, Ontario, in 1984. I got to know the trade issue well, and also found myself called upon to represent the "no" side in various debates.

In the 1993 election, because of our support for the failed Charlottetown Accord the year before, the Reform Party won a lot of formerly NDP territory by accusing the NDP of siding with the political elite. My view is that when it comes to criticizing the politics of elite accommodation, criticizing the politics of Canadian constitution-making is at worst a deliberate diversion, and at best a case of straining at gnats while swallowing a camel (Matthew 23:24). Only the NDP has been willing to challenge the interests of the real elite, the economic elite—and an increasingly global one that has no national or community loyalties. When push comes to shove, the corporate elite do not care about bilingualism, multiculturalism, how we deal with young offenders, the gun registry, same-sex marriage, abortion, MPs' pensions, giving in to Quebec, or any of the other issues that the populist right uses, too often with help from poorly considered tactics on the left, to lure working people away from their traditional defenders. The global corporate elite only care about how easy it is to make a profit. Indeed, one cannot help but think that their fondest hope is that politics will always be about issues other than their powerful role in the world.

Anyone who seeks to convince Canadians that the real elite in Canada is the political class obscures, deliberately or otherwise, the ability to discern who is really running the country—and the world—and for what ends. In *For the Common Good*, John Cobb and Herman Daly argue that while the goal of building global community should be embraced, we should not succumb to a fraudulent globalism that asks nations with a strong sense of community and social equality to sacrifice their achievements and the well-being of their working or middle classes, in order to compete with countries that have no such social and economic culture. This would be to destroy existing community in the name of a broader world community that does not really exist. What exists is a smaller global community of wealth and privilege, a global class that through its various national branches has been able to muster huge resources to advocate or defend its world view when necessary.

In *A Theology for the Social Gospel,* Walter Rauschenbusch made a distinction between having one government on paper and another in fact. Stanley Knowles, long-time NDP member for Winnipeg North Centre, used to talk about the visible government and the invisible government. As I see it, the work of left-wing politics is to make the invisible visible, and thereby accountable and challenged. The work of our opponents is to keep everyone talking about something else, usually with the aid of the media. Yet politicians are one of the last defences, if not always the strongest defence, against corporate interests that see national, regional, or community-based arguments as something to be disdained or treated as out of date.

The election of 1988, in which free trade came to the forefront, is officially remembered in NDP circles as the election in which we won a record 43 seats in the House of Commons. This positive narrative, though, obscures the reality that the election was a hugely negative watershed for the federal NDP. Even the math is somewhat misleading; we lost previously safe seats to the Liberals in Manitoba, as well as two of the three seats we had won in the 1987 by-elections. And nearly half of the 43 seats we won were from British Columbia, where the provincial politics of sending Social Credit Premier Bill Vander Zalm a message played a big part in the outcome. Shortly after the election, Ed Broadbent announced that he would step down as party leader.

The NDP caucus would grow to 44 when Phil Edmonston won a by-election in 1990 in Chambly, thus becoming the first NDP MP from Quebec. But Edmonston did not run for re-election of 1993. Quebec would remain barren for the NDP for another decade and a half, until Thomas Mulcair won an Outremont by-election in 2007, and then made history as the first Quebec NDP member to win a seat in a general election in 2008. The Outremont by-election was a matter of great family pride, as it was in no small part due to the work of my daughter Rebecca as the provincial NDP organizer in Quebec.

Rebecca Blaikie spent several years in Quebec, before returning to Winnipeg in 2008. In 2004 she was the NDP candidate in the Montreal riding of LaSalle–Émard, running against the Liberal incumbent, Prime Minister Martin. In the election of May 2, 2011, she was the NDP candidate in the riding of Winnipeg North, and lost by a heartbreaking 44 votes. Ironically, her work in Quebec bore fruit in 2011, and had she run in LaSalle–Émard instead of in what was regarded as NDP heartland, she would have been elected with dozens of other new NDP MPs from Quebec.

There was much recrimination within the party after the 1988 election. People who had been part of making the electoral strategy with their party hats on immediately afterwards put on their labour hats and, criticizing the leader and the strategy, behaved as if they had not been in the room when decisions were made. This was a feature of the party's relationship with the labour movement that I often found difficult—it was okay for them to change hats and criticize the party, but if anyone in the party dared criticize labour, that was a violation of the expected solidarity. In my view the recriminations contributed to the premature departure of Broadbent, who should have at least stayed until the party had the opportunity to take the measure of all the new MPs who had been elected in 1988.

For me there was a terrible irony at work in the 1988 election. I had spent the 1980s, along with others, trying to get the party to campaign on the environment. And so it was at first with satisfaction that I observed the wonderful ad with our party leader and a child, near a pond, talking about that very issue. But then with growing anxiety, I began to realize that the election would be about the Free Trade Agreement and little else. Any other focus was tragically counterproductive, and left us open to the charge that we did not care enough about the FTA or appreciate its significance. This perception was exacerbated by two factors, one arising from principle, and one from strategy.

The first had to do with our position on the Senate. When the Liberal-dominated Senate threatened to obstruct the trade deal that had been passed by the House, Broadbent expressed the long-held NDP view, based on a matter of democratic principle, that the unelected Senate had no right to obstruct the will of the elected House of Commons. This stance was reinforced by the view, though it may seem incredible in hindsight, that we had a chance of winning the election. With a chance to win, the last thing we needed to do was to legitimize an unelected Senate, with no NDP representation, potentially holding up the will of an NDP Parliament. The Liberals had no such anxiety, principled or otherwise, about the Senate. They used the issue to portray us as soft on the free trade deal when we were, more accurately, being hard on the Senate.

Our second vulnerability was also related to the perception that we had a chance of winning. Winning the election meant winning in Quebec, where our numbers and our expectations were high. Winning in the rest of the country meant making the ballot question a non-economic one, or so the theory went, as the NDP was seen to be weak on economic issues. Hence the environment ad, for example. Also, the free trade deal was less unpopular in Quebec than in the rest of Canada, so our strategy there was not to lead with it, although contrary to the conventional wisdom I am told by people who were there that Broadbent did mention the Free Trade Agreement in Quebec on the opening day of the election. As always, parties are held responsible for what is reported, not for what actually happens.

And winning the election was not just a matter of winning for its own sake. We were convinced, and I think time has borne this out abundantly, that the only way to stop the Free Trade Agreement was for the NDP to form the government. We did not believe, despite a certain personal sincerity about the deal on Liberal leader John Turner's part, that the Liberals could be trusted on the issue.

That decision to focus on issues other than free trade has become part of a liberal-left narrative that some recount to this day to suggest that the NDP was responsible for the 1988 outcome. It is added that particularly toward the end of the campaign, we attacked the credibility of the Liberals and were unwilling to co-operate with them in unnamed ways. The Liberals had no interest in co-operating either and didn't hesitate to attack us, we had entered the election with equally strong prospects, and time has exposed the Liberals' true colours on the issue—but none of that seems to matter.

This is more than a grumpy historical footnote—this narrative has contemporary manifestations. The same narrative blames the NDP for the defeat of Paul Martin's minority government in the fall of 2005. We did indeed arrange to defeat the government in the House, causing the election of January 2006. But we did not lose the election for the Liberals. They lost it, and helped precipitate the election, by not working with us in the House. Barring a miracle, our party was hoping for another Liberal minority in which NDP MPs would hold the balance of power, a position we had been only a few seats short of after the 2004 election. When Michael Ignatieff spurned the idea of a coalition in 2008, he was simply baring the real soul of the Liberals, Stéphane Dion's willingness notwithstanding. Lovers of the blame-the-NDP narrative, take note.

It will be interesting to observe the debate about the relationship between the NDP and the Liberals in the aftermath of the 2011 election that saw the NDP become the Official Opposition. As for me and my house, I have never accepted, at least since 1984, that there was anything left of centre in the Liberal Party to relate to, notwithstanding a few individuals who are clearly to the left of their party.

Had we won enough seats to stop the FTA in 1988, the same strategy that is now derided would be lauded. Honestly doing what we thought would increase our chances of winning the election, we may have employed the wrong strategy, but that's not the same as being on the side of wrong. Had the strategy worked, it would have made us heroes instead of bums. But when it became clear that the election was narrowing to a free trade election, it was unfortunate that we were unable to shift gears and run harder on the issue. Repeated calls to shift gears, on my part and those of others, went unanswered, a particularly painful case of the party organization's culture of unwillingness to take feedback from candidates seriously.

In Winnipeg Transcona my team ran hard against free trade. It was not uncommon, however, to knock on a door and have someone tell you that though they usually voted NDP, this time they were voting Liberal to stop the trade deal. Or at the very next door to have someone tell you that though they usually voted Liberal, this time they were voting NDP because they were opposed to the FTA and only the NDP had a chance of beating the Tory candidate in the riding. In the end all the strategic voters must have cancelled each other out, as we won the riding with the usual plurality.

My Liberal opponent was Shirley Timm-Rudolph, a local city councillor whom I had once endorsed when she first ran for council, unsuccessfully, as a

New Democrat. The Progressive Conservative candidate was Mike Thompson, a Transcona teacher. Thompson had a bad habit that I appreciated greatly. At election debates held in high schools, he would say that I was misleading the students and taking advantage of them because they were young and uninformed. My response, to the effect that he was insulting their intelligence, never failed to get a rousing round of applause. But he did this school after school. Our youngest daughter, Tessa, was born during the election and Thompson thoughtfully sent Brenda flowers.

Sometime in the year previous to the election, Thompson had come to Ottawa. He looked up his MP, and I took him to the parliamentary dining room. I guess he liked the place. I had no idea I was hosting my future opponent. It reminds me of a conversation I had in the Winnipeg airport in 1974 with the newly elected Tory MP Dean Whiteway. Neither of us could have guessed that I would be running against him some day, although fortunately the story ended differently for me than it did for Mike Thompson.

————

Cross-Canada hearings on the Canada–U.S. Free Trade Agreement were conducted before the election by the Standing Committee on External Affairs and International Trade, chaired by Bill Winegard, a Tory with a distinguished academic and naval record, having been at one time the youngest officer in the Canadian Navy and later the President of Guelph University. My own approach to the agreement was rooted in a deep suspicion of anything Brian Mulroney was up to, as well as an ideological prejudice against such idolatry of the market. But I also wanted to do more than simply denounce the deal. I was pleased, therefore, to read in *Wrestling with the Elephant*, a memoir by Gordon Ritchie, Deputy Chief Negotiator of the FTA, that in the hearings I was a "quite impressive" committee member and came to epitomize for him "some of the best traditions of Canadian public discourse" for having given "every evidence of genuinely seeking to determine the truth in these complex matters." He also said my questions "were usually the most challenging."

The hearings were by nature an exercise in repetition, as the same groups representing the same positions came forward in each city. But they provided some memorable moments. In Nova Scotia, I first encountered quite an instructive way of thinking about the deal. One witness called our attention to a Robert Burns poem entitled "Such a Parcel of Rogues in a Nation," about how Scotland was sold out by its ruling class. The second verse tells it best:

What force or guile could not subdue,
Thru many warlike ages
Is wrought now by a coward few,
For hireling traitors wages
The English steel we could disdain,
Secure in valour's station
But English gold has been our bane—
Such a parcel of rogues in a nation

The parallel with what was happening to our country, having won the War of 1812 only to be sold out in 1988 for American gold, fortified my already raised hackles. It must have done the same for Maude Barlow, since she wrote a book about the free trade deal called *Parcel of Rogues*. In my case it led to an article in *The Canadian Forum*, in which I compared the trade deal to the Highland clearances in the late 1700s and early 1800s whereby a way of life was destroyed so that the powerful could make more money. The FTA, in my view, was all about making Canada gradually conform to American social and economic policy, thus creating greater disparities between rich and poor and paving the way for increased foreign ownership of the Canadian economy.

My Scottish hackles would be raised again years later, when right after watching *Braveheart*, I had to vote late one June night in 1995 on the privatization of CN, which transferred a huge piece of public infrastructure from the Canadian people to American shareholders. I used the power of one to deny the unanimous consent that was sought to dispose of the votes quickly. It was the rage of the powerless, raging against what I still regard as an act of treason by the Liberals. Turning CN over to American shareholders, and then through the merger with Illinois Central a few years later to American management, would have been unthinkable before 1988, but it was not unthinkable in the wake of the paradigm shift brought in by Brian Mulroney.

Mulroney had grown up in a one-industry pulp-and-paper town, Baie-Comeau, where the industry was owned—in fact the town had been created in the first place, in 1937—by American newspaper baron Colonel Robert McCormick. The colonel, a conservative Republican and staunch opponent of Roosevelt's New Deal, came to visit once in a while, and an eight-year-old Brian apparently once sang for him. I, too, grew up in a one-industry town, Transcona, founded in 1911, where the industry, the Canadian National Railway shops, was owned by the people of Canada. I never would have guessed that my experience and that of my community would be regarded as somehow inferior and destined for elimination, albeit by the Liberals, in 1995.

Perhaps I should have seen the writing on the wall at the Shamrock

Summit in 1985, when Brian was singing for Ronnie. By 1988, anything was permissible. Even Wayne Gretzky was traded to the Americans by another Tory, Peter Pocklington, whose low-wage meat-packing business in Edmonton was a significant element in the destruction of the well-paid meat-packing industry that once flourished in Winnipeg.

———

Not everything that opponents of the free trade deal predicted has come true, but much has. Some of our worries were dealt with by the way that NAFTA superseded the FTA when it took effect in 1994. In the FTA there had been an agreement to take five years, and another two if needed, to define what was to be considered a subsidy. Our worry was that medicare, for example, might come to be defined as a subsidy to Canadian businesses. The subsidy definition process never happened, but medicare continues to be vulnerable because of free trade and particularly Chapter 11 of NAFTA, whereby any privatization of health care that came to be owned by an American corporation would be very difficult to reverse through the mandated investor-state dispute settlement. Canada came close to inviting this scenario when Alberta contemplated making it easier for private for-profit hospitals to come into being in the late 1990s. I argued strenuously in the House that what they were contemplating was not only wrong on its own merits, but thanks to NAFTA, also a danger to the entire Canadian health care system.

Another worry that did not materialize was that the Canadian wine industry would go under. But the debate about its future did occasion some levity. When we heard from Mordecai Richler on cultural matters in the Ottawa hearing, he added, vis-à-vis Canadian wine, that there was only so much "schlock" that one should be expected to drink for one's country. That same evening we also heard from Margaret Atwood, who was opposed to the FTA and who was given a very rough time by some of the Tory MPs on the committee. I intervened on her behalf, although she was quite capable of defending herself. An account of this event is found in Robert Mason Lee's *One Hundred Monkeys*, where I am referred to as "a lunch bucket social democrat" from Winnipeg. I take this description as a compliment, intended or not, and have often used it in speeches.

The most revealing moment of the hearings came when Peter Lougheed, former premier of Alberta, testified before the committee. I had not realized the extent to which the Free Trade Agreement had its origin for some in the fight against the Trudeau government's National Energy Program of the early 1980s, which was seen by many in Western Canada as an attempt by central Canada to unfairly capture more than its fair share of the revenue generated by oil and gas. This element of the FTA is still underappreciated. Ironically, the original recommendation for such an agreement came out of the Royal Commission on the Economic Union and Development Prospects for Canada created by Pierre Trudeau in 1982 and headed by a former Liberal finance minister, Donald Macdonald. The commission reported to Brian Mulroney in 1985 and he ran with it. This is not something that is part of the Liberal narrative on free trade.

Early in the development of the Free Trade Agreement, Canadians did not envision energy as part of the equation, but it is hard to believe that the Americans did not envision including energy all along. In any event, many in Canada were surprised at the inclusion of energy in the deal, and even more so, at the particular provisions relevant to energy. But perhaps not everyone was surprised, especially those who saw the trade negotiations as an opportunity to close, by taking it out of the political arena, what should have continued to be an important debate about the proper stewardship of Canada's fossil fuel resources.

Lougheed was very honest about it when in response to a question I put to him, he said very clearly that what he liked best about the FTA was that it made any new national energy policy virtually impossible. When I followed up with the observation that this seemed to mean he would rather have energy policy made in Washington than in Ottawa, it was clear that he was not bothered by such an attack on the national government's power to regulate a vital sector in the larger national public interest. It was revelations like this that I futilely hoped would be reported on. I had always found Peter Lougheed likeable. After that exchange, my fondest wish was that other proponents of the deal could have been half as honest as he was about what was really going on.

The FTA provisions on energy and on foreign investment constituted the most obvious sellout of Canadian interests. The deregulation of oil and gas exports, the emasculation of the National Energy Board, the abandonment of the idea that Canada should keep a 25-year supply of natural gas for its own needs—all this happened even before the FTA. The FTA added permanent insult to temporary injury by making it impossible to ever have a Canadian price for Canadian energy, guaranteeing the Americans a proportional share in perpetuity of Canadian energy supplies, and prohibiting export taxes as a source of revenue.

This surrender of sovereignty, and uncritical embrace of a continental energy policy, was made more wrong by putting these policies in an agreement in such a way that they could only be changed by abrogating the whole agreement. The same could be said of the provisions on foreign investment. Instead of an ongoing debate about the appropriate levels and rules of foreign ownership, the FTA committed future generations to an ideological monoculture on these issues.

As a result, questions about Canadian energy security and foreign ownership of the Canadian economy came to be seldom raised. When they were brought up, generally by the NDP, they were experienced as questions from a bygone era, instead of a living alternative to present policies. The cheerleaders for unrestricted foreign ownership may not be so cheery when the Canadian economy is owned, not by their American friends, but by state-sponsored Chinese and other forms of foreign investment not foreseen at the time.

At least Mexico had the self-respect, in NAFTA, not to sell out its energy sovereignty in the same way. The FTA, in my view, could well have been the backdrop, had he not supported it, for Lucien Bouchard's claim that Canada is not a real country. I remember infuriating John Crosbie, the Tory Trade Minister, who I knew had been for Newfoundland joining the United States in 1949 instead of Canada, when I suggested that perhaps it was too bad he failed then, as he wouldn't now be dragging the rest of us along with him in this continental experiment.

Bouchard left the Tories shortly after the FTA. It would be a whole decade later, at the Free Trade Area of the Americas summit in Quebec City, before the Bloc Québécois, which Bouchard founded after leaving the Tories, finally realized that the free trade agenda was a threat to Quebec sovereignty. It was not just something that weakened Canada, or something that they had to approve of in order to not frighten the Americans about what approach an independent Quebec might take. I used to go after the Bloc on this, but I was glad when they got on board. Unfortunately it was a little late, given that many of them probably supported Mulroney in 1988, where Quebec made the difference in deciding the immediate future of the Free Trade Agreement.

In my closing speech of the free trade debate I expressed the view that much more was at stake than the debate had acknowledged, and that even those who supported the FTA might come to regret the consequences someday. I believe the agreement changed, and is still changing, the way we imagine our country. It affects how much control we have, and expect to have, over what kind of economy we want and, therefore, over what level of economic justice we can achieve. The other watershed in the debate, despite John Turner's performance and even genuine passion in the 1998 TV debate, is that its aftermath marked the passage of the Liberal Party of Canada from a party that could reasonably claim a heritage of sticking up for the Canadian middle class to a party that was willing to sell them down the river rather than stand up to corporate Canada. The Canadian middle class is not alone in having been betrayed this way. The year before the Canadian Liberals came to power, the American Democrats did the same with Bill Clinton. And so it was that Democrats and Liberals together implemented, enshrined, and politically neutralized the ideological dreams of their Republican and Conservative opponents. Shame on both their houses.

CHAPTER

16

Globalization and the WTO

Speaker after speaker said that trade must be
made clean, green, and fair, and that nations that
act to make trade clean, green, and fair should not
have their laws struck down.

As NDP Trade Critic from 1995 to 2000, I would again encounter the free
trade agenda in the guise of the World Trade Organization (WTO), the
Multilateral Agreement on Investment (MAI), and the Free Trade Area of the
Americas (FTAA).

When the first ministerial meeting of the WTO took place in Singapore
in December 1996, Trade Minister Art Eggleton, now a senator, invited
opposition trade critics to be part of the Canadian parliamentary delegation.
I was grateful to attend, along with Charlie Penson of the Reform Party and
Benoît Sauvageau of the Bloc Québécois. We weren't staying far from the
historic colonial Raffles Hotel, where the first Singapore sling was poured.
A visit to the patio there was an occasion for the kind of political ecumenism
that our country needs more of.

Tragically, Sauvageau was killed on August 28, 2006, when he drove
into a tow truck while distracted by his cellphone. His funeral mass, which
I attended, was conducted by Father Raymond Gravel, who would succeed
him as the MP for Repentigny, much to the puzzlement of those who still
lamented that Father Bob Ogle had been forbidden to run in 1984. Within
a couple of years, Gravel was forced to choose between the priesthood and

politics, too, but that was because he openly disagreed with the church on gay marriage and abortion. Ogle had been faithful to the positions of the church, and still had to leave politics.

In addition to the fellowship with other MPs, international gatherings are good opportunities for networking with various Canadian non-governmental organization leaders. Ironically, it would be very difficult in Canada to assemble as many Canadian activists in one place. Among the activists I met in Singapore was Elizabeth May, then Executive Director of the Sierra Club. I had known May since the 1980s when we worked together on saving South Moresby Island, and always hoped that she would someday run for the NDP. May would support my bid for the federal leadership, but shortly thereafter emerged as the leader of the Green Party of Canada, winning the first ever parliamentary seat for that party in the federal election of 2011.

Singapore was a superb choice for the WTO conference—it had an economic culture devoted to the ideology of the market and an authoritarian political culture that tolerated only minimal opposition. Singapore was also admired by some Reform MPs, particularly Art Hanger, for its generous use of various forms of corporal punishment. An article I read in a Singapore paper about rising juvenile crime rates suggested to me that such methods were perhaps not as effective as some would have had us believe, however politically effective talking about them might be for right-wing politicians.

An early draft of the declaration issued in Singapore began by recalling that all members of the WTO subscribed to the Universal Declaration of Human Rights. This sentence was the first casualty of the negotiations; its loss signified the extent to which the WTO needed to deny the connection between core labour standards and human rights. Admitting the connection would have inserted a moral dimension into an endless discourse about capital being able to flow more efficiently to wherever it will yield the best returns.

Shortly thereafter, an Asia-Pacific Economic Cooperation summit in Vancouver in 1997 saw no effort by the Canadian government to include labour rights on the agenda. Instead of APEC being remembered for a breakthrough on labour rights, it is remembered for the violation of civil rights and the needless pepper spraying of protesters. It also led to the resignation of Attorney General Andy Scott, whom I knew to be a decent man, after he was overheard on a plane by New Democratic MP Dick Proctor explaining that the RCMP sergeant in charge of the pepper spraying would take the fall at the end of the public inquiry that had ensued.

I again joined the Canadian delegation for the second ministerial meeting of the WTO in Geneva in 1998. There had been few protesters in Singapore; there were about 10,000 at this meeting, but it would prove to only be a foreshadowing of what was to come at the third ministerial in Seattle. In Geneva I heard speeches by international heavy hitters including Nelson Mandela, Bill Clinton, Tony Blair, and Fidel Castro.

Mandela said it was important to start with "a reaffirmation that the building of a multilateral-based system is fundamentally correct." He was right to emphasize that point, because so often critics of the corporate model of globalization that the WTO enshrines are portrayed as narrow nationalists who do not understand that the world is now global. This criticism shows how those who control the language control the debate. In the 1980s the churches and others had called for a new, just, participatory, and sustainable international order. But in the 1990s the corporate world seized the language of globalization for its own purposes, and its critics were accused of thinking small and being throwbacks to some kind of narrow nationalism.

The reaction to Castro was fascinating. As he entered the plenary session and proceeded down the aisle to his seat, the whole room progressively rose to give him a standing ovation—except the American delegation, who seemed stunned by it all. Castro proceeded to trash the WTO as well as the Multilateral Agreement on Investment, a hot topic at the time, but that did not seem to matter. The whole world seemed momentarily united, despite the legitimate criticisms that can be made of Castro's regime, in strange awe of someone who had stood up for so many years to the United States, as many of them were now trying to do in their own way in the trade negotiations.

A boat cruise I took on Lake Geneva had a communist tie-in as well; one site that was pointed out to tourists is where Vladimir Lenin lived prior to the Russian Revolution. I remember the cruise with laughter, as Charlie Penson and I were waiting at the wrong place and almost missed the boat we had bought tickets for earlier in the day. It dawned on us just in time that the boat we were watching with great interest was the one we were both waiting for. I hesitate to speculate on what political lessons may be lurking herein.

————

In Singapore and Geneva, and later in Seattle and Cancun, I would participate in meetings with European politicians on agricultural subsidies. I always felt awkward because I had much more sympathy for elements of the European position than the rest of my Canadian counterparts, who only seemed to be able to talk about seeking greater efficiencies. The Europeans saw agricultural policy as part of a larger social policy that took into account the value of preserving their smaller farms and villages, as a way of life as well as for tourism. Not all of their subsidies, particularly on exports, were necessarily justified, but the Canadian inability to get the social argument often meant that it was a dialogue of the deaf.

The other reality behind the European position was the need for food security. Europe remembers a time when its people did not have enough food, a memory that kept its negotiators from succumbing to blandishments about letting others grow things because they can do it more efficiently. I was first introduced to this perspective by Vic Althouse, an NDP MP from Saskatchewan. Althouse was a farmer himself, and in my view knew more about agriculture than anyone else in the House of Commons. Between him and other Saskatchewan members like Les Benjamin and Stan Hovdebo, who had won Prince Albert in the by-election precipitated by John Diefenbaker's death in 1979, the NDP caucus was rich in knowledge of rural Saskatchewan and the co-operative values that had taken root there in the dirty thirties.

The European position was reminiscent of the NDP's approach in the battles over Canadian agriculture, particularly in Western Canada. From the effect of rail line abandonment on small Prairie communities to the abolition of the statutory Crow Rate for transporting Western Canadian grain, we had always argued that there was a bigger set of books to keep than those kept by the railways or grain companies. But just as corporate interests were not motivated by what was good for rural communities or for farmers, they were also not motivated by what was good for working people in their own countries or by what was good for democracy.

The debate over the Crow Rate in the early 1980s created one of the more difficult moments in my political life. The railways had done a pretty good job of persuading many railroaders that if the rate was abolished the increased profits would be invested in new plants and machinery. In Transcona the promise was a new diesel or motive power shop. When I was invited to speak at a meeting convened by the rail unions in the basement of the Princess Hotel just down the street from the CN shop gate, I was given a hard time for opposing the change. I replied that I had defended railroaders against farmers when I thought they were right and I would do the same for farmers when I thought they were right, and if the rail unions thought they could find a better friend than me they were welcome to try.

The political challenge, of course, was that there were hundreds of railroaders and no farmers in my riding. In any event, my unabashed defence of my position won the day. I continued to have their support. The Canadian National Railway never did build that new diesel shop. Years later, after the abolition of the Crow Rate, and after the abolition of its successor, the Crow Benefit, in the 1990s, as Minister of Conservation in Manitoba I would have to deal with the environmental consequences of the hog industry that was spawned by these measures, but that is a story for another day.

The silence on human and labour rights in the new WTO trading rules not only threatens the integrity of established democracies, it also inhibits the social and political progress of less-developed societies. By leaving these rights outside of the enforceable rules, the WTO gives authoritarianism the competitive advantage of cheap, compliant labour markets. The NDP view is that trade should be part of the process of building democracy rather than defeating it. Or as I liked to say by way of summary, wars may have been fought to make the world safe *for* democracy, but recent trade agreements seem designed to make the world safe *from* democracy. And indeed, formal democracies have grown in number as trade agreements replace the need for other ways of conforming the world to the corporate agenda.

The political response in North America to the insecurity and declining living standards offered up by globalization was somewhat surprising and politically varied. In Canada, it was the NDP that took up the critique of the new global economy; in the United States, it was often the populist right.

Pat Buchanan did surprisingly well in the Republican primaries in 1992 on an anti-NAFTA platform, using a dangerous vocabulary of chauvinist nationalism, religious intolerance, and fortress America protectionism. Vulnerable sections of the middle class were rightly feeling abandoned, cornered, and insecure about their declining living standards, while the CEOs of the companies that had just laid them off were making record salaries and bonuses. But Buchanan's first principle was restoration of American economic domination and sovereignty. He resisted the very idea of a global order, whether just or unjust.

The NDP also spoke for and to the increasingly stressed middle class, but for us Canadian nationalism is a means to an end, not an end in itself. We are critical of free trade and globalization because it does not provide a level playing field between communities of citizens and multinational corporations. Our concerns are part and parcel of our long-standing concerns about the way unfettered, unaccountable markets work. Domestically and internationally, we don't think that communities have to accept the gross inequalities of wealth produced by the market, be it the gap between the minimum wage and the skyrocketing salaries of corporate executives in Canada, or the gap between the living standards of workers in the developing world and the shareholders of the multinationals and their contractors.

Until the international trading system protects human rights, labour rights, and the environment, and provides for some democratic accountability, the power of national governments should be preserved as a vehicle for people to have a significant say about what kind of world they want to live in. The NDP believes that trade can be an effective way of raising living standards in the developing world, as long as the world economy is designed to allow incomes in the developing world to rise.

U.S. opposition to NAFTA also came in the form of Ross Perot, an independent presidential candidate in 1992. Perot was famous for predicting that after NAFTA, Americans would hear the giant sucking sound of jobs being drained out of the United States and into Mexico. I managed to get the quote of the day in *The Globe and Mail* early in 1994 when I said that the giant sucking sound Canadians could hear was the sound of the Liberals swallowing themselves whole on NAFTA.

———

In 1995, I was invited, as NDP Trade Critic, to join a Canadian Auto Workers delegation led by union President Buzz Hargrove to Mexico City. I was very appreciative of the opportunity, as in the years 1993 to 1997, when the NDP had lost party status, the nine of us who were still in office were largely ignored. We seemed to exist only to be critiqued for our inability to get any media attention, something that was hard to do when you only had three or four questions a week and they all happened just before the end of question period after the press gallery had already left.

I had met Hargrove before, but this was my first opportunity to get to know him a bit, and to hear him out privately about his unhappiness with the provincial NDP government led by my former Commons seatmate Bob Rae. I listened sympathetically, but the problem seemed to be as much about poor communication and poorly tended relationships as about substantive policy disagreements. Some years later, perhaps out of his obsessive anger with Rae, Hargrove became an unrelenting and unfair critic of the federal NDP and Alexa McDonough's leadership. Hargrove's critique of the party culminated in his support for the New Politics Initiative proposal to merge the NDP with antiglobalization social movements in 2001, which I opposed, and our relationship never recovered. Ironically, given Hargrove's critique of the NDP for not being radical enough, Hargrove and Rae would end up together again as supporters of Paul Martin's Liberals.

In Mexico we met with the President of the Confederación de Trabajadores de México, Mexico's oldest and largest union. We were led into a darkened boardroom to await the arrival of Don Fidel. It felt like a scene in a movie in which one was meeting the godfather. Fidel Velásquez Sánchez was 95 years old, and was certainly not intimidated by his Canadian trade union counterparts who were there to share their critique of NAFTA. He calmly explained that he thought the benefits for his members, in terms of increased job opportunities, were a good reason to support NAFTA and wished us well.

Fortunately for us, and for Mexican workers, there were other Mexican unions, politicians, and human rights activists to meet with who could see that whatever the short-term benefits were, NAFTA was part of a larger corporate strategy that would be harmful to Mexican workers. They might win the race to the bottom for a while, but not for long.

———

During the 1988 and 1993 elections, the NDP clearly opposed the FTA and NAFTA. In 1988 the Liberals had also campaigned against the FTA, but in 1993 they sought to have it both ways. Although they ran against the agreement, at the same time Liberal leader Jean Chrétien told Canadians that if they were opposed to NAFTA they should vote NDP. This moment of political clarity should have attracted more attention. Despite claiming during the election that they wanted iron-clad assurances on labour and environmental standards before they signed NAFTA, the fact was that the Liberals, going forward from their 1990 policy conference in Aylmer, Quebec, had adopted a position on trade that fully embraced the spirit of NAFTA and the corporate model of globalization. The weakness of the side accords on environment and labour that they obtained reflected this reality.

The extent to which the Liberals had joined the ranks of the globalizing elites could be seen at the Miami Summit of the Americas in 1994, where negotiations began toward a Free Trade Area of the Americas. The FTAA has yet to be realized. The original target completion date was 2005. In discussing the possibility of free trade with Chile, Chrétien claimed that a trade deal with Chile would lead to cheaper bananas for Canadians. Someone in the

Department of International Trade forgot to tell him that Chile, in Latin America but not a tropical country, does not actually produce bananas.

This revealing gaffe was characteristic of the way that the Liberals went bananas about free trade after the 1993 election, blindly accepting or at least repeating all the mantras about the benefits of unrestrained globalization. They ratified NAFTA, they helped negotiate the new WTO, they signed on to free trade timetables in APEC and the FTAA, they negotiated a NAFTA-like agreement with Chile, and they would have signed on to the Multilateral Agreement on Investment in the late 1990s, if it had not been killed for other reasons.

The MAI came to light in early 1997, but it had been under negotiation for three years before that. It was to have been an agreement among the 29 member countries of the Organization for Economic Co-operation and Development. Its purpose was to replicate NAFTA at the level of the OECD, in the hope that this agreement would be a stepping stone toward subsequently replicating the deal at the level of the World Trade Organization. At the WTO, developing countries objected to liberalized investment rules that would hamstring their governments' ability to make sure foreign investment served the public interest. But the more powerful countries of the world, urged on by the international investment community, wanted to be able to present the MAI as an established fact that poorer countries would abstain from joining at their peril.

The most significant right the MAI would have entrenched would enable investors to take governments to a dispute settlement process. Pursuant to a similar provision in Chapter 11 of NAFTA, in 1997 the U.S.-based Ethyl Corporation sued the Canadian government for profits lost due to the banning of the toxic gasoline additive MMT, claiming that the environmentally motivated legislation was "tantamount to expropriation." In 1998 the Liberal government caved, cancelled the ban, paid Ethyl's costs, and prevented the matter from coming to a conclusion. In the view of NAFTA's critics, the reason for this had a lot to do with the likelihood of Ethyl being successful and NAFTA being clearly exposed as a threat to the public interest. The MAI would have made matters worse by expanding the definition of *expropriation* beyond tangible assets, such as property or money, to include measures having "equivalent economic effect" and for which payment of "prompt, adequate, effective compensation" was required. This expansion treated a comprehensive range of what are properly domestic political choices as objects of binding international arbitration.

In addition to the inappropriate legal status that this process gives corporations, it also has a chilling effect. Governments may, out of fear of such litigation, refrain from legislative actions deemed to be in the public interest but unhelpful to corporate profit. It would definitely be thinking outside of the corporate model to imagine provisions by which a trade union or an environmental group could take a government to a binding settlement process. But for enforceability of investor rights, the sky was to be the limit. To make matters worse, the MAI was to bind countries for a 20-year period, through several parliaments.

A sub-committee of the Standing Committee on International Trade held hearings on the MAI, and alternate hearings were sponsored across the country by an anti-MAI coalition. I participated in both sets of hearings, and produced an NDP minority report for the sub-committee. One particular exchange made it onto the evening news. After establishing with a witness from the business community that Canadian companies wanted the MAI so that they could more easily make money in other countries, I asked him where he got the nerve to ask his country to become more vulnerable just so that he could make more money elsewhere. The question was not appreciated.

Fortunately, the MAI did not happen. Credit must be given to the international movement that was organized to oppose it, with groups like the Council of Canadians playing a significant role, not just nationally but internationally as well. At the end of the day, however, it was killed by a government, not a movement. It was the Socialist government of France that ultimately scuttled the deal, largely because of the deal's ramifications on the government's ability to protect French culture. No social movement by itself could have killed the MAI. Certainly not in Canada, where a reluctance to support the NDP is combined with an infinite capacity to forgive and forget who the Liberals really are. Although the 2011 election may hopefully signal the beginning of a new era, Canadian activism, when it comes to the Liberals, has too often been like Charlie Brown hoping that this time Lucy will not pull away the football before he kicks it.

The biggest challenge in building a more democratic international community is to ensure that international trade agreements require the respect of human rights, including basic labour rights, to ensure that economic decision-making allows workers to negotiate the terms on which they participate in the global economy. Trade rules are remarkably one-sided in their defence of the rights of investors. They pretend that labour, social security, and the environment are not trade issues. They are eloquent about the multinationals' rights to intellectual property and to the free movement of capital, but say nothing about workers' rights to form trade unions or to have a safe workplace. They speak loudly about level playing fields, but are silent about the most important playing field of all, the one between employers and employees.

An unregulated global market effectively allows the multinationals to hold an auction to see which countries will bid the cheapest and least-regulated labour, the lowest corporate taxes, and the most lax environmental standards. In response to these kinds of concerns about the market that arose in the context of the European Union, a Social Charter was called for by a resolution of the European Parliament in March 1989. Having just come through our own free trade debate, I was interested in the debate within the European community about this idea. In the fall of 1989, I participated in the European Community Visitors Program, which allowed me to visit Denmark and Ireland to talk to people about the proposed Social Charter, as well as to Scotland to inquire into the possibility of a Scottish parliament, which would come to pass a decade later.

The European Social Charter was adopted in December 1989. It would be followed in 2000 by a broader Charter of Fundamental Rights, which became enforceable in 2007. The Social Charter defined rights that are not to be put in jeopardy by the pressures of competition brought on by the European single market. It guards things like health and safety in the workplace, freedom of association and collective bargaining, and protection of children.

Worldwide, one of the most pressing manifestations of the effects of globalization has been the growing plague of child labour. While the international effort to combat child labour must operate on many fronts—better labelling of products to allow for consumer pressure, increased development assistance for education, helping governments build up their own regulatory systems—international trade rules must be put at the service of this fight. In 1994, when the WTO was ratified in the House of Commons, by a vote of 185 to 7, I had moved amendments on behalf of the NDP to enforce the rights of children and amend our own customs laws to prohibit imports of goods made with child labour. When these amendments were defeated by the Liberal and Reform parties, I introduced a private member's motion on child labour, but the Liberals used their majority to keep the motion from coming to a vote. Around this time I had the pleasure of meeting in my parliamentary office with a very young man named Craig Kielburger, who at 12 years of age in 1995 had initiated a campaign to call attention to victims of child labour around the world. The organization that he founded at that time, Free the Children, continues to do much-needed work on this issue.

One of my most irritating days in the House of Commons was the day that British Prime Minister Blair spoke to the House and sang the praises of free trade and deregulation in 2001. He talked as if there were no significant differences between free trade within the European Union and within NAFTA, though the European community's recognition of the social dimension of the market stands in marked contrast to the continental and global markets created by NAFTA or the WTO. It had been unpleasant enough on a previous occasion to be lectured in the House by British Prime Minister Thatcher, but Tony Blair's intellectual dishonesty in ignoring the differences between a market with a Social Charter and a market without one left me fuming.

Fortunately, I was able to unburden myself about Blair's speech to the House when I was interviewed later that day by Don Newman, host of CBC Newsworld's daily politics show. Newman was my favourite national broadcaster of that time. I always enjoyed being on his show, on a panel or individually, and valued the institutional memory he brought to the interview, even when it was an inconvenient memory. As fellow alumni of the University of Winnipeg, Newman and I both received honorary degrees from that institution in 2007.

On this occasion, I told Newman that I found Blair's rhetoric particularly galling in light of the fact that he had campaigned on the need to recognize the social dimension of the single European market and sign the charter. The British Conservatives had refused to sign the Social Charter; Blair signed it in 1998. In addition, Europe does not suffer the asymmetrical relationship that exists in NAFTA between the United States and the other two amigos. It is hard to imagine anyone associating the two situations in the uncritical way that Blair did that day in the House.

My disappointment with Blair would only grow as the years went by. I supported his policies on devolution in Scotland and Wales, but New Labour's embrace of the Third Way always seemed to me to be a fancy name for a form of accommodation or capitulation to the neo-liberal corporate agenda. I had become aware of Blair early in his parliamentary life through my interest in the Christian Socialist group in the United Kingdom that he was once a part of, along with John Smith, the Labour leader whose premature death in 1994 while hiking in the Scottish hills had set the stage for Blair.

In the summer of 1997, just after the spring election that brought Blair to power, I was in Scotland with my daughter Jessica and son, Daniel, both of whom played the pipes with the Transcona Youth Pipe Band. We visited the island of Iona. The Christian community located there is known for its commitment to connecting the life of faith with the struggle for social justice, so it seemed no coincidence when I happened upon the grave of Labour leader John Smith, who is buried in the old Iona graveyard with several ancient Scottish kings.

The other problem with Blair was his affinity for American foreign policy, particularly under George W. Bush. Labour MPs were not always happy with their leader; some explained to me at parliamentary gatherings that he was staying close to the Americans to make sure he had the influence to prevent them from doing the wrong thing, but there is little or no evidence for this argument. What he did not prevent is all we have to go on, and the memoirs of his former ministers, notably Robin Cook, who resigned as Foreign Affairs Minister over the decision to participate in the invasion of Iraq.

The irony is that the federal NDP was often accused by its critics on the left of seeking to embrace the Third Way, or wanting to imitate Blair's New Labour. Nothing could have been further from the truth. It would have been more accurate to have described us as the last, best left, compared to most of our sister parties in the Socialist International. Very few other trade critics, if any, at meetings of the WTO felt, as I did, more comfortable with most of the protesters than with the politicians inside the security perimeter.

I had the historic privilege of being in Seattle in November 1999 for the third ministerial meeting of the World Trade Organization, an event that precipitated what came to be known as the Battle in Seattle. As NDP Trade Critic I was a member of the Canadian delegation led by Liberal Trade Minister Pierre Pettigrew. The meeting was supposed to be the launch of what was then called the Millennium Round of negotiations. Instead it became the last big protest of the century—and the place where I had my first taste of tear gas, albeit at a distance.

The protest was remarkable not for its violence; that was a small and over-reported dimension of the event. It was remarkable for its effectiveness in initially preventing the WTO meeting from opening, and for its unity in bringing so many people and causes together from around the world. The protest was remarkable for its success in profiling the issues, putting the WTO debate on the map, and humbling those who thought their corporate agenda could go on indefinitely without serious challenge.

It is no accident that democracy was the theme that united the diverse group of protesters in Seattle. The protesters wanted a world in which the democratic decisions of various nation-states are not trumped by a global organization that judges every policy by the benchmark of whether it impedes trade or not. They were calling for an entirely new set of multilateral trade rules in which the market ethic and corporate interests are subordinate to democracy, social justice, environmental integrity, and cultural diversity, with democracy being the overriding value. It is, after all, through the democratic process that we pursue the common good.

Renato Ruggiero, a former director general of the WTO, once said that they were "writing the constitution of a single global economy," echoing Ronald Reagan's reference to NAFTA as an economic constitution for North America. At the People's Rally and March for Fair Trade, on November 30, 1999, a Tuesday, 50,000 people joined together to say that they wanted their so-called economic constitution to reflect certain values. I was in the stands with the hundreds of Canadians who came to Seattle to participate, as speaker after speaker said that trade must be made clean, green, and fair, and that nations that act to make trade clean, green, and fair should not have their laws struck down. The director general by the time Seattle rolled around was a man by the name of Michael Moore, which was the cause of much irony. Activist filmmaker Michael Moore was also at Seattle, where he hosted a welcoming event for protesters on the Monday at a Seattle arena.

The rally was accompanied by a march, and it was wonderful to see trade unionists, environmentalists, farmers, Aboriginal people, food safety activists, and many others, including many from various churches, united by their common perception of the WTO as a threat to democracy and the common good. It is when democracies act in the interest of the common good— elevating labour and human rights, environmental and health concerns, and cultural diversity over corporate power and commercial interests—that they come into conflict with the WTO.

One highlight was a press conference on the democratic deficit at the WTO that I participated in. Organized by Velma Veloria, the first Filipino American elected to a state legislature, it included Congressman Peter DeFazio, chair of the Progressive Congressional Caucus, and Tom Hayden, a California state senator. Hayden had been one of the infamous Chicago Seven who were tried for organizing anti–Vietnam War protests at the Democratic National Convention in 1968. It was a treat to be standing beside someone who was part of a story that had inspired me as a youth. Hayden's other claim to fame is that he was once married to Jane Fonda.

Earlier in my life I had another opportunity to meet someone who was part of the Chicago '68 story, when I was waiting to go on the Jack Webster show in Vancouver in 1982. Webster, a legendary curmudgeonly Glaswegian journalist, had agreed to interview me on his TV show because I was in town to speak at an NDP Burns Night in the riding of Vancouver Kingsway, a seat held by another Canadian of Glaswegian origin, Ian Waddell. I found myself waiting backstage with William Kuntsler, the American lawyer who had become famous defending the Chicago Seven. I had a conversation with Kuntsler as we waited our turns, but Webster was so interested in him when he finally got on that I only ended up with a couple of minutes on the air at the end of the show.

Tom Hayden's view of Seattle was that the young people and activists were dealing with an issue bigger than the Vietnam War. They were confronting the "very nature of the way economics, environmentalism, and human rights are going to be shaped for the rest of our lives.... The Vietnam War was going to end eventually, but the new world order will not."

On November 29, I sat on the People's Tribunal on the Human Face of Trade with the Belgian Minister of Consumer Protection, Magda Aelvoet, and American Congresswoman Maxine Waters, a Democrat. The event, chaired by Congressman George Miller, a Democrat and the ranking minority member of the Committee on Resources in the U.S. House of Representatives, was held at First United Methodist Church, and I got a laugh out of the crowd by remarking how disorienting it was, amid the massive outpouring of opposition to the WTO, for us habitual critics of the WTO to feel like we were on the winning side for a change.

Later that same day I was one of six parliamentarians to speak at a reception held by GLOBE USA, an association of members of Congress committed to international environmental issues. The other speakers were Caroline Lucas, the first Green member of the European Parliament from the United Kingdom; John Gummer, former minister of the environment in the government of Margaret Thatcher; and Wakako Hironaka, former minister of the environment in Japan; as well as two American Congressmen, George Miller and Barney Frank.

In addition to such alternative forums, I participated in bilateral meetings set up between Canadian MPs and elected representatives from other countries. One such meeting happened to be in the hotel where the American delegation was staying, and we all got caught in a lockdown of the hotel, as protesters had gathered nearby and the hotel had been surrounded by buses to create a security perimeter. We were eventually allowed to leave the hotel, but for a while we wondered how long we might have to stay there.

But that was nothing compared to the deliberate detention of many innocent protesters by the Seattle police and those who were called in to help them. By the next afternoon, the initially tolerant response of the Seattle police was disappearing, partly as a result of the violence of a few, which was focused on by the media and actively opposed by many protesters. It probably also arose from the sheer success of those protesters who had organized themselves to non-violently disrupt the conference and the pressure to prevent any further obstruction of the meeting.

Tuesday night a curfew was imposed, a state of emergency was declared, downtown Seattle was declared a no-protest zone, and the tear gassing had begun. When protesters tried to do again on Wednesday what they had successfully done on Tuesday, the use of tear gas and batons began in earnest and so did the arrests. Many non-violent protesters were mistreated. Many innocent non-protesting citizens of Seattle were also hurt by police. And many protesters were arrested and held for some time, including Elizabeth Carlyle from the University of Winnipeg, there on behalf of the Canadian Federation of Students, who was held from Wednesday to Friday.

The hotel where I was staying with others of the Canadian delegation was right beside a marshalling point for the police. From my window it was disturbing to observe the police lined up, loudly tapping their batons in unison. I was more disturbed when events after Seattle reproduced a pattern of police behaviour that raises lots of questions, including what happened later in Quebec City at the FTAA Summit in April 2001 when non-violent, non-obstructing protesters would be on the receiving end of rubber bullets.

———

Beyond the debate about police behaviour I was and am more interested in questions of police attitude. I grew up in an environment that was respectful and appreciative of police. My maternal grandfather was the Chief of Police in Transcona and his son, my uncle, was in the RCMP for 25 years before heading up the National Harbour Police in Halifax after his retirement. My involvement in the piping and drumming community has also been a connection to the military and police community. I do not enjoy being critical of the police, and when I am, it is definitely more out of sorrow than anger.

The challenge for police is to do their job with discernment, discerning not only who should be treated a particular way and who shouldn't, but also discerning the value of legitimate peaceful dissent in a democracy and not taking political sides in the situations they are called into. I remember reading in the *Canadian Police Magazine* about the police success in managing the protests at the meeting of the Organization of American States in Windsor in June 2000. I can see some pride being taken in a job well done, but I did not like the language used to caricature and demonize the protesters as an assortment of obvious subversives. I raised this with a delegation of police from Winnipeg lobbying in Ottawa, reminding them that one of the things that anti–free trade protesters were concerned about was free trade in services, something that could lead to job losses if policing services were contracted out to multinational firms. Unfortunately, if the way peaceful protesters were treated at the G20 in Toronto in 2010 is any indication, there is still much work to do in changing the police culture that takes over when such events occur. In saying this I have had the benefit not only of media reports, but first-hand eye-witness accounts from my youngest daughter, Tessa, who was one of those who were peacefully protesting at the event.

After my time as Trade Critic, in 2000 I became one of the few MPs to be made their party's Justice Critic without also being a lawyer. I was soon back into reflecting on the nature of legitimate dissent in a democratic society when after September 11, 2001, as a member of the Standing Committee on Justice of the House of Commons, I was in the middle of a hurried attempt on the part of the Chrétien government to bring in Bill C-36, the antiterrorism legislation. C-36 was part of the Canadian government's response to the call by the United Nations after 9/11 for all countries to implement antiterrorist legislation and to implement relevant UN conventions on the prevention of terrorism within 90 days.

Unfortunately, the debate about C-36 happened not just in the context of what al Qaeda had done. It also happened in the context of many Canadians having very fresh memories of how they or their fellow citizens had been treated at APEC, at the OAS meeting, and at the FTAA meeting in Quebec City. Assurances that the legislation was not intended for lawful advocacy, protest, or dissent were of little comfort to those who had recently had their lawful behaviours treated as if they were unlawful. As NDP Justice Critic I gave voice to such concerns in the debate over C-36.

The intersection of debates about democracy and dissent, free trade versus fair trade, global community versus global marketplace, and global environmental integrity versus global corporate profit strategies made being the NDP Trade Critic one of the most interesting of the critic portfolios I had during my many years as an opposition MP. The issues are still there, even if the debate has died away. Bilateral free trade agreements have become the strategy now, along with larger proposals like the one for free trade with the European Union, a deal that will magnify the already weak ability of Canadian governments at all levels to defend the public interest.

CHAPTER

17

A Passion for Justice

The confession of Jesus Christ as Lord is also a
statement about what is not sovereign.

When I began my federal political life in the fall of 1977 by seeking the
nomination in the new riding of Winnipeg–Birds Hill, I was excited about
what I saw as an emerging convergence of Protestants and Catholics. Christians
were being brought together in part by a revival of the Protestant social gospel
tradition, and by the liberation theology movement in Latin America, with
both of these trends being informed by other political theologies from Black
theologies to feminist theologies. Not to mention by a series of statements by
Canadian Catholic bishops in the 1970s that were very clear about how action
on behalf of justice and societal transformation was a constitutive element
of the Christian life. This convergence could already be seen in a dozen
ecumenical coalitions that addressed such issues as northern development,
international trade, peace, and human rights in Latin America, to name a few.

One could still dream of this unity in 1983 when the Canadian Conference
of Catholic Bishops made their controversial statement on the economy. The
bishops' statement was a highlight of a lost era, an era brought to an end by
the culture wars, by the onslaught of free trade and globalization, and by
events in the wider church's own life. These events ranged from preoccupation

with internal debate over sexual orientation issues in some churches, like my own, to the harm inflicted on the reputation of the mainstream churches in Canada by the residential school saga, not to mention the crisis over child sexual abuse by priests in the Catholic Church.

Those of us on the religious left might be forgiven if we look back somewhat nostalgically on a time when genuine controversy could erupt over an ecclesiastical declaration, especially one that proclaimed:

> The needs of the poor have priority over the wants of the rich, the rights of workers are more important than the maximization of profits, and the participation of marginalized groups takes precedence over the preservation of a system that excludes them.

The dream of a unified religious left was eventually replaced with a new convergence, one between older sources of diversity and disagreement, that took place between evangelical Protestants and Catholics over issues like abortion and marriage. Not that the convergence has produced any policy victories as such. As Noah Feldman argues in *Divided by God*—in an analysis of the last 25 years of American politics that has Canadian parallels—the liberals have been winning the culture wars (even more so in Canada), while the conservatives have been winning the war over economics.

There are a number of ironies in this analysis. The first is that the political right's exploitation and manipulation of the culture wars has certainly assisted the economic right to succeed politically. Meanwhile, the culture wars, however useful to the political right, have been won by the left in any event, but in the courts rather than at the polls. To the extent that social conservatives have lined up with the corporate agenda, they often made alliances with folks who worked in the unfettered marketplace to stimulate and commercialize the very instincts and modes of thought that they say they are concerned about. Television advertising is a good example. Viewing this strictly private sector activity for a single night is much more challenging to conservative values than anything the left could generate. But free enterprise must not be interfered with or criticized.

A second irony is the actual similarity between the winning side in the culture wars and the winning side in the economic wars. Both partake in their own way of an expanded liberal, individualist, or autonomist view of human life. In one, personal choice is exercised over values; in the other, over consumption of products and services. This similarity is articulated well by theologian Stanley Hauerwas, in a 2007 article in the journal *First Things*. When talking about the philosopher Alasdair MacIntyre, author of the book *After Virtue,* Hauerwas says:

> [MacIntyre] makes clear that his problem with most forms of con-
> temporary conservatism is that conservatives mirror the fundamental
> characteristics of liberalism. The conservative commitment to a way
> of life structured by a free market results in an individualism, and in
> particular a moral psychology, that is as antithetical to the tradition of
> the virtues as is liberalism.

Or as antithetical to the core economic message of the Bible, I would add. Or to the core idea of democratic socialism. Theologian Paul Tillich argued in *The Socialist Decision* that the challenge of socialism was not to return to some pre-liberal social unity based on tribe or race or nation, like certain forms of conservatism. Rather, the challenge is to go beyond liberalism, while incorporating the progress in human freedom that liberalism represented, to achieve a new, more conscious social unity that would permit the fullness of humanity to be realized.

In my inaugural speech in the House of Commons on October 19, 1979, I said, of the NDP, in an attempt to both provoke and reveal something I profoundly believed, "We are the true conservatives." I believe that democratic socialists are better conservatives than the conservatives, who would sacrifice everything else they say they believe in on the altar of their market idol. A conservative who is willing to think and act critically toward the market, who has a more organic and less individualistic view of society, is what is meant by the term *Red Tory*. It does not only or necessarily mean a conservative who is more progressive on controversial social issues, although it is sometimes used that way. Unfortunately, Red Tories are virtually an extinct political species. The late Senator Heath MacQuarrie was one of the last, and he entitled his memoir *Red Tory Blues.*

———

Christopher Hitchens's book *God Is Not Great* claims to redefine the debate about religion in public life by addressing what is alleged to be the most urgent issue of the present age, the "malignant force of religion in the world." Religion "poisons everything," according to Hitchens. I prefer the analysis of his believing brother, Peter Hitchens, who says, in a competing book entitled *The Rage against God*, that conflicts fought in the name of religion often disgust the most faithful and enthuse the least religious. Nevertheless, while I disagree with Christopher Hitchens and find his atheism to be shallow and intellectually dishonest, I have sometimes had feelings similar to his about religious input into political debate.

There is a way of doing theology, or of putting forward religiously derived positions in political or public debates, that can be poisonous to the process, to relationships between people of faith and non-faith, and to relationships between members of the same faith, in my case the Christian community. If I had a dime for every time I had to deal with the charge that began "I thought you were a Christian, until…" or "I thought as a United Church minister you would never hold such a despicable view.…" The latter charge was the more mysterious, because I was hardly ever even minimally at odds with the teachings of The United Church of Canada.

When I was not being emotionally assaulted or eternally judged by fellow Christians, I often had to endure the attitude from colleagues on the left that religiously derived criticism could be dismissed outright—as "religious," as a category—regardless of the actual merit of the policies being advocated. At such times, I often wondered how those of us who came to our left-wing views through our faith were supposed to feel. Was it just a matter of tactical convenience that some of the religiously deluded had fortunately deluded themselves into holding the same position as the non-deluded on the left? Or did it ever occur to the so-called non-deluded that this might be cause for a less simplistic analysis of religion and its place in the public realm? As theologian Walter Wink points out in *Naming the Powers,* secular activists too often dismiss the hymns, gospel songs, eucharists, and prayers of a Martin Luther King or a César Chávez, as "merely a shrewd accommodation to the subcultures with which they worked" instead of a larger statement about what kind of struggle was really at hand.

Despite the resurgent, even militant atheism of authors like Richard Dawkins and Christopher Hitchens, the fact is that God has not died the death predicted by so many. Much of the discourse about faith and politics in a previous era involved an assumption that faith was on its way out. Instead, unlike the expectations that inspired a book title like *The Politics at God's Funeral*, written 25 years ago by the great American socialist Michael Harrington, we are all challenged by the politics of God's persistence. Just as we should also continue to be challenged by Harrington, who called for an alliance between faith and antifaith against the corrupting hedonism of late-20th-century capitalism.

Journalists John Micklethwait and Adrian Wooldridge, authors of *God Is Back,* make a case for the view that, far from being the enemy of religion, as modernity was thought traditionally to be, modernity and its hallmarks democracy, markets, technology, and reason are leading to a kind of pluralism in which religion is thriving, with the possible exception of in Europe. Peter Berger, the iconic sociologist of religion, is cited as admitting to the mistake of assuming that modernization was connected to secularization, when it is actually connected to pluralism. This pluralism includes non-belief, but it is characterized by an explosion of faith types that seek to provide meaning and guidance in the meaninglessness created by the modern world. The Americanization of the global culture, and of the global economy, so goes the argument, creates the opportunity for the spread of American religion, as one form of Americanization seeks to solve the problems created by the other.

At first glance, this doesn't seem to be the opportunity a social gospeller would be looking for. But what some have called the resetting of the faith dialogue within America itself as a result of Barack Obama is to be welcomed. This is a U.S. president who seems to understand that religion is a significant factor in how the world works, locally and globally, and that any political agenda wanting support will include a commitment to deepening our understanding of faith and enhancing our ability to talk about it, without excommunicating the other when we don't agree.

The authors of *God Is Back* refer to the "new, new religious right, and a newly emergent religious left." The new, new religious right has to do in part with the expansion of evangelical Christian political consciousness to include issues beyond the customary short list—issues like global poverty, HIV-AIDS, and climate change are increasingly on the evangelical radar. In the United States, the symbol of this new evangelical consciousness is Saddleback Church pastor Rick Warren, who offered one of the prayers at President Obama's inaugural ceremony.

There is no Canadian Rick Warren yet. But I believe that there is a growing desire on the part of a younger generation of evangelical Canadian Christians to grow beyond the confines of an earlier generation. They may recover the imagination of even earlier generations of evangelicals who were part of the social gospel, or who even earlier, in the United Kingdom for example, took on slavery. The story of William Wilberforce, portrayed in the movie *Amazing Grace*, has become part of the evangelical narrative for growing numbers of Canadians. I do not share Marci McDonald's view, expressed in *The*

Armageddon Factor, that the main lesson evangelicals are being encouraged to learn from the Wilberforce story is how to make Parliament do something it did not intend. I found the story of how Wilberforce outsmarted the slave trade parliamentarians to be a joyful one, rather than a suspicious prelude to tactics employed by 21st-century right-wing parliamentarians.

———

In the spring of 2006 in Ottawa, I was invited to an event sponsored by the Manning Centre to debate and discuss the social gospel with Preston Manning. At the end of the meeting, I expressed the view that the growth of evangelical Christianity didn't bother me as much as they might think, because I saw it as creating the spiritual capital of the next social gospel. It was an observation that puzzled some of the Conservatives in the room. My observation was rooted in the belief that as a younger generation of evangelicals begin to explore the systemic causes of the problems they wish to address and the powerful interests that stand in the way of needed changes, as they begin to see that there are sinful structures and not just sinful people, they will have entered into the social gospel, whether they immediately recognize it as such or not.

At that same meeting, I had occasion to respond to a common criticism that the religious right offers the religious left. It is said that we are too preoccupied with the horizontal dimension of reality, with the world that is, and pay too little attention to the vertical, to our relationship with God. My response to this charge is twofold. First of all, it presupposes that those of us on the Christian left have a flawed or somewhat inadequate spirituality. The sheer self-righteousness of this criticism is irritating enough.

Second, I would argue that one of the major signs of having your vertical relationship right is how much attention you pay to the world, how much you are obedient to the commandment to seek first the kingdom of God and its justice (Matthew 6:33). As Gregory Baum noted in his book *The Social Imperative,* the watershed Third Synod of Bishops, convened in Rome in 1971, marked a turning point. It recognized the reality of "social sin" and rejected the distinction between the vertical and the horizontal dimension of the faithful life that rendered engagement with the struggle for social justice a second-class spiritual activity.

With regard to the newly emergent religious left, there is a movement south of the border of progressive Americans whose politics is motivated by their spirituality, a spirituality either progressively understood, or even understood from a theologically traditional standpoint. The first is represented by Rabbi Michael Lerner, for example, the leader of the Network of Spiritual Progressives, founder of *Tikkun* magazine, and author of a book entitled *The Left Hand of God*. The second group is represented by Jim Wallis of the Sojourners Community in Washington, author of *God's Politics: Why the Right Gets It Wrong and the Left Doesn't Get It*. I had the opportunity to meet both of them at a Politics of Meaning Summit in Washington in 1995, and have subsequently worked with Rabbi Lerner on one occasion.

One of the three tenets of Lerner's Network of Spiritual Progressives is entitled "Challenging the Anti-religious and Anti-spiritual Biases within Liberal Culture," a tenet that seeks to educate liberals and progressives to carefully distinguish between their legitimate critiques of the religious right and their illegitimate generalizations about all religious and spiritual beliefs, with a view to helping social change activists become more conscious of, and less afraid to affirm, their own spiritual inclinations. The same tenet challenges the elitist notion that secular people are intellectually or morally on a higher plane than people who believe in God or participate in spiritual or religious communities.

Where is evidence of a similar Canadian phenomenon?

Actually, in the NDP. A few years ago I heard a young woman recount to an NDP meeting that when she told some New Democrats that she had just been at church, they were astonished and asked her how she could be in both the party and the church. And at her church, when she mentioned that she had been at an NDP event, they too were astonished and asked her the same question. It is reasonable to claim that at one time this question might not have been asked, at least not in the same way as it came to be after a generation of associating religion with the political right.

What we recently did in the NDP, as a result of an initiative that originated with some caucus members, was to start a faith and justice caucus that met regularly to discuss the relationship between our faith and our politics. We went on, with party members at large, to create the Faith and Justice Commission of the party. This made a statement about the history, the present, and the future of left-wing politics in Canada, and also created a venue in which party members could come to know each other as fellow faith-inspired political colleagues. At a noon workshop held at a national convention a few years ago, it was like a giant coming-out party where people who had worked together politically for years became aware of each other as fellow people of faith. Given the unique character of the debate about secularism in Quebec, the presence in 2011 of so many new NDP MPs from Quebec may well contribute a new dimension to the NDP's ongoing understanding of the relationship between faith and politics.

At a certain time in the past, such a meeting at an NDP convention would not have been necessary in the same way. In the more recent past, it might even have been objected to. The fact that it was accepted, even welcomed, is part of a larger unfolding story that is far from over. Contrary to the claim made by Marci McDonald in *The Armageddon Factor,* this is not an attempt "to build a religious left," something she describes as an "unsettling development." It is an attempt to recognize something that is already there, with a view to breaking the perceived monopoly of the religious right when religion and the public square are talked about.

This is only worrisome if you desire a public square in which all reference to religious belief is inadmissible. It is not worrisome if you see the appropriate secular society not as secularist in an ideologically confining way, but rather as one in which healthy debate can take place between faiths, and between faith and antifaith, as to what public policy should be on any given issue, and how we can identify and integrate the strands of solidarity that will be needed to make pluralism work. This, I believe, is the direction that Charles Taylor advocates in *A Secular Age* and subsequent reflections. While addressing the necessary question of how to have a society that does not privilege one belief over another, Taylor is also concerned about how to not privilege unbelief over belief. Even unbelief represents a particular world view that should not be imposed on those who do not subscribe to it, particularly in a democracy. Taylor's gift is his consistent putting of these questions in the context of what is good for societies that are democratic and want to remain healthily so. As he wrote in a September 2010 opinion piece in *The Globe and Mail,* he is concerned about a challenge unprecedented in our history, the need to create "a powerful political ethic of solidarity self-consciously grounded on the presence and acceptance of very different views."

Having said this, the one issue on which I fully share McDonald's alarm is the prospect, hopefully slight, of a foreign policy based on a geopolitical analysis that claims to make sense of current realities on the basis of a particular reading of the Book of Revelation. This is not even biblical literalism. It is biblical speculation that has no place in public policy, or in a proper reading of the text itself for that matter.

Another possible contribution to a different future for the relationship between faith and politics is a stronger re-engagement of the Catholic community with questions of economic justice. Such a possibility may hopefully now be discerned in the 2009 encyclical of Pope Benedict XVI entitled *Caritas in Veritate*—On Integral Human Development in Charity and Truth. Pope Benedict's analysis of globalization is not dissimilar in many ways from that offered on the political left. This has caused a bit of a debate within the Catholic Church, with right-wing Catholic thinkers like George Weigel, associated with the late Richard John Neuhaus, founder of the journal *First Things* and a leading conservative Catholic commentator in America, reported to suspect that somehow Pope Benedict mistakenly allowed the justice and peace types in the church to subversively insert passages into the encyclical.

Passages, I presume, like the one that seems to take aim at the free market fundamentalism of the last two decades, when Pope Benedict says that the "conviction that the economy must be autonomous, that it must be shielded from 'influences' of a moral character, has led man to abuse the economic process in a thoroughly destructive way." Benedict is saying what others have said before, including another German theologian, Karl Barth, whose repudiation of capitalism was simple: A system based on the promotion of selfishness produces neither justice nor a proper Christian orientation.

I remember an exchange I had with Neuhaus at an event in Ottawa in the 1990s when I questioned him as to why someone who had written a book called *The Naked Public Square,* a book that lamented the absence of biblical values in the public square, didn't simultaneously lament the absence of biblical values in the marketplace. In answering he spoke about the economy as an autonomous reality, properly beyond politics. Pope Benedict seems to share the left's concern about the notion of an amoral economy, lamenting the downsizing of social security systems, and calling for the strengthening of trade unions, among other things.

In *Tommy Douglas: The Road to Jerusalem,* the biography by Douglas's close friend and adviser Tommy McLeod, the author notes on the last page that Douglas hoped MP Bill Blaikie "would carry on the mission of the social gospel in Canadian left-wing politics." This is a hope that I have done my best to live up to, not always knowing for sure what the mission was calling me to do at certain points in my political life. Whether Douglas would always have agreed with me, I do not know. I have always tried to avoid, particularly in the context of new questions that have arisen, the hubris of claiming to know what he would have thought, a tactic that enrages me when employed by others.

What I do know is that there will always be a role for people of all faiths to speak out of their prophetic, justice-seeking traditions. This role will challenge the rulers of their day to do justice, to love kindness and mercy, and to measure their political choices not in terms of how they help the rich and already powerful, but rather by how they help the hungry, the poor, the vulnerable, the marginalized, the excluded, and the environment that future generations will have to live in.

What I hope for is that it's out of each faith's prophetic tradition that the needed unity can emerge, that out of a united ethical vision, peace and justice between religious communities can be more hopefully pursued, even as important differences continue to be identified and better understood. The challenge for Christians in such a context is to find the sweet spot in the dialogue. It should enable the distinctiveness of the gospel to be confessed in a way that does not partake of the arrogant exclusivism associated with Christendom. Nor confessed in a way that loses what has sometimes been called the "scandal of particularity" in various blends of pluralism, universalism, and inclusivism that rob faith of the call to involvement, and replaces it with disinterested tolerance and observation. Canadian theologian Douglas John Hall explains this better than I in a chapter he wrote for *Many Voices, One God: Being Faithful in a Pluralistic World*. Hall argues that the world of post-Christendom pluralism, of Christianity as one faith among many, is more biblically normal, and therefore more open to biblical instruction.

The social gospel is suited to such a context, despite its roots in Christendom. The confession of Jesus Christ as Lord is also a statement about what is not sovereign. There is a political choice to be made as to where we look for authority. Will we seek it in the power and wealth of Herod and Caesar of old, of the global corporate powers and profit strategies of this age? Or in the life and teachings of a Galilean peasant rabbi who challenged the domination system of his time, was crucified for it, and whose disciples went on to proclaim that oppression does not have the last word, that God's passion for justice is the last word? This is a passion that asks the faithful to resist the temptation to divide the world up into believers and non-believers, and instead to see the world as a place where the faithful are called to work with all those who hunger and thirst after justice.

NDP Members of Parliament, 1979 to 2008

Althouse, Vic
Anguish, Doug
Angus, Charlie
Angus, Iain
Atamanenko, Alex
Axworthy, Chris
Barrett, Dave
Bell, Catherine
Benjamin, Les
Bevington, Dennis
Black, Dawn
Blackburn, Derek
Blaikie, Bill
Breaugh, Mike
Brewin, John
Broadbent, Ed
Butland, Steve
Cassidy, Michael
Charlton, Chris
Chow, Olivia
Christopherson, David
Comartin, Joe
Crowder, Jean
Cullen, Nathan
Davies, Libby
de Jong, Simon
Deans, Ian
Desjarlais, Bev

Dewar, Marion
Dewar, Paul
Dockrill, Michelle
Earle, Gordon
Edmonston, Phil
Epp, Ernie
Faour, Fonse
Fisher, Ron
Fulton, Jim
Funk, Ray
Gardiner, Brian
Godin, Yvon
Gruending, Dennis
Hardy, Louise
Harris, Jack
Harvey, Ross
Heap, Dan
Hogan, Andy
Hovdebo, Stan
Hunter, Lynn
Ittinuar, Peter
Jewett, Pauline
Julian, Peter
Karpoff, Jim
Keeper, Cyril
Knowles, Stanley
Kristiansen, Lyle
Laliberte, Rick

Langan, Joy
Langdon, Steven
Laporte, Rod
Layton, Jack
Lewycky, Laverne
Lill, Wendy
MacWilliam, Lyle
Mancini, Peter
Manly, Jim
Marston, Wayne
Martin, Pat
Martin, Tony
Masse, Brian
Mathyssen, Irene
McCurdy, Howard
McDonald, Lynn
McDonough, Alexa
McLaughlin, Audrey
Miller, Ted
Mitchell, Margaret
Mulcair, Thomas
Murphy, Rod
Nash, Peggy
Nystrom, Lorne
Ogle, Bob
Orlikow, David
Parker, Sid
Parry, John

Peters, Arnold
Priddy, Penny
Proctor, Dick
Rae, Bob
Riis, Nelson
Robinson, Svend
Rodriguez, John
Rose, Mark
Samson, Cid

Sargeant, Terry
Savoie, Denise
Siksay, Bill
Skelly, Bob
Skelly, Ray
Solomon, John
Stoffer, Peter
Stupich, Dave
Symes, Cyril

Taylor, Len
Vautour, Angela
Waddell, Ian
Wasylycia-Leis, Judy
Whittaker, Jack
Young, Neil

Notes

Chapter 2. The Social Gospel

15 *many leftists in Canada...*   Ian McKay, *Rebels, Reds, Radicals: Rethinking Canada's Left History* (Toronto: Between the Lines, 2005), p. 43.

17 *Predatory profit or graft...*   Walter Rauschenbusch, *A Theology for the Social Gospel* (New York: Abington Press, 1945), p. 73.

Chapter 4. Growing Up Political in Transcona

38 *When the workday...*   Henry Duckworth, *One Version of the Facts: My Life in the Ivory Tower* (Winnipeg: University of Manitoba Press, 2000), p. 6. Reprinted with permission.

Chapter 5. The Prophetic Tradition

57 *[The church] is, however, entitled...*   William Temple, *Christianity and Social Order* (Harmondsworth, Middlesex, England; New York, N.Y.: Penguin Books, 1942), p. 32.

Chapter 6. Seeking the Welfare of the City

60 *Under [Woodsworth] the mission...*   Allen Mills, *Fool for Christ: The Political Thought of J.S. Woodsworth* (Toronto: University of Toronto Press, 1991), p. 36. © University of Toronto Press. Reprinted with permission of the publisher.

Chapter 7. First Peoples and Constitutional Debates

72 *We have never had to determine...*   Justice Thomas Berger, *Northern Frontier, Northern Homeland: The Report of the Mackenzie Valley Pipeline Inquiry*, 1977, p. 200. Reprinted with permission.

78 *To a great extent...*   Proceedings of the House of Commons ("Hansard"). December 1, 1981. Reprinted with permission.

Chapter 8. An Effective Electorate

88 *The readiness to use...*   George F. Kennan, *The Nuclear Delusion: Soviet-American Relations in the Atomic Age* (New York: Pantheon Books, 1982), pp. 206–207.

92 *win enough seats...*   Stanley Knowles, *The New Party* (Toronto: McClelland and Stewart, 1961), p. 29.

Chapter 9. The Medicare Crisis

101   *if extra-billing is permitted...* Emmett M. Hall, 1898–. *Canada's national-provincial health program for the 1980's* / [Emmett M. Hall] – [Ottawa : Health and Welfare Canada, 1980.] – viii, 101, 102, vii p.; 28 cm. – AMICUS No. 2279972, p. 27. © Government of Canada. Reproduced with the permission of the Minister of Public Works and Government Services Canada (2011).

102   *Canadians understand the full meaning...* Hall, p. 6. Reproduced with permission.

104   *Bill Blaikie, my NDP counterpart...* Monique Bégin, *Medicare: Canada's Right to Health* (Montreal: Optimum Publishing International, 1988), p. 91. Reprinted with permission.

Chapter 10. Parliamentary Reform

120   *Allow me, Mr. Speaker...* Hansard, June 25, 1987. Reprinted with permission.

125   *Delay is one of the features...* Hansard, April 10, 1991. Reprinted with permission.

Chapter 11. Our Environmental Deficit

127   *being carried to the brink...* Barry Commoner, *The Closing Circle: Nature, Man and Technology* (New York: Knopf, 1971), p. 299.

Chapter 12. Hope in the Post-Cold War Era

146   *It is...of paramount importance...* *Common Security: A Programme for Disarmament,* The Report of the Independent Commission on Disarmament and Security Issues (London, Sydney: Pan, 1982), p. ix. Reprinted with permission.

Chapter 15. Free Trade—A Chosen Powerlessness

187   *spring into action...* Elaine Bernard, "The Battle in Seattle: What Was That All About?" *Washington Post*, December 5, 1999. Reprinted with permission.

192   *quite impressive...* Gordon Ritchie, *Wrestling with the Elephant: The Inside Story of the Canada-US Trade Wars* (Toronto: Macfarlane Walter & Ross, 1997), p. 161. Reprinted with permission.

Chapter 17. A Passion for Justice

216   *The needs of the poor...* Excerpt from the *Ethical Reflections on the Economic Crisis* by the Episcopal Commission for Social Affairs, copyright © Concacan Inc., 1983. All rights reserved. Used with permission of the Canadian Conference of Catholic Bishops. cccbpublications.ca

217   *[MacIntyre] makes clear...* Stanley Hauerwas, "The Virtues of Alasdair MacIntyre," *First Things*, October 2007 (www.firstthings.com). Reprinted with permission.

218   *merely a shrewd accommodation...* Walter Wink, *Naming the Powers* (Philadelphia: Fortress Press, 1984), p. 117.

222   *a powerful political ethic...* Charles Taylor, "All for One, and One for All," *The Globe and Mail*, September 29, 2010. Reprinted with permission.

223   *conviction that the economy...* *Caritas in Veritate*—On Integral Human Development in Charity and Truth. Encyclical letter of Pope Benedict XVI, 2009. © Libreria Editrice Vaticana. Reprinted with permission.

223   *would carry on...* Thomas H. McLeod and Ian McLeod, *Tommy Douglas: The Road to Jerusalem* (Edmonton: Hurtig, 1987), p. 309.

Index

A

ability to begin anew, 156, 160
Aboriginal people, 71–79, 82–84
   Constitution (1982), 77–79
   defence of rights, 73, 76–78
   Meech Lake Accord, 79
   Quebec, 78–79, 83–84
   religion, 12
   residential schools, 69, 72, 78, 216
   White Paper (1969), 73
   in Winnipeg, 68, 69, 71
abortion, 23–25, 27–29
acid rain, 129–30
Action Canada Network, 90, 94
Adams, Gerry, 163, 165
Adams, Peter, 176
Afghanistan, 155, 172, 173
African National Congress, 144
agricultural policy, 200–201
Alexander, Lincoln, 43
All People's Mission, 60
Allen, Richard, 14
Allmand, Warren, 87, 171
Althouse, Vic, 201
Angus, Adam, 117
Angus, Iain, 112, 117, 144
Antigonish Movement, 102
antiterrorist laws, 213
arctic environment conference, 138, 174
Arias, Oscar (Costa Rica), 178

arms trade, 169
Asia-Pacific Economic Cooperation, 199
atheism, 218
Atleo, Shawn (AFN), 74
Atwood, Margaret, 194
Austin, Senator Jack, 180
auto emission regulations, 130
Axworthy, Lloyd, 4, 146, 177
Axworthy, Tom, 41

B

Bachand, Claude, 123
Badertscher, John, 51, 52, 56
bagpipes, 40, 47, 48, 62, 117, 162, 164
Bailey, Ron, 23
Bain, Sir George, 164–65
Baird, Vaughan, 43
Baker, Walter (Tory House Leader), 111
Ballistic Missile Defense, 173
Baltic states, 158–60
Bank of Canada, 96
Barlow, Maude, 94–95, 133, 193
Barth, Karl, 22, 223
Baum, Gregory, 56, 220
Bégin, Monique, 101, 103, 104
Belfast meetings, 163–64
Benedict XVI, Pope, 162, 223
Benjamin, Les, 201
Berger, Justice Thomas, 72, 73
Berger, Peter (sociologist), 219

Berger Report, 72–73, 74
Berlin Wall removal, 174
Bernard, Elaine, 93–94, 187
Berrigan, Daniel (activist), 51
Berrigan, Phil (activist), 53
Best, Ernie (prof.), 57
Bible books
  Book of Revelation, 222
  Deuteronomy, 87
  Genesis, 134
  Habakkuk, 59
  Jeremiah, 59, 69–70, 89
  John, 67
  Luke, 22
  Matthew, 58, 187, 220
biblical literalism, 29
Biggar, Saskatchewan, 47
Bihun, Bill (Brenda's father), 46, 47
Bihun, Brenda (later Blaikie), 46, 47
Bird, Bud, 177
Black, Dawn, 144
Blaikie, Bill
  Aboriginal people, 71–79, 82–84
  abortion issue, 23–25, 27–29
  bagpipes, 40, 47, 48, 62, 117, 162, 164
  Conservation Min, Manitoba, 4, 134,
    202
  Defence Critic (2004–08), 122–23, 154
  Deputy Speaker, 1
  early political experience, 42–46, 49
  Environment Critic (1984–87), 127–34
  External Affairs Critic, 128, 143–44,
    156–66, 169–81
  first election as MP, 23, 71, 120
  Health Critic, 98, 101, 103, 104
  inner-city ministry, 59–64, 67–70
  Justice Critic, 213–14
  Lefebvre and McGrath Committees,
    109–16, 126
  marriage, 52
  NDP House Leader, 180–81
  NDP Parliamentary Leader, 126, 173
  ordained, 54, 75

  race to lead NDP, 5, 62, 84, 97
  retirement from federal politics, 1, 3
  social gospel tradition, 7–10, 16, 20.
  supporting peace activists, 174–75,
    177–78
  Tax Critic (1990–93), 65–66, 143
  theological studies, 52–58
  trade critic, 181–82, 184, 198, 203,
    209, 214
  University of Winnipeg, 49, 50–52
  upbringing, 37–39, 42, 50
Blaikie, Bob, Jr. (father), 35, 48, 150
Blaikie, Bob, Sr. (grandfather), 47
Blaikie, Bobby (brother), 8, 180
Blaikie, Brenda (wife, née Bihun), 41, 46,
    52, 53, 54, 64, 116, 128, 129, 163,
    165, 167
Blaikie, Daniel (son), 209
Blaikie, Jessica (daughter), 209
Blaikie, Jim (great-uncle), 47
Blaikie, Kathleen (mother), 24–25, 39, 48,
    72, 162
Blaikie, Rebecca (daughter), 189
Blaikie, Tessa (daughter), 192, 213
Blair, Tony, 97, 208, 209
Blais-Grenier, Suzanne, 129, 130
Blakeney, Allan, 78, 108, 132
Bland, Salem (social gospeller), 14
Blenkarn, Don (fed-prov task), 105
Blix, Hans (UN weapons insp), 172
Bloc Québécois, 81, 123, 176, 196
Boag, Helen (grandmother), 48
Bonhoeffer, Dietrich, 21, 85
Borg, Marcus, 51
Bosc, Marc, 1
Bosley, John, 112, 177, 178
Bouchard, Lucien, 84, 196
Bourassa, Robert, 106, 133
Bourgault, Lise (McGrath comm), 111
Boyce, Greer (prof), 58
Brandt Report (1980), 148
Brandt, Willy, 148
Breau, Herb (fed-prov task), 105

Bretton Woods agreement, 18

Broadbent, Ed, 143, 148, 190
  Aboriginal issues, 77, 79
  leaves as NDP leader, 188, 189
  NDP policy on NATO, 149

Brown, Dee (author), 73

Brundtland, Gro Harlem, 137

Brundtland Report (1987), 137

Buchanan, Pat, 202

Bund (socialist movement), 17

Burns, Robert, 62, 82, 112–13, 192–93

Burns Supper, 112–13

Bush, George (the first), 130

Bush, George W., 53, 172, 173

C

Caccia, Charles (acid rain), 130, 138

Cadman, Chuck (independent), 167

Cadman, Dona, 167

Câmara, Bishop Dom Hélder, 55–56

Camp, Dalton, 39

Campbell, Douglas, 82

Campbell, Kim, 33

Canada
  Common Security (NDP), 145–46,
    148, 149
  postwar achievements, 18

Canada-China Business Council, 180

Canada-China Legislative Assn, 180–81

Canada Day, 115

Canada Health Act, 98, 101, 105, 106–7

Canada Health and Social Transfer, 107

Canada-UK Parliamentary Assn, 163

Canada-US Air Quality Agreement, 130

Canada-US Free Trade Agreement, 90, 144
  1988 election, 189–90
  and democracy, 183, 185
  energy policy, 195–96
  hearings, 187, 192–93, 194, 195
  original recommendation, 195
  results, 194, 196–97

Canadian Action Party, 95–96

Canadian Alliance, 6, 42, 116, 172, 176

Canadian Arctic Gas Pipeline Ltd., 72

Canadian Auto Workers, 47, 203–4

Canadian Coalition on Acid Rain, 130

Canadian Health Coalition, 98, 101, 102

Canadian Labour Congress, 101, 102

Canadian Medical Association, 99

Canadian National Railway, 37, 47, 201–2
  privatization, 154, 193

Canadian Nurses Association, 106

Canadian Wheat Board, 186

Cantelon, Bill (house church), 53

capital punishment, 26, 115–16, 120–21

capitalism, 22, 56, 139, 140, 175

Cardenal, Ernesto and Fernando, 177

Cardinal, Harold (author), 73

Carlyle, Elizabeth (Seattle), 212

Carr, Shirley, 148

Castro, Fidel, 200

Catholic Church
  activist priests, 102–3, 177, 178
  Canadian Catholic Bishops, 12, 215–16
  family relationship, 162
  papal encyclicals, 10, 22, 223
  social concerns, 7–10, 29, 99, 222–23
  Vatican, 9

cellphones, 119, 125

Cellucci, Paul (US ambassador), 173

Central America, 10, 144, 170, 177–78

Cerilli, Al (union), 46

Cerilli, Joanne, 46

CF-18 controversy, 81, 87

Charest, Jean (Quebec premier), 3

Charlottetown Accord, 81–82

Charter of Rights and Freedoms, 78
  notwithstanding clause, 40, 78
  and religion, 12
  role of Parliament, 125

Chávez, César, 54, 218

Checkpoint Charlie, 174

Chernobyl nuclear disaster, 138

Chiang Kai-shek, 160

child care plan, 2, 29–30
child labour, 187, 207–8
China, 178–79, 180–82
    admission to WTO, 169, 181, 187
    human rights abuses, 180, 181–82, 187
    supression of protest, 181
    trip to mainland China, 180
choice as a right, 27–28, 216–17
Chomiak, Dave (NDP Man), 46
Chrétien, Jean, 3, 30, 66, 82
    acts after Quebec referendum, 80–81
    free trade, 90–91, 134, 204–5
    inaction on environment, 128
    Iraq decision, 171–72, 173
    liberal leadership, 79–80, 166
    relations with China, 180
Christian realism, 20
Christian Week, 6–7
Christianity
    Bible see Bible books; biblical literalism
    confessing Jesus as Lord, 224
    culture wars and see culture wars
    diversity within, 11, 15–16, 25
    ecumenical movement, 19, 56, 215
    Emmanuel College, 53, 54, 56, 58
    evangelicals, 11, 26, 216, 219
    Faith and Justice Commission of NDP,
        221–22
    Knowles-Woodsworth Centre, 4
    left-wing see religious left
    pluralism, 13, 219, 222, 223–24
    politics and see faith and politics
    prophetic tradition, 50–58, 67, 68, 143
    right-wing see religious right
    Roman Catholics see Catholic Church
    secular society and, 11, 12–13
    a social religion, 50–51, 57, 215–16
    stewardship of creation, 134–36, 141
    theological studies, 49–58
    Toronto School of Theology, 52–58
    United Church see United Church of
        Canada

University of Winnipeg, 4, 49–52
    see also social gospel
Christie, Jim, 4
church, role in politics, 121
cities, 59–70
civil rights movement, 17, 218
civility in Parliament, 125, 129
Clarity Act (Bill C-20), 82–84
Clark, Gen. Wesley, 164
Clark, Joe (PM), 42, 116, 156, 160
    collegiality, 124
    government, 80, 111
Clarkson, Adrienne (Gov Gen), 175, 176
class consciousness and NDP, 90
class differences, 66
climate change, 136–38
Clinton, Bill, 97, 197
Clinton, Senator Hillary, 154
Club of Rome report (1972), 136
co-operation, 15, 57
Coady, Father Moses, 102
coalitions
    Canadian Health, 98, 101, 102
    government, planned, 3, 191
    social issues see social movements
Cobb, John (author), 188
Cold War, 18, 144, 146
Coldwell, M.J., 11, 42, 48
collective bargaining, 18
Collier, Ken (Transcona), 45
Committee of Concerned Citizens, 132
committees
    attempts at reform, 114
    dysfunctionality, 3
    effective working, 122–23
common security, 145–46, 147
Commoner, Barry, 127, 137
communism in Soviet Union, 138, 139,
    175
Connors, Kathleen (Nurses), 106
conservatism, 217
constituents and MP's role, 119–21

Constitution and First Nations, 77–79
Contras, 177
Cook, Jeff (UCC), 55
Cook, Robin (UK), 209
Cooper, Albert (McGrath comm), 111
Cooperative Commonwealth Federation
    (CCF)
    backer of public health, 98–99
    founding of party, 7, 16–17, 19
    internationalist view, 145
    see also New Democratic Party (NDP)
Copps, Sheila, 126
corporations, 18, 50, 51, 136, 140
    multinational, 183, 184–86
    see also free trade; globalization
corruption, 126
Costa Rica, 177–78
Council of Canadians, 94, 95, 206
courts and Parliament, 78
Cristiani, Alfredo, 177
Crombie, David (Health Min), 100
Crosbie, John, 150, 179, 196
Crossan, John Dominic, 51
Crow Rate, 201–2
cruise missile, 86–87, 147
Cuban missile crisis, 49
culture wars, 25–36, 216–17
    abortion, 23–25, 27, 28, 29
    capital punishment, 26, 115–16,
        120–21
    gun control, 32–33
    gun registry, 34–36
    prayer breakfast, 34
    right to choose, 28
    same-sex marriage, 30–31
    United States, 26
Cureatz, Sam, 159-60
Cyprus, 165, 166

D
Dalai Lama, 181
Daly, Herman (author), 188

Danis, Marcel (Quebec Tory), 112
Darling, Stan (Acid Rain), 130
Davies, Libby (NDP), 168
Davis, Bill (Ont premier), 130
Dawkins, Richard (author), 218
Day, Dorothy, 102
Day, Stockwell, 6, 7
de Bruyn, Hank, 67–68
de Chastelain, Gen. John, 164
de Jong, Simon (NDP), 73, 136
De Roo, Bishop Remi, 56
Deans, Ian, 112
defence, Bill Blaikie as Defence Critic,
    122–23, 154
delay, seen as unproductive, 125
Deloria, Vine, Jr. (author), 73
DeMarsh, Roy (NDP), 103
democracy
    hurt by globalization, 183, 185–87
    and protest, 210
den Hertog, Johanna, 148
Deng Xiaoping, 181
D'Escoto, Father Miguel, 10, 177, 178
Desjarlais, Bev (NDP), 30–31
Diefenbaker, John (PM), 4, 8, 28, 43
Dieppe veterans' medal, 117
Dingwall, David, 150
Dinsdale, Walter (PC), 43
Dion, Stéphane (Lib), 3, 83–84, 191
disabled child, 32
diversity among Christians, 11, 15–16, 25
Doer, Gary (Man), 4, 35, 46, 128
Domino, Leonard (Transcona), 42, 45
Domm, Bill, 115
Doody, Sen. Bill, 179
Douglas, Shirley, 62
Douglas, Tommy, 42, 57, 61, 113, 147
    memorial service, 61–62
    patriation and Charter, 78
    public health care, 99, 101, 106
    social gospel, 9, 11, 223
drug companies, 28, 108, 186

drug legislation, 18, 185–86
Dryden, Ken (Lib), 2
Duckworth, Dr. Henry, 38
Dzyndra, Bill (Transcona), 40

E
Earth Summit in Rio (1992), 137
East Timor, 170
economic elite, 187–88
economic equality, 64–65
economy, a moral issue, 50–51, 217
ecumenical movement, 19, 56, 215
Edmonston, Phil (Quebec NDP), 189
education, public, 18
Eggleton, Art (Trade Min), 198
El Salvador, 177
elections
    (1963), 28
    (1979) 23, 71, 120
    (1984), 85–86, 90–91, 127
    (1988), 149, 188, 189–90, 191
    (1993), 92, 187
    (2004), 1, 122
    (2006), 2, 26, 191
    (2008), 26, 123
    (2011), 3, 84, 124, 191
Eliason, Magnus (NDP), 45
Elliott, Cliff (prof), 54
Ellis, Jack (McGrath comm), 111
Ellul, Jacques (author), 66
Emmanuel College, 53, 54, 56, 58
Endicott, James (missionary), 179
Enns, Harry (PC), 44
environmental issues, 127–42
    changing or dying, 140–42
    cutbacks to programs, 130
    energy policy, 54, 195–96
    free trade and, 133, 195–96
    greenhouse gas, climate change, 136–37
    stewardship of creation, 74, 134–36,
        141–42
    sustainable development, 137
    threat to security, 145

Epp, Jake (PC), 24, 27, 45
Erasmus, Georges (AFN), 76
Established Programs Financing, 101, 105,
    106
Ethyl Corporation, 205
Europa Hotel (Belfast), 163–64
European Social Charter, 207, 208
evangelicals, 11, 26
    see also religious right
External Affairs Committee, 85, 174–75,
    187, 192
extra-billing (doctors), 100, 103, 106

F
Faith and Justice Commission of NDP,
    221–22
faith and politics, 4–13, 16–18, 148, 218,
    222
    Barack Obama and, 219
    Bonhoeffer on, 21
    freedom to participate, 22, 121
    political choices for Christians, 22
    politics of the Bible stories, 51
    see also culture wars; social gospel
Faith Today, 6, 10
Falls, Admiral Robert, 149–50
family allowance, 18
Fawcett, Vernon (prof), 58
Fed-Prov Fiscal Arrangements, 105–6
Feldman, Noah (author), 216
Fiddler, Annanias, 75
financial agreements, 121
firefighters, 117–18
First Ministers, 125
Fletcher, Carol (UCC), 55
food banks, 63
foreign investment, 18
foreign ownership, 37, 196
foreign policy issues, 143–55
    Afghanistan, 155, 172, 173
    common security, 145–47
    end of the Cold War, 144, 146, 174
    Gulf Wars, 169–73

Kosovo intervention, 152–53
NATO, 147, 149, 152, 154–55
nuclear weapons, 146, 147
see also free trade
Fraser, John (Speaker), 112–13, 131
Free the Children, 208
free trade, 183–97
  1988 election, 189–90, 191
  drug licensing, 185–86
  environment and, 133, 140, 195–96
  FTA *see* Canada-US Free Trade
    Agreement
  human rights, 186–87, 206–7
  nations weak, 183–86, 195–96, 203,
    214
  North America *see* NAFTA
  Quebec and, 196
  results, 194–97
  theological and justice issue, 121
  trade tribunals, 122, 185
  water, 132–34
  see also globalization
Free Trade Area of the Americas, 183, 196
  Quebec protest (2001), 212
Friesen, Benno (McGrath comm), 111
Fulford, Gordon (UCC), 55
Fulton, Jim, 77, 128–29, 131, 136, 142

G

G-20 protest in Toronto (2010), 213
Galbraith, John Kenneth, 139
Gandhi, Indira (India), 179–80
Gandhi, Mahatma, 179
Garden Hill First Nation, 75
General Agreement on Tariffs and Trade,
  185
generic drug legislation, 18
Gibeau, Marie (Namibia), 157, 158
Glass, Dr. Helen (CDN Nurses), 106
globalization, 17–18, 140
  capital flows, 184
  declining living standards, 202
  economic elite, 187–88

enemy of democracy, 183, 184–86
human rights, 186–87, 199, 202
labour and, 184, 186, 187
multinational corporations, 183,
  184–86
protests against *see* Seattle protest
  (1999)
responsibilities, 184–85
trade agreements *see* free trade
WTO and *see* World Trade Organization
GLOBE USA, 211
God
  persistence of, 218
  relationship with, 220
Gorbachev, Mikhail, 158–59, 160, 175
Gorbachev, Raisa, 175
Gordon, King (CCF), 62
Graham, Alex (Pipe Major), 117
Graham, Bill (Defence Min), 154
Graham, Billy (preacher), 10
Graham, Peter (Man Tory), 42
GRAND Canal project, 132–33
Grant, George (author), 28
Grant, John Webster, 56, 58
Gravel, Father Raymond, 198–99
Gray, Aunty Bea, 48
Green Party of Canada, 199
Greenaway, Richard, 45
greenhouse gas effect, 136–37
Gruending, Dennis (author), 99
Guenther, Heinz (prof), 58
Gulf War, First, 169–71, 172
Gulf War, Second, 171, 172–73
gun control, 32–33
gun registry, 33, 34–36
Gunn-Walberg, Ken (Man), 42
Gushowaty, Brent (friend), 150–51, 162

H

Haig, Graeme (Winnipeg), 42
Hall Commission (1964), 99
Hall, Douglas John (theologian), 56, 224
Hall, Justice Emmett

Hall Commission (1964), 99
second report (1980), 100–101
Hancock, Ken (house church), 53
Hargrove, Buzz (CAW), 47, 203–4
Harper, Elijah, 79
Harper, Stephen (PM), 1, 74, 92
2008 call for election, 3
Afghanistan, 172
attitude to NDP and UCC, 104
Christian Right, 6
contempt of Parliament, 122
on controversial issues, 26–27, 116
formation of Conservative Party, 42
social spending, 167–68
suspicion of environmentalism, 137
Harrington, Michael (author), 218
Harvard, John (Lib), 166
Hauerwas, Stanley (theologian), 217
Havel, Václav (Czech), 153
Hayden, Tom (Chicago Seven), 210, 211
health care see public health insurance
Heap, Dan (worker priest), 7, 64
Hellyer, Paul (Cdn Action), 95–96
Herbert, Hal (Canada Day), 115
Heshka, George (principal), 68
Hickerson, Bill (UCC), 55
Hitchens, Christopher, 217, 218
Hitchens, Peter (author), 218
Hitler, Adolf, 154
HMCS Chicoutimi, 122–23
hockey, 53, 66, 165
Hogan, Father Andy (NDP), 7, 102
Hong Kong, 179
hospital user fees, 100, 101, 103, 106
housing policies, 18, 70
Hovdebo, Stan (Sask NDP), 8, 201
human rights, 145, 153
abuses in China, 180, 181–82
free trade attack on, 186–87, 206–7
ignored by WTO, 186, 187, 199, 202
Hurley, Adele (acid rain), 130
Hurtig, Mel (National Party), 95

Hussein, Saddam, 169, 170, 172
Hutchinson, Roger (Emmanuel), 11, 56

I

Ignatieff, Michael (Lib), 191
India, 179–80
inner-city ministry, 59–70
Iona, 282
Iraq
attack on Kuwait, response, 169–71
US-led invasion of, 171–73
Ireland see Northern Ireland (Ulster)
Irish Republican Army, 164
Israel, 165–66
Ittinuar, Peter (NDP), 77
Ivens, Rev. William, 61

J

Jamieson, Don, 179
Japanese Canadians, 92–93
Jay, Douglas (prof), 56
Jesus Christ, 17, 22, 29, 120
confessing Jesus as Lord, 224
economics and, 51, 57, 68
Jewett, Pauline (NDP), 86, 144
jobs and environmental policies, 141
John Paul II, Pope, 10, 15
John XXIII, Pope, 99
Johnson, Gen. Leonard V., 149
Johnston, Don (Cyprus), 166
Johnston, Richard (trip), 159
justice, 17, 20, 22, 28, 220, 223–24

K

KAIROS, 104
Kaunda, Kenneth (Zambia), 158
Keenan, Brian (prof), 51
Keeper, Cyril (NDP), 77
Kelowna Agreement, 2
Kennan, George (diplomat), 88
Kennedy, Robert F., 40–41
Kenney, Jason (Tory), 104, 165

Kielburger, Craig, 207–8
Kierans, Thomas, 133
King, Martin Luther, 16, 40, 218
Kinnock, Neil (UK), 171
Knowles, Stanley, 42, 188
    memorial service, 62–63
    MP, 38, 39, 55, 92
    social gospel, 4, 7
Knowles-Woodsworth Centre, 4
Kosovo, NATO and, 152–53, 172
Kostyra, Eugene (1994 renewal), 93, 94
Kuntsler, William, 211
Kuwait, invasion by Iraq, 169–71
Kyoto Accord (1997), 2, 137

L
labour laws, 18, 186–87
Lacayo, Sergio (Nicaragua), 178
land mines, 146
Langdon, Steven (NDP), 187
Laporte, Pierre, 47
Latimer, Robert, 32
Layton, Jack, 1, 31, 110, 122
Lefebvre Committee, 110
Leibovitch, Peter (renewal), 93, 94
Leningrad, mass graves from war, 175
Leo, Y-S Columbus, 161
Lerner, Rabbi Michael, 221
Levan, Chris (house church), 53
Lewis, David (NDP), 17, 42, 73
Liberal Party of Canada
    1995 budget, 94
    and corporate power, 197
    free trade position, 204–5
    sponsorship scandal, 2
liberation theology, 215
Lincoln, Abraham, 113, 255
Lithuania, 158–60, 174
Lloyd, Woodrow (Sask), 48
Loney, James (Iraq hostage), 25
Long, Harry (Dieppe vet), 117
Lougheed, Peter, 194, 195

love, 20
Lowe, Monty (teacher), 41
Lyon, Premier Sterling (Man), 67, 78

M
MacDonald, Alex (Cyprus), 166
MacDonald, David (Tory MP), 157
Macdonald, Ian (North End), 60
MacDonald, Jim (CLC), 102
MacEachen, Allan, 105, 113
MacKay, Elmer (Tory), 103
MacKay, Peter, 42–43
MacKenzie, Randy, 53
Mackenzie Valley Pipeline, 54
Mackenzie Valley Pipeline Inquiry, 72–73
Macmillan, Harold (UK), 154
MacNamara, Sister Geraldine, 68
MacQuarrie, Senator Heath, 217
Magnificat of Mary, 22
Mandela, Nelson, 144, 200
Manitoba Indian Brotherhood, 76
Manitoba Inter-Church Coalition, 75
Manitoba Telephone System, 154
Manly, Jim (NDP), 7, 77
Manning, Preston, 32, 92, 220
Marchi, Sergio (Lib), 134
market ethic, 53, 122, 139, 140, 217, 223
marketing systems, 18
Martin, Keith (Parl Sec), 123
Martin, Paul (PM), 79–80, 107, 118, 122, 189
    2005 budget, 2, 167
    military decisions, 173
    minority government, 191
Martindale, Doug (house church), 53
Maurice, Frederick Denison, 57
May, Elizabeth, 130–31, 199
McCormick, Col. Robert, 193
McCullum, Hugh (journalist), 75
McDonald, Lynn (NDP), 118
McDonald, Marci, 31, 219–20, 222
McDonough, Alexa, 31, 35, 83, 148, 171

McEwen, Gary (teacher), 41
McGovern, George (US Sen), 49
McGrath Committee, 109, 111–16, 123
  committees, power and makeup, 114
  private members' business, 114–19
  Speaker's role, 111–13
McGrath, Father Des, 102
McGrath, Jim (committee chair), 109, 111
McKay, Ian (author), 15
McKay, Stan, Jr., 75
McKay, Stan, Sr. (North End), 63
McKay, Verna (North End), 63
McKenna, Frank (NB Lib.), 80
McKibben, Bill (author), 136
McLaughlin, Audrey, 34–35, 79, 143, 171
McLean, Walter, 86, 87, 157–58, 161, 175
McLeod, Bruce (UCC), 161
McMillan, Tom (Env Min), 130–31
McMurtry, Doug (UCC), 55
McNally, Fred (North End), 60
McRae, Paul (minority report), 86, 87
McTeer, Maureen, 167
media dimension, 126, 129
medicare see public health insurance
Meech Lake Accord, 79–81, 80–81
  absence of Aboriginal rights, 79
members and constituents, 119–21
merchant navy veterans, 117
Mercredi, Grand Chief Ovide, 81
Merrithew, Gerry (Defence), 117
Methodism, 50
Mexico, 196, 203–4
Michael, Lorraine (NDP), 102–3
Micklethwait, John (author), 219
middle class, 197, 202
Miki, Art (Japanese Cdn), 92–93
military alliances, 144
Millar, Bill (UCC), 46
Miller, Bob (writer), 157, 177
Miller, George, 211
Miller, Lynette (UCC), 55
Milliken, Peter, 1, 149

Mills, Allen (biographer), 60
Mills, Dennis (Lib), 133
Mills, Howie (prof), 54, 55
Milosevic, Slobodan, 153
Minority Report on disarmament (1982), 85–86
Molgat, Gil (Manitoba senator), 40
Moore, Michael (activist), 210
Moore, Michael (WTO), 210
Morgentaler, Dr. Henry, 27
Morris, Barry (UCC), 64
Mulcair, Thomas (Quebec NDP), 189
Mulroney, Brian (PM), 62, 93, 127
  animosity toward, 79, 81, 192
  environment, 128, 129–30, 137–38
  free trade, 186, 193–94, 195, 196
  medicare, 103, 134
  Meech Lake Accord, 79, 79–80
  military action, 152, 170–71
  parliamentary reform, 110–11, 115–16
Multilateral Agreement on Investment, 183, 205–6
multinational corporations, 183, 184–86, 205
Munich conference on security (2005), 154
Murphy, Rod (NDP), 77, 118

N
NAFTA, 90, 121, 186, 194, 196, 203, 205, 208
Namibia, 156–58
National Energy Program, 110, 195
National Party, 95
NATO, 147–49, 151–52, 154–55
  intervention in Kosovo, 152–53
Nehru, Jawaharlal (India), 179
neo-conservative (neo-liberal), 65
Neuhaus, Richard John, 223
New Democratic Party (NDP)
  agricultural policy, 201
  class consciousness and, 90
  Faith and Justice Commission, 221–22

foreign policy approach, 143–49,
    151–52, 171
importance of, 97
leadership race (2002–3), 5, 36, 62,
    84, 97
Official Opposition, 191
opposition to globalization, 202–3, 204
position on NATO, 147–49, 151–52
renewal conference (1994), 93–94
social gospel tradition, 7, 221, 223–24
see also Cooperative Commonwealth
    Federation (CCF)
New Politics Initiative, 96–97, 203–4
Newcombe, Charlie (prof), 51
Newman, Cardinal John Henry, 162
Newman, Don (CBC), 208
Nicaragua, 177, 178
Nicholson, Rob (Justice Minister), 27
Niebuhr, H. Richard (theologian), 50
Niebuhr, Reinhold (theologian), 19, 20
Nisga'a Treaty, 82
non-tariff barriers, 185
NORAD agreement, 174
North American Free Trade see NAFTA
North Atlantic Assembly, 147, 151, 152
North End Community Ministry, 63,
    67–68, 71
Northern Ireland (Ulster), 162–65
Norway, 137
notwithstanding clause, 27, 78
nuclear arms race, 145, 147
nuclear disarmament, 50, 146, 155
    specific pledges, 86, 89, 90
nuclear power, 118, 131–32
nuclear waste, 132
nuclear weapons, 146, 147, 155, 173
Nujoma, Sam (Namibia), 157
Nunziata, John, 126

O

Obama, Barack, 30, 219
O'Brien, Audrey (Clerk), 1
O'Brien, Pat (sub inquiry), 123

Ogle, Father Bob, 7, 9, 10, 198–99
oil and politics, 169
oil spills, 64, 129
Okimaw, Chief Moses, 76
Olds, Father Fred (Transcona), 10
Oleksas, Josas (Lithuania), 160
opposition, role of, 124
Orlikow, David (NDP), 45
Ortega, Daniel (Nicaragua), 177, 178
Ostpolitik, 148
Ouellet, André (McGrath comm), 111

P

pacifism, 20, 21, 57
Paisley, Ian (Ireland), 162, 165
Palme Report, 145–46
Parasiuk, Willie, 41, 164
Parasiuk, Wilma (nee Hewitson), 41
Parent, Gib (Speaker), 34
Parizeau, Jacques, 106
Parliament
    abdication of powers, 122
    and the courts, 78
    importance, 91–92
parliamentary calendar, fixed, 110
Parliamentary Centre, 157, 177
parliamentary committees, 110, 122–23
parliamentary issues, 123–26
    Charter and role of Parliament, 125
    collegiality, 124, 125
    First Ministers, 125
    isolation of members, 125
    media dimension, 126, 129
    opposition, 124
    parliamentary decorum, 125–26
    public opinion polling, 125
parliamentary reform, 109–26
    Lefebvre Committee, 110
    McGrath Committee, 109–12, 169
    see also Lefebvre Committee; McGrath
        Committee
parliamentary secretaries, 114, 123
parliamentary travel, 150, 152, 176

party discipline, 109
Paulley, Russ (MLA, NDP), 39, 42, 44, 45
Pawley, Howard, 31, 46, 80, 81, 132
PCB spill, 129
peace initiative by Trudeau, 88–89
peace movement, 85–90
Peltier, Leonard (activist), 119
Penikett, Tony, 148
Penson, Charlie, 198, 200
Perley, Michael (acid rain), 130
Perot, Ross, 203
Perry, Jack, 40
Peterson, Jim (Taiwan), 161
Pettigrew, Pierre (Trade), 209
Petursson, Rev. Philip, 45
Phipps, Bill (UCC), 54, 104
physicians, extra-billing, 100, 101, 103,
    106
pluralism, 13, 219, 222, 223–24
Pocklington, Peter, 194
Point Douglas, 59, 61
police and demonstrators, 212–13
political parties
    and voters, 85–87, 89–92, 94–95
    see also elections
poverty and debt, 139, 145
prayer breakfast, 34, 68
Prime Minister's Office, 109
private members' business, 114–19
privatization
    of health care, 107
    of public assets, 153–54
    of religion, 12
pro-life movement, 23, 24, 27, 29
Proctor, Dick (NDP), 148, 199
profit motive, 14
Progressive Conservatives
    1984 election, 85–86, 90
    Bill Blaikie's activity in, 42–44
progressive tax system, 18
Project North, 74–76
prophetic tradition, 50–58, 67, 68, 143

corporations and, 50, 51
social democracy, 68–69
University of Winnipeg, 50–52
proportional representation, 2
prorogation of Parliament, 3
public control of utilities, 18
public health insurance, 18, 98–108
    concerns, 100, 194
    continuing pressures on, 107–8
    extra-billing, user fees, 100, 101, 103,
        106
    funding, 100–101, 107–8
    Saskatchewan, 99
    social determinants of health, 108
public opinion polling, 125, 137
public pension, 18
Putin, President Vladimir, 176

Q
Quebec
    Aboriginal people, 82–84
    and free trade, 196
    national election (2011), 84
    NDP seats in, 189, 190
    party politics, 79–80
    patriation of Constitution, 78–79
    referendum on separation (1995),
        80–81
question period, 126, 129

R
Rae, Bob, 136, 159, 203, 204
rail line abandonment, 137–38, 201
Rambouillet accord (1999), 153
Rauschenbusch, Walter, 16–17, 19, 188
Reagan, Ronald, 129, 136, 140, 210
Red Tory, 217
referendums, 119, 121
Reform Party
    opinions, 24, 73–74, 109, 152
    parliament and, 109, 116–17, 119, 121,
        125

rise of party, 81, 82, 87, 92, 94, 187
Reid, Daryl (NDP), 42
Reisman, Simon (FTA), 133
religion
  pluralism, 13, 219, 222, 224
  and politics see faith and politics
  privatization of, 12
  and the state, 13
religious left, 4, 5, 7–10, 11
  newly emergent, 219, 220–22
  social justice, 14–18, 57, 216, 223–24
religious right, 6–7, 8–9, 15, 26, 219–20
Reshaur, John (YPC), 45
residential schools, 69, 72, 78, 216
Responsibility to Protect (R2P), 153
Revenue Guarantee, transfer payments,
  105
Richler, Mordecai, 194
Ridd, Carl (prof), 51, 52, 60
right to choose, 28
Ritchie, Gordon (FTA), 192
Robarts, John (premier ON), 106
Robbins, Walt, 132
Robertson, Colin, 134
Robertson House, 71
Robichaud, Louis (premier NB), 106
Robinson, Svend (NDP), 35, 77, 97, 136,
  153
Roblin, Duff, 43, 44, 105
Roche, Doug (activist, MP), 87
role of an MP, 119–21
Roman Catholics see Catholic Church
Romero, Archbishop Oscar, 177
Rose, Mark (Canada Day), 115
Rossbrook House, 68
Rowland, Doug (NDP 1974), 23
Royal Commission on Health Services, 99
Ruggiero, Renato (WTO), 210
Rumsfeld, Donald, 154
Russia, 175–76
  see also Soviet Union
Ryan, Father Tim, 55

S
same-sex marriage, 7, 26–27, 30–31, 116
Sánchez, Don Fidel Velásquez, 204
Sandinistas, 177, 178
Sanger, Clyde (journalist), 145
Sargeant, Terry (NDP), 77, 86, 90
Saul, John Ralston (author), 176
Sauvageau, Benoît, 198
scandal, preoccupation with, 65, 124, 126
Schreyer, Ed (Gov Gen), 40, 45, 46, 167
Schulz, Randy, 46
Scott, Andy (Att Gen), 199
Seattle protest (1999), 96, 209–12
Second World War, 21
security
  NDP paper on, 145, 146, 148, 149
  threats to, 145
Selinger, Greg, 46, 68, 134
Senate, NDP position on, 189–90
Shamrock Summit (1985), 129, 193–94
Shelef, Yitzhak (Israel), 165
Sherman, Bud (Winnipeg), 49
Shevardnadze, Eduard, 175
Short, Peter (UCC), 53
Siberian gulag, 176
Sikh community, 118
sin
  as a social reality, 20, 220
  forgiveness and choice, 22
Slovo, Joe (activist), 158
Smith, John (UK Labour), 208, 209
Smith, Smokey (Vic Cross), 44
smoking, 118
social gospel, 5, 7–11, 14–22, 121
  activist priests, 7–10, 102, 177
  NDP and, 7, 221, 223–24
  recent years, 219–24
  revival, 1970s–1980s, 64, 215–16
  roots in inner cities, 69
  spirit of optimism, 19
  struggling with war, 21–22

social movements, 67, 85–94
  and political choices, 85–86, 91–92
socialism, 22, 56, 217
Socialist International, 148
Socialist Party (Debs), 20
Solidarity, 10
Solzhenitsyn, Aleksandr, 175
South Moresby Island, 131
Soviet Union
  collapse of, 169, 174
  communist system in, 138, 139, 176
  visits to, 174–76
  see also Lithuania; Russia
Speaker's role (McGrath), 111–13
Speller, Bob (Namibia), 157, 158
Spivak, Senator Mira, 44
Spivak, Sidney (PC), 44
Stainton, Michael (trip), 161
Stanfield, Robert, 105
stem cell research, 32
stewardship of creation, 74, 134–36,
  141–42
Stewart, Ian (author), 80
Stotsky, Karen (researcher), 101
Strahl, Chuck (Reform/Cons), 82
Stringfellow, William, 51–52
Strong, Maurice, 137
submarines purchased from UK, 122–23
Sullivan, Father Emmanuel, 162
Summit of the Americas (1994), 204
sustainable development, 137
Sutherland Mission (Winnipeg), 59–61
Suzuki, David, 142

T
Taiwan trip, 160–61
taxation, 65–66
Taylor, Alex (grandfather), 44, 162
Taylor, Charles, 28, 222
Taylor, Margaret (great-aunt), 162
Taylor, Mary (grandmother), 162
television advertising, 216

Temple, Archbishop William, 57
Thatcher, Margaret (UK), 66, 140, 166
theological studies, 52–58
Third Way, 97, 208
Thompson, Dudley (North End), 61
Thompson, Eleanor (North End), 61
Thompson, Mike (PC), 192
Tibet, 181
Tillich, Paul (theologian), 217
Timm-Rudolph, Shirley, 191–92
Tobin, Brian (Lib), 126, 131
Tompkins, Father Jimmy, 102
Toronto School of Theology, 52–58
Transcona, Manitoba, 37–39
Transcona Memorial United Church, 25,
  37, 52, 55
transportation changes, 137–38, 201
Trimble, David, 163
Trudeau, Margaret, 180
Trudeau, Michel, 180
Trudeau, Pierre, 80, 109, 124, 132, 144,
  147, 167, 180
  peace initiative, 88–89
Tulchinsky, Ted, 61
Turner, John (PM), 4, 124, 190, 197

U
Uhrich, Jim (UCC), 55
United Church of Canada, 19, 30, 218
  apology to Aboriginals, 72
  formation, 19
  and NDP, 11, 55, 104
  support of public health care, 102
United Nations, 152, 155, 172
  Disarmament Special Session (1982), 85
  Gulf Wars, 169–73
  Responsibility to Protect (R2P), 153
United States
  attitude to UN, 152
  backing dictatorships, 147, 177–78
  Canada-US FTA, 90, 144, 183, 185,
    190, 192–93, 196–97

culture wars, 26
Gulf Wars, 170, 172–73
lack of interest in Canada, 154
Vietnam War, 20, 41, 50, 64, 147
University of Winnipeg, 4, 49–52
uranium mining in Saskatchewan, 132
Urban Circle, 61
user fees (hosp), 101, 103, 106

V
Vandezande, Gerald, 75
Veloria, Velma, 210
veterans, 117, 179
Vietnam War, 20, 41, 50, 64, 147
voters and social movements, 85–87,
   90–92, 94

W
Waddell, Ian, 77, 112–13, 131–32, 211
Walding, Jim (Man MLA), 80
Wałęsa, Lech (Solidarity), 10
Walker, Michael (Fraser Inst), 47, 65
Wallis, Jim, 52, 221
The Walrus magazine, 6
war
   and capitalism, 21–22
   and social gospel, 21–22, 57
war cemeteries, 150–51
War Measures Act, 144
Warren, John (author), 152
Warren, Peter (radio), 120
Warren, Rick (pastor), 219
Wasylycia-Leis, Judy (NDP), 118
water exports, 132–34
weapons of mass destruction, 172
Webster, Jack (journalist), 211
Weigel, George, 223
Weir, Walter (Man premier), 43
Weisgerber, Archbishop James, 25
Wesley, John (Methodism), 50
Westworth United Church, 60
Whitehead, Dr. Ray, 178

Whiteway, Dean, 23–24, 192
Wilberforce, William, 219
Wilson, Michael (Tory), 66
wine industry, Canadian, 194
Winegard, Bill (Trade chair), 192
Wink, Walter (theologian), 218
Winnipeg-Bird's Hill riding, 39, 42, 215
Winnipeg General Strike, 61
Witer, Andrew (Cyprus), 166
Wogaman, J. Philip, 141
Wolfe, Bernie (Man), 40
Woodsworth, J.S., 4, 7, 16, 21, 39, 57, 60,
   61, 69
Wooldridge, Adrian, 219
World Health Organization, 104–5
World Trade Organization, 154, 183,
   198–200
   admission of China, 169, 181, 187
   child labour, 207–8
   culture and trade rules, 186
   Geneva (1998), 200
   human rights ignored, 186, 187, 199,
      202
   Seattle protest (1999), 209–12
   Singapore (1996), 198–99
   threat to democracy, 210
Wright, Art (Man), 44
Wright, Phil (prof), 51

Y
Young, Neil, 113

Z
Zambia, 158
Zentner, Harry, 41
Zhou Enlai, 4

"In *The Blaikie Report,* Bill Blaikie captures 30 years of Canadian political history with a generous reflection on the intersection of faith and political action. *The Blaikie Report* makes an important contribution to both. A very good read!"

—Lorne Calvert, Principal, St. Andrew's College;
Premier of Saskatchewan, 2001–2007

"*The Blaikie Report* is a story worth telling, and Blaikie tells it well. For three decades at the intersection of faith and politics, Bill Blaikie has accrued a wealth of knowledge and insight which he shares with clarity and grace. His story captures the changes in the public arena over three tumultuous decades. This is essential reading for students of parliamentary democracy and people of any and all faiths who wish to learn how to walk the walk."

—Jim Christie, Director, Ridd Institute for Religion & Global Policy;
President, Canadian Council of Churches, 2006–2009

"An elemental threat to Canada's democracy is the growing caricature that parliamentarians are typically self-serving and powerless. Bill Blaikie proves the contrary. He was a highly-respected MP for 30 years, driven by a profound commitment to civility and social democracy, and setting a clear example of how significantly one person can advance the public interest. He offers solid advice on how to improve our Parliament which he describes, sadly but aptly, as 'a case of good people falling into a toxic culture.'"

—Joe Clark, Prime Minister of Canada, 1979–1980

"Throughout his impressive parliamentary career, Bill Blaikie stood tall among his political peers as an ethical and intellectual force to be reckoned with. This fascinating book is more than a chronicle of past events—it is a moral compass for those who aspire to practise principled politics in a complex and challenging world."

—Alexa McDonough, NDP Leader, 1995–2003

"This is a book I have been waiting for. Bill Blaikie has occupied a unique position on the faith and political landscape for over 30 years. I have always admired his unabashed and unapologetic rooting of his politics in his faith and the Social Gospel tradition…. This book is a wonderful weaving together of political insight, fascinating personal stories, and theological analysis. With humility and clarity, Bill casts a special light on the past 35 years of Canadian history. For people who care about Canadian politics and the role of one's faith, this book will inform, refresh, inspire, and challenge. It is a very special gift to all Canadians."

—Bill Phipps, Moderator, The United Church of Canada, 1997–2000

"Always an inveterate partisan of the ideological left, at times scandalized at how life's particularities set him at odds with party line, Bill Blaikie is a fine example of a man in his right mind. Here is passion without presumption, commitment without credulity and loss without despair. There is plenty of information and political anecdote but even more important, there is insight into the underground stream of faith that nourishes a lifetime of struggle and hope. *The Blaikie Report* is a treasury of Canadian political analysis and a treasure for all of us who long to understand vocation to God's world."

—Peter Short, Moderator, The United Church of Canada, 2003–2006